Advance Praise for

Monkey Morales

"Anyone who knows anything about Miami's mythic webs of intrigue knows Monkey Morales lay at the heart of them all. Finally, a pacy biography that sorts fact from fiction—and needless to say the facts are much, much stranger than the tallest of tales."
— Nicholas Griffin, author of *The Year of Dangerous Days: Riots, Refugees, and Cocaine in Miami 1980*

"John le Carré and Ian Fleming together could not have invented a more compelling real life spook than what is found here in the pages of this definitive biography of the legendary Ricardo 'Monkey' Morales. His most closely guarded secrets and undercover exploits in espionage all are revealed here for the first time, finally providing the missing puzzle pieces that help resolve some of the biggest historical jigsaws of 20th century spy craft."
— Fernand Amandi, MSNBC analyst

"I've been trying to understand Ricardo Monkey Morales for thirty years. He left us all these clues—in police records, on the lips of exiles, across international press, in hours of surreal testimony. Fact. Fiction. Hyperbole. Heartbreak. You could never quite put his story down. Finally, Rick, Jr. and Sean Oliver connect it all for me. This book—decades overdue—is a gift."
— Roben Farzad, author of *Hotel Scarface: Where Cocaine Cowboys Partied and Plotted to Control Miami*, CNN, NPR Radio

"The authors have done a masterful job putting all these elements together so cogently; I don't know how anyone could've done it, but they've certainly done the job. I can't say enough how impressed I am. Masterful job, just outstanding, masterful...over and over."
— Jerome Sanford, former Assistant US Attorney

Also by Sean Oliver

Tod is God: The Authorized Story of How I Created Extreme Championship Wrestling

MONKEY MORALES

The True Story of a Mythic Cuban Exile, Assassin, CIA Operative, FBI Informant, Smuggler, and Dad

SEAN OLIVER and
RICARDO MORALES, JR.

Post Hill Press

A POST HILL PRESS BOOK
ISBN: 979-8-88845-859-4
ISBN (eBook): 979-8-88845-860-0

Monkey Morales:
The True Story of a Mythic Cuban Exile, Assassin, CIA Operative, FBI Informant, Smuggler, and Dad

Cover design by Cody Corcoran

This book, as well as any other Post Hill Press publications, may be purchased in bulk quantities at a special discounted rate. Contact orders@posthillpress.com for more information.

This is a work of nonfiction. All people, locations, events, and situations are portrayed to the best of the author's memory and knowledge. Although adequate research was undergone concerning criminal cases, real-life people and perceptions, and authentic situations and incidents, the author and publisher do not assume and hereby disclaim any liability concerning any legal or criminal details present in this book.

Post Hill Press
New York • Nashville
posthillpress.com

Published in the United States of America
1 2 3 4 5 6 7 8 9 10

For Roberto.

Table of Contents

PART ONE

RICARDO

The Players

Ball, Joe: FBI agent, one of Monkey's handlers

Becerra, Humberto "Super Papi": Enforcer in Carlene Quesada's smuggling operation

Bosch, Annette: Monkey's niece

Bosch, Lynette: Monkey's niece

Bosch, Dr. Orlando: Anti-Castro bombing group organizer, pediatrician

Cid, Juan: Pot dealer and silent partner in Roger's on the Green

Cook, John Clarence: Miami-based jewel thief connected to Chicago mafia

Cornillot, Hector: Anti-Castro bombing group organizer, Monkey's brother-in-law

Costanzo, Aton "Atomico": Exile and would-be assassin

Davis, George: FBI agent, one of Monkey's handlers

Diaz, Raul: Metro-Dade detective assigned to Monkey

Garcia Vasquez, Orlando: CIA asset and commanding officer in Venezuela's DISIP intelligence agency

Lamazares Cid, Nancy: Widow of German Lamazares, later ex-wife of Juan Cid, companion of Monkey

Lamazares, German: Drug dealer, DEA informant, and business partner of Eladio Armando Ruiz

Martinez, Raul: City of Miami, detective

Morales Despau, Raul: Monkey's father, court justice in Havana

Morales, Ines: Monkey's mother

Morales, Magda: Monkey's first wife, mother of Raul, Rick, and Sylvia

Morales, Mimi: Monkey's second wife, mother of Roberto

Morales, Raul: Monkey's oldest child

Morales, Rick, Jr.: Monkey's second child

Morales, Roberto: Monkey's fourth child

Morales, Rolando "Pucho": Monkey's brother

Morales, Sylvia: Monkey's third child

Morales, Yolanda: Monkey's sister

Novo, Rogelio: Part owner of Roger's on the Green with Juan Cid

Otero, Rolando: Terrorist bomber known as "The Condor"

Pérez, Carlos Andrés: President of Venezuela 1974-79, 1989-93

Posada, Luis: Bomber, CIA Operation 40 veteran, and Venezuela DISIP intelligence agency officer

Quesada, Carlos "Carlene": Head of narcotics smuggling organization; former partner of Rudy Rodriguez

Robertson, William "Rip": "Wild Geese" squad commander in CIA's Congo operation

Rodriguez, Rudy: Head of narcotics smuggling organization; former partner of Carlene Quesada

Rosenthal, Frank "Lefty": Ran bookmaking operation in Miami for the Chicago mafia

Ruiz, Eladio Armando: Anti-Castro group member, drug dealer, and would-be assassin

Sanford, Jerome: Former Assistant US Attorney, associate, and confidant of Monkey

Sanjenis, Joaquín: Recruiter of Cuban exiles for CIA's Operation 40

Scruggs, Mollie: Mutiny Club waitress, friend of Monkey

Sturgis, Frank: Anti-Castro CIA operative

Torres, Orlando: Armed security at Roger's on the Green

Introduction

It was South Florida's trial of the century.

The colorful players in this theatre of intrigue had been gracing the covers of local newspapers for years, but the seductive headlines never came close to the real stories of the people on center stage. The national media was drowned out by the local population, which was much more closely connected to this trial. For many, their culture was intertwined in the riveting tale. Everything being reported had happened on their own streets with ties to the country from which they'd come. The community had ties to the participants mentioned in the depositions and hearings on both sides of the law. Even that divide had become a little blurry in the past couple of weeks. Then there was the defendant who'd recently gone missing on the high seas off the Bahamas, a beloved figure who'd run a community center for refugees.

It had more explosive content than anything in the cinema in 1982.

Bombs. Cocaine. Murder. Spies.

Though unlike the silver screen, this stuff was all true, and the finale hadn't even been staged yet. But it was to happen that Wednesday morning when the packed courtroom brimmed with anticipation for the final act, now about to start. It was dead quiet as everyone just waited for the curtain.

It would shortchange the event to say they awaited the entrance of a person. They more sought to be an eyewitness to the iconic centerpiece of a spellbinding tale about to deliver on its dramatic promise.

Victor Hugo's barricade, Andrew Lloyd Weber's chandelier.

Eight weeks of testimony[1] in Judge Gerald Kogan's Miami courtroom had seemingly come to this appearance. Over a thousand hours of FBI wiretaps were produced for what had come to be known as the "Tick Talks" trial, so named for the recording device planted in drug kingpin Carlos "Carlene" Quesada's clock. The enigma responsible for the wiretaps was about to enter the courtroom, called to validate everything caught on the tapes and stick the State's charges to the thirty defendants that day in late May 1982. He was, in essence, the whole case.

High profile entanglements with the law and its agencies were nothing new to the State's star witness, as the Miami media had been showcasing for years. There was nary a time he wasn't actively involved in committing crimes, whether in the name of self-manufactured justice or informing on someone else's misdeeds. Both prosecution and defense teams knew that and were prepared to move forward. It seemed everyone on all tiers of law enforcement knew it, too.

Tales of "The Monkey" had become mythic.

Known widely by this moniker, Ricardo Morales Navarrete had spent more than twenty years telling tales far taller than his five foot eight frame for others to circulate. But unlike those attributed to James Bond or any other international spy of fiction, these were true.

He worked for Castro's G-2 secret police and escaped Cuba in 1960, only to land in the hands of the CIA during their construction of an elite division of mercenaries to neutralize Fidel Castro. In his forty-three years, he'd been shot in the back while freeing captured missionaries in the Belgian Congo, shot in the head on a Miami street, and blown up in a rental car. The Cuban exile had also been a prolific bomber-for-hire in Miami, a paid contract agent for the FBI and CIA, an informant for the DEA and Miami-Dade police, a commissioner of counterintelligence for Venezuela's secret police, and a drug dealer during Miami's booming narcotics renaissance.

It was that last part that had drawn everyone to the courtroom on this occasion. After nearly two months[2] of wrangling between State Attorney Janet Reno's prosecution team, the defense attorneys, and Judge Kogan, the boards would now be cleared for the most notorious informant in the world's arena. Morales's gregarious, presentational nature was sure to entertain; he wasn't the strong silent type typified by secret agents of fiction. He was a wordsmith, highly intelligent with a near photographic memory. This famously allowed him to never write down one detail, from names to license plates, in all his years of working for agencies. The show was about to begin.

It was a show that law enforcement was growing tired of, despite Morales's position on the side of the prosecution. The complicated rabble-rouser was a roller coaster for anyone he dealt with. He tested everyone, trusted no one, and kept the world guessing whose side he was actually on. Eventually, everyone would come to the same conclusion—Ricardo Morales was on the side of Ricardo Morales.

"I don't play to win or lose," he once said. "I play to stay in the game."[3] He saw everyone as his chess pieces.

Courtroom procedure was altered for the day.[4] The premises were searched thoroughly, and all attendees were frisked upon entry. The star witness of the Tick Talks trial had made enemies all over the world on both sides of the law which, as Morales would continually point out, was gauged on a sliding scale anyway.

The defense tables were comprised of many men from Morales's past. Some he fought beside in Cuba and the Congo, and others he'd known since his childhood days in Havana. Defense attorneys for the individuals facing the drug trafficking charges had tried for weeks to suppress the damning recordings on which prosecutors had hinged their entire case. Morales would be Assistant State Attorney Rina Cohan's knockout blow when he recounted all the events in which he participated, corroborating what the jury would soon hear on the tapes. Judge Kogan announced to the court that Morales was presently being brought in, led by police escort.

There he was: the legend of South Florida. The entire room sat up upon his entrance, finally beholding the man *Time* and *Fortune* columnist John Rothchild said was conducting both sides of this trial like "a patient who directs his own gallbladder operation."[5] The folkloric force loomed larger than what his pedestrian sweater and blue jeans might suggest. Morales raised his right hand for the ceremonial pledge then sat before the assembled throngs and prepared to open his infamous mouth one more time.

But nothing in Monkey Morales's sphere ever went according to plan.

Chapter One

Cuba (–1960)

August 30, 1960.[6]

It was not the kind of wedding the bride or groom had imagined. Circumstance had made Ricardo and Magda act with pragmatism, standing before a justice wanting simply to get this event on paper. Every other couple's daydream was now a formality to the new Mr. and Mrs. Ricardo Morales, and there was hardly any time for celebration for the young couple, she eighteen years old and he just having turned twenty-one. A lot was going on, and more was coming down the pike.

Maria Magdalena Cornillot's family was already heading to the United States in small groups, with her father, Hector Sr., having already landed in Forest Hills, Queens, New York.[7] He secured a factory job and awaited the rest of his family's entry into the country. Ricardo's family was on their way out of Cuba as well. His brother Rolando, more commonly known as "Pucho," had been in the US for over a year, and his mother and sister were standing by, awaiting their exit.

A fire was lit beneath Ricardo and Magda. Her travel papers had been approved, and her flight was just days away. Morales's situation was not as simple; the Castro government would prefer to give him a bullet before travel papers.

Now, he needed to get the fuck out too.

Morales had been serving the Castro regime in an official capacity for nearly a year, though informally well before that. He was compelled to follow his older brother Pucho, who had become active in anti-Batista outings in Havana. Young Ricardo was arrested twice for "conspiring against Batista," once while only fifteen years old, then again at eighteen.[8] He was like many idealistic, politically aware young men in Cuba at the time who were eager to look beyond Colonel Fulgencio Batista toward newer, more equitable ideas that better represented Cuba's working class.

Ricardo Morales had been studying law at the University of Havana when his friend Raul Arguiles, a major in the intelligence department of the Cuban National Police, recommended him for the military.[9] That vote of confidence from a high-ranking officer encouraged the twenty-year-old to leave law school and enlist with DIER (Department of Intelligence of the Rebel Army, translated), which later changed its name to G-2. Castro, despite taking over the country and commanding its national army, propagated the illusion of a democratic government with this term—"rebel army."

In plain terms, G-2 was the political police force tasked with uncovering subversive actions that served any interests other than the new regime's. G-2's chief, Commander Ramiro Valdez Menendez, operated out of the general staff headquarters on La Avenida del Puerto on Havana's northern coast, where he managed the administrative and political business.[10] The Operations Section of G-2 was headquartered not far from there, at 5th Avenue and 14th in the Miramar section of Havana, and it housed the lieutenants overseeing the prisons, workshops, radio patrols, and general police corps.

The G-2 agency operated smaller operational offices and outposts in locations like Havana Port and Rancho Boyeros Airport, now José Martí International Airport, where Ricardo Morales was stationed under Lt. Rolando Matos Bozan. Agents were assigned customary job titles like flight dispatchers and customs inspectors but also more curious positions like "airplane guards" and "passenger checkers."[11]

"My position," Morales later said, "was to uncover subversive organizations, especially members of the overthrown dictatorship of General Batista."[12]

The installation of Castro's military system featured an overhaul of Cuban courts. After the Cuban revolution, he enacted a new military tribunal court, wherein anyone suspected of engaging in conduct deemed oppositive to the regime was brought before the bench.[13] The tribunal would decide the charges as evidence was presented against the accused, including testimony from officers of the secret police who'd brought the accused before the court. That was Castro's military court, hearing the charges leveled by Castro's military police. These proceedings paved a very narrow, one-way street for the accused, or "kangaroo trials," as Morales himself put it.[14]

In September 1959, Morales enlisted for service and began training on the outskirts of Havana, which consisted of the very basics of investigative procedures. No one he knew in the revolutionary army was qualified to teach advanced and tested tactics, so Morales began his on the job training when handed a badge, gun, and little else. But Ricardo considered himself streetwise and was undaunted by figuring it all out on his own.

Shifting politics signaled increasing danger for Morales and anyone with ties to Batista. Castro's grip on the country was tightening, partially due to the elimination or exit of those opposed to his regime, by means both natural and otherwise. Added to that was a wrinkle in the Morales family's past, namely his father's and grandfather's positions under Batista. His father, Raul Morales Despau, was an appointed justice in Batista's courts for over forty years, and his grandfather was the chief justice of the Province of Havana. By contemporary standards in a free society, a federal judge is only marginally colored by his appointing body, but in military dictatorships all are subject to orders from the dictator. Morales Despau, for instance, was a justice whom Batista's military officers would visit at all hours for signatures on death certificates. Well into the night, on more than one occasion, ranking military officials would ring Morales Despau's bell with the death certificate of a man riddled with bullet holes, on which the judge would write "heart attack" before signing the document.

Pucho's flight out exemplified the Morales family's connection to the Batista regime. Ricardo's brother left Cuba in January 1958 courtesy of a special passport letter hand-signed by José Manuel Cortina, Cuba's Secretary of State and an influential member of Batista's administration. On January 20, Pucho entered Paraguay wielding the document that ordered unquestioned, unfettered passage through the country and into Chile. He made it through Paraguay, Chile, and into the United States courtesy of a letter only the eldest son of a federal justice in a dictator's court might possess.

But that brand of influence became a grave liability after Fidel Castro's overthrow of the Batista regime in 1959. The ragtag assembly of the G-2 police force may have allowed Ricardo's family lineage to go undetected at first, but it would certainly fall under the microscope during his tenure in Castro's G-2. And, while allowing the exodus of those opposed to his policy was a key tactic in Castro's garnering control, families of those linked to Batista's regime underwent a different fate.[15]

By 1959, six hundred people found to have worked for the Batista government had been put to death by Castro's courts.[16] Morales, serving Castro's secret police, had been part of that system, all the while concealing the secret of the Morales men before him that would no doubt begin to sound more loudly. By 1963, the CIA estimate of political executions under the Castro administration was 2,500, though only eight hundred were publicly announced by the regime.[17]

Morales felt a clock ticking with every day that went by. He'd seen what the Cuban revolution had become, and he'd witnessed the punishment meted out for anyone opposing Castro. And one's family having close ties with the Batista government was as good as pointing a gun at The Beard.

★★★

"This is a fine young man, and a very smart young man."[18]

Ed Sullivan, the trusted icon stamping approval on entertainers and pop culture figures on TV for over twenty years, had just given his seal of approval to a thirty-two year old man that many watching had only cursory knowledge of. He'd just sat with Sullivan for a pre-taped interview segment that aired on the January 11, 1959 *Ed Sullivan Show* broadcast. The bearded guest spoke of himself, of his country, and of America and its citizens.

"The people of the United States," Sullivan began, "have great admiration for you and your men. Because you are in the real American tradition of a George Washington."[19]

To millions of Americans, this was their first exposure to Fidel Castro. That televised endorsement may be shocking, but in the context of the time it wasn't. Castro was a master of many things, not the least of which was his use of populism as a device to rise to power. It had worked in Cuba, and that hoodwinking had clearly enraptured an American institution like Ed Sullivan.

Col. Batista, after having first served President Carlos Mendieta as Chief of Staff and then serving the two subsequent presidents Jose Barnet y Viageras (1935–36) and Federico Laredo Brú (1936–40), won his first presidential term in 1940.[20] After leaving the country in 1944, he returned and ran again in 1952. When his loss appeared inevitable, he staged an overthrow of the government and closed elections until 1954, wherein he was elected president after running unopposed. Batista's official four-year term began on February 24, 1955.

Fulgencio Batista's Cuba saw growing discontent from the working class and rural farmworkers.[21] By contrast, Castro's vague rhetoric, crafted to infuse non-specific but electrically charged proclamations to the disenfranchised masses, won him popularity among those disgusted with Batista's catering to the aristocracy and outside interests. The political corruption and rigged elections under Batista gave little hope to the majority who felt overlooked that anything would ever change. Castro rode in with the promise of righting the wrongs of the Batista government and, in the most populist terms, giving the country back to its working people. But his 1959 victory was not easily won; his revolution began years before.

Fidel Castro was a law school graduate from the University of Havana.[22] He was a candidate for the Cuban People's Party in 1952, but that election was postponed by Batista. Undaunted, Castro led more than 150 men on an attack of a provincial army post on July 26, 1953. Despite his intention to trigger an uprising against Batista, most of the attackers were killed and Fidel and his brother Raul were captured and imprisoned.

After his release and exile to Mexico, Castro partnered with Ernesto "Che" Guevara to organize a smaller group of guerrillas for another attempt at Batista's army. On December 2, 1956, a group of eighty-one rebels boarded the vessel *Granma* and sailed to the eastern coast of Cuba where all but twelve men were killed or captured.[23] Fidel, Raul, and Che were among the survivors who bolted to the Sierra Maestra mountains where they regrouped. They dubbed themselves the "26th of July Movement," assuming the moniker taken from the date of the original offensive on the Batista regime.

At the same time, the country was falling into chaos. Student insurrectionists waged a bloody revolt on the presidential palace, trade unionists organized strikes, and the economy was in shambles. Batista suspended any form of free assembly, speech, or expression on August 1, 1957.[24] Meanwhile in the mountains, Castro's rebel army had grown from a dozen men to a couple thousand. They set their sights on a violent return, rife with the rhetoric Castro knew would galvanize many more Cubans.

Castro made a direct appeal to the most marginalized individuals, who were also far more likely to take arms. He denounced the capitalist scourge of Batista allowing foreign investment in the country, and he spotlighted the dictator's closure of universities, dissolution of the Senate, and rigged elections as justification for his ousting. Castro touted the nationalization of electricity and telephone services, and he proposed a revolution of inclusivity with redistribution of once-private land. Result-based quotes with no proposed plan, like stating such redistribution would make unemployment "automatically disappear," pumped the starving lower and working classes full of adrenaline. He poured questionable statistics around the simmering peasants like gasoline, claiming 2,800,000 of them lacked electricity due to the corporate control of public services, and that 85 percent of small farmers that paid rent were facing eviction.[25] They didn't need to be told to hate Batista; they just needed an alternative to him.

Revolutionary forces amped up the aggression, and soon there was widespread violence tearing the country apart. Sugar mills and plantations burned as rebel activity further crippled the economy. Batista seized upon the tumult and called for the postponement of the 1958 presidential election from June to November, giving him more time to figure out a plan. Meanwhile, his military took the fight to Castro's rebel forces headquartered in the Sierra Maestra in July, but they were successfully deterred by the 26th of July Movement forces, causing the Cuban army to retreat.

Castro ensured that the rest of the world didn't ignore his proposed revolution. His forces kidnapped American and Canadian workers from the Freeport Sulphur company's mining headquarters and twenty eight US sailors from the Guantanamo Bay base, only to release them days later.[26] Their release wasn't inconsequential, either—he'd accomplished his goal of garnering attention from his northern neighbors.

As the November 3 election drew nearer, Castro threatened violence against both candidates and voters. Ultimately, Batista's chosen successor, Andrés Rivero Agüero, was awarded the presidency. The more moderate Carlos Márquez Sterling won provinces where the votes were certified and supervised, but unchecked ballots elbowed him out of the picture, and Batista's choice was declared the winner. That, for many Cubans, was the final straw.

The US arms embargo resulted in the Cuban army's weapons supply drying up, which equipped Castro's rebel forces to match the army more evenly. Additionally, on December 27, 1958, Che Guevara led the capturing of an armored train filled with weaponry destined for the Cuban army.[27] With their new cache of armaments and the army's evaporated supply, the 26th of July Movement was poised to eradicate those foolish enough to stay and fight.

On the morning of January 1, 1959, Batista fled the country for the Dominican Republic and relinquished the presidency of Cuba. A temporary junta was put in place to govern the country, though Castro's regime ignored it completely, proclaiming victory from the balcony of Santiago de Cuba city hall. On January 8, Castro was prime minister of Cuba.

Castro effected total control by employing more than just his rhetoric. He encouraged mass exodus of those opposed to his rule, largely the older, more affluent citizens. In his first decade in power, somewhere between five hundred thousand and seven hundred thousand took advantage of that, with thousands more bailing out via the Varadero-Miami airlift, small private boats, and even jumping the fence at the US Naval base in Guantanamo.[28] This proved a remarkably effective strategy for Castro, as the median age of the country fell so drastically that by January of 1969, 55 percent of the country was under twenty-five years old. The oldest of that 55 percent had been drinking the Castro Kool-Aid since they were fourteen years old.

On the political front, the new Cuba pledged to remain neutral in the US's conflict with the Soviet Union, though that soon became moot as Cuba's dilapidated economy couldn't function without support. Unemployment and falling prices of Cuban-produced commodities necessitated a mentor with money and resources, and Castro found one in Soviet Prime Minister Nikita Khruschev. In 1960, Cuba signed a trade pact with the USSR and officially got in bed with the Soviets.

Castro's pledge to "give the land to those who till it" hadn't played out as promised.[29] Castro soon began seizing private assets in the name of the government. Almost all farms and ranches were nationalized and converted to state ownership, and by 1969 small farm owners working 30 percent of the land in Cuba were the only private property owners in the country.

The seizure of farms and private land came first, but a more complete assessment came into focus shortly after Castro came to power, when the US Justice Department established the Foreign Claims Settlement Commission. American citizens and companies whose properties were confiscated filed 5,913 claims worth $1.9 billion, roughly $7 billion today.[30] That figure doesn't include thousands of Cuban Americans whose property was confiscated before they fled. US companies with seized assets included Coca-Cola, PepsiCo, Colgate-Palmolive, Texaco, and movie studios Universal and 20th Century Fox. Personal property included homes, ranches, farms, vehicles, cattle, horses, and a Holocaust memorial library in New York City.[31]

But before any of that, in January 1959, sharing the airwaves with acrobats, a comedian, Gaelic singers, and a poodle fashion show, Fidel

Castro got the nod from the trendsetting show that would break the Beatles in the United States.

"With the help of God and our prayers," Ed Sullivan said, "and with the help of the American government, he will come up with the sort of democracy down there that America should have."[32]

★★★

Ricardo Anibal Morales Navarrete was born to Raul Anibal Morales Despau, the judge, and Ines Navarrete Gonzalez, a housewife, on June 14, 1939 in Havana. He was preceded by a sister and brother, Yolanda and Pucho, fourteen years and eleven years his senior, respectively, making Ricardo the miracle baby of the family. Ines was thirty-six when she gave birth to the fairest skinned of all the children—a detail important to Cubans at the time. His father Raul was stately, tall, thin, and stern. He was quick to scold the children at high volume, as was the chain-smoking Ines, though she laughed a lot more than Raul.[33] His position in the courts provided them a comfortable life in Bejucal in a large home that featured Raul's prized aviary, and they remained there until the older children were out of the house.

Raul, Ines, and young Ricardo then moved from rural Bejucal to upscale, urban Vedado Nuevo, into a large floor-through apartment in an impressive building with a colonial/classical style facade and stone-framed windows with pediments above. The entrance was adorned with marble, including the staircases which supported large wooden banisters.

Their apartment featured oversized wooden furniture below gold-framed Cubano impressionist landscapes and a cubist style portrait of Raul playing dominos with friends. Large, majestic Spanish planters stood in the corners of the spacious rooms, and young Ricardo's feet traipsed the marble, tile, and granite floors. The grand apartment overlooked a busy street and was the picture of Cuba that travelers had in mind when imagining the romance of the island. Their housekeeper, Antonio, cleaned, shopped, gardened, and took care of the spoiled miracle boy. It was the embodiment of upper-middle-class life under Batista; the abode of someone of status working in his government.

In 1954, at age fifteen, Ricardo was admitted to St. George School, an exclusive, high-tuition private school located a ten minute walk from the Morales's apartment. Ricardo passed the school's notoriously rigorous entrance exam known to turn away other children of wealthy families. The school itself was in a villa-style mansion outfitted with Victorian furniture and an expansive atrium with gardens. The curriculum centered around international languages, and students were only permitted to speak the language on campus correlating to their grade. Students began with English, then French, German, and Latin; Spanish was forbidden altogether. Ricardo graduated and began law studies at the University of Havana in 1958.

It's hard not to imagine Ricardo having had a tainted view of law as he'd come to know it in Raul Morales Despau's home. Raul had once become embroiled in scandal when he refused to give false testimony on behalf of the state, and the governing law body tried to have him removed from the bench. He fought the accusations and proved he was being framed, which resulted in the crooked legal panel being removed from their posts. Ricardo was also witness to the late night visits from soldiers and the fudged death certificates his father was providing. Those forgeries were preferable to the ones wherein Raul was rousted from bed and brought to the lagoon in Havana where mass executions were carried out by Batista's forces. Raul was called upon to report "natural death" on the spot. None of the above escaped young Ricardo.

The stress of such a job caught up with Raul when he succumbed to a heart attack in 1957. His death before the regime change precipitated a drastic change in the family's status. He'd worked up to his last day, "dying on the bench" as they say, and the elimination of his salary forced Ines to live on his pittance of a pension. All of the children were out of the home by that time, and she sold much of what the family had accumulated over the years and moved from El Vedado Nuevo to El Vedado Viejo which, by comparison, was a more run-down section of the city. She liquidated everything and moved into a small fourth floor walk-up apartment with a single window. Gone were the vases, fine China, artwork, silver, and nearly everything else—Ines's apartment didn't even have a drape covering for the sole window, though she kept the painting of Raul playing dominos.

Yolanda, Ricardo, and Pucho were an aggressive crew, though Yolanda's daughter Lynette described the dynamic more crudely, attributing their outlier behavior to a lineage of warrior blood. "We descend from one of two brothers in the Spanish Reconquista at the Battle of Covadonga in the Year 792 who hacked their way through the opposition army," she said. "When their swords broke they skewered foes with mulberry branches they tore from a tree with their bare hands. You understand we are all *totally* those guys, adjusted for whatever is going on. Every one of us is fundamentally uncivilized. Those are the Morales. We are not polite."[34]

Bearing that in mind, it is no surprise Ricardo would exchange law school for a badge and gun from the revolutionary army. He was an intelligent student but an active child, always on the move, questioning everything and everyone.

"Richard and Pucho were the embodiment of those original Morales brothers who hacked up the opposition with mulberry branches," Lynette said. "My mother [their sister] was the female version of that. That is the image to keep in mind. Normal people puzzle us. We live among them and have learned their ways, but they are as pale shadows to us."[35]

Ines quickly aged beyond her years after Raul's passing, morphing into a shuffling, somber soul with a hunched posture, sheet white hair, and house dresses that became her uniform. A collection of saints watched the apartment from all corners, gazing out from candle holders and statuettes as solemnly as their host who fed them water and sugar. Ines was excessively dramatic and always sorrowful about something, usually the adventures of her restless sons in whose veins coursed the Morales blood. She could sense where their brand of adventure would eventually lead as she heard more and more bombing in the streets.

★★★

While Ricardo was working for G-2, he and Magda's brother, Hector Cornillot, who was working at the Ministry of Commerce, found they were both struggling to resist the same insurrectionist impulses.[36] They began having talks about subverting the Castro regime from the inside and opened their circle a bit as they heard similar sentiments among others. In all, Ricardo and Hector assembled a collective of six or seven willing young men, including César Vega, owner of the popular Havana nightclub Cabaret Las Vegas. The lively spot located near the University of Havana was frequented by college students and Havana's young hipsters.

Vega had been a schoolmate of Fidel Castro and maintained a friendship with him until November 1959 when the adventure-seeking Vega went to Panama to assist in a rebellion.[37] This is said to have fractured the relationship between the two former comrades in revolution. Dissatisfaction with Castro was becoming more commonplace within his government, though any overt signs of subversion were remedied handily by G-2. Such talk needed to be done in dark corners and barely above a whisper. Hector and friends chose Mocambo, a café on the main drag La Rampa to host such talks.

"Americano," Morales's partner on the G-2 police force, was one of those voices with whom Morales was secretly conspiring.[38] Morales brought him to a meeting and introduced him to Hector and the others. They sat around Mocambo, planning options to incite rebellion within the Castro regime. They'd outlined some activities, including setting fire to specific Castro assets and deciding which people would need to be dropped. No one at the table balked when the topic of killing was broached.

Morales needed to get the ball rolling fast. He was concerned that his family's lineage in Batista's government would be found out, but an even more pressing issue arose within G-2. Morales showed up at Hector's house in the summer of 1960, jittery and nervous, which was unusual for him.

"What's wrong?" Hector asked.

"We're being investigated," Morales told him. He'd gotten word that his own intelligence agency was examining both him and Hector. "I'm gonna go find out what's going on." He told his future brother-in-law to have their group start planning their individual exits. Hector wondered aloud how they'd landed on G-2's radar.

"Americano is working against us," Morales confessed.

Americano, the fucking traitor; the one outsider in the circle who Morales had trusted and brought in. He was angry, but he understood business.

"Well," Hector said with a shrug. "You gotta 'off' Americano."

Within days, Morales drew his service pistol while he was patrolling alone with Americano and shot him to death. The discovery of his body drew G-2 investigators' eyes to the Mocambo crew; their days were numbered.

Morales continued to work for G-2 with his head on a swivel, aware that his own people would come for him at any moment. He made sure not to be alone with them at any moment. One afternoon, Morales's patrol car was involved in a crash. He was injured and placed in the hospital with a broken pelvis, under the watchful eye of G-2, who always had a presence in the location. Morales lay incapacitated and largely at the mercy of the secret police; he was sure that would be his end. A local priest he knew well, Father Villaverde, even began visiting and taking his confession.[39] The Villaverdes had grown up a half block from the Woolworth 5 and 10 store, a favorite hangout for the neighborhood kids, young Ricardo included. It was there he befriended the Villaverde brothers, Rafael and Raul, with whom he'd be connected for years.

During his hospital stay, Morales was formally charged with "conspiring against Castro."[40] That charge, coupled with the inevitable revelation that he'd descended from a line of Batista justices, meant a death sentence. There was no proof he'd killed Americano, but it didn't matter in Havana. Father Villaverde must've begun taking his confession because he knew a dead man was laying in that bed, and during one such visit in late July, 1960, Morales said as much to the priest. Villaverde blessed him, assuring him that Jesus Christ absolved him of all sin, and was prepared to walk with him. Morales, though, was ready to walk a different route.

Pucho waited in his idling car at the hospital service entrance as he was instructed by his brother. Upstairs, Morales waited for G-2 to be clear of his room and pulled himself out of bed. He struggled down the corridor to the stairwell, steadying himself on the walls and shuffling across the slick tile as fast as he could before patrol returned to his side of the floor. He ambled down the stairs as the sounds of confusion and chaos rose behind him, and was soon out the service door beside the garbage and laundry. He collapsed in Pucho's backseat as his brother sped out of the loading zone and around the block.

Morales's break from Castro's G-2 meant he'd need to go underground. The agency pursued him for weeks, and he spent August bouncing around safe houses maintained by other Castro dissenters.

"They were chasing me all over Havana," Morales later said.

Everyone else in the Mocambo Cafe rebellion clique realized they were in mortal danger when they heard about Americano's murder. Hector immediately used his travel papers and flew to Mexico. César Vega bailed on his club, heading first to Costa Rica and then Puerto Rico, before settling in Miami.

With Hector already gone, the rest of Magda's family's got their travel papers approved, and things accelerated. Morales had no chance of legally escaping the country, so he told Magda to go with no guarantee when he'd be able to join her. But there was one matter they had to handle first.

On August 30, 1960, Magda and Ricardo were quietly married by a justice of the peace at the courthouse—no family, no guests, no fanfare. The newly married couple would not celebrate with a party or even consummation, rather with Magda's flight to Miami and Morales's escape to the Brazilian embassy, crouched down in Pucho's backseat yet again.

★★★

In early September, Morales entered the Brazilian Embassy in Havana seeking political asylum, beginning an eighty-two day stay he described as a "nightmare."[41] He and the other assembled defectors endured constant harassment while awaiting judgement on their fate in the confines of the majestic, six-story fortress of concrete and stone overlooking the waterfront.

Morales recalled, "There were militia people marching around the embassy compound screaming, '*Paredón*! *Paredón*!'" This expression, translated as "Wall! Wall!", was a reference how Castro's police executed traitors, standing them at a wall while a firing squad ventilated their bodies. It was being made clear they'd be waiting for those seeking to escape Cuba.[42] Each day holed up in the embassy was nerve-wracking, but a return to the streets of Castro's Havana after a failed escape attempt was not an option.

After two and a half months, on November 29, 1960, Morales and five others were granted a tourism visa, and he took a Pan Am flight to Miami. His family, as well as Magda and the Cornillots, had already settled in the city, with some of the men in Magda's family already settled in New York to secure factory work. Hector had flown to Miami via Mexico just after the breakup of the Mocambo gang, and Yolanda and mother Ines set up in a ground floor apartment in a two-story project building on the downtown end of 8th Street in Little Havana. Morales moved in with Magda and her family.

Morales's waiting family wasn't the only group anticipating his arrival in the US. Upon his entry into the Brazilian Embassy in Havana, the Rio de Janiero office of the CIA sent a cable to the agency director stating, "Six Cubans, including Ricardo Anibal Morales y Navarrete, granted asylum [in] Brazilian Embassy, Havana."

His position in G-2 and the uncertainty of his status with Castro's government led to him being singled out and personally tracked. On January 11, 1961, an internal memo was sent to the CIA's Miami training facility, codenamed JMWAVE, spotlighting those very concerns. Their memo expressed that "...Morales has recently joined AMIRON and is a Castro G-2 agent. [We] suggest every effort be made to determine whether this is a penetration attempt."[43] AMIRON was the CIA codename for the Cuban Democratic Revolutionary Front, a centralized organization of anti-Castro exiles that would soon play a much larger role in the US-Cuban conflict.

The Cuban Democratic Revolutionary Front, known as FRD for the untranslated Frente Revolucionario Democrático, was formed to consolidate exiles and form a militia capable of military strikes against Castro.[44] It was initially headed by the leaders of five exile groups—Aureliano Sanchez Arango of Triple A group, Justo Carrillo of Montecristi, Manuel Artime of Revolutionary Recovery Movement (MRR), Ignacio Rasco of the Christian Democratic Movement, and Antonio de Varona of Rescate. They named their military arm Brigade 2506.

The CIA's notifying their JMWAVE training facility of Morales's arrival in the country was particularly noteworthy. JMWAVE had begun covertly working with the FRD exiles, and Morales was a significant prospective asset. The CIA's caution about Morales's G-2 position was coupled with interest in its potential benefits. His first-hand experience in Castro's secret police would be a rare advantage; they'd proceed with caution, but proceed nonetheless.

Morales had not yet attempted to enlist in the FRD, and none of the agencies knew his whereabouts once entering the country. Yet they actively looked for him; on January 20, the CIA confirmed in a dispatch that the recruiter for JMWAVE had already heard of Morales's arrival and alerted the FRD organization.[45] This recruiter was Joaquin Sanjenis Perdomo, known within the agency by his cryptonym AMOT-2. He was the former Chief of Police in Havana under Batista's predecessor Carlos Píro Socarrás, and he was now living in exile in Miami and putting together an elite assassination squad for the CIA.

Chapter Two

Operation 40 (1961)

"The overwhelming majority of anti-Castro exiles in this country hope for an early overthrow of the Castro regime. The exiles feel and believe that this is realizable; thus they are prepared, each on his own level, to contribute to and participate in actions necessary to achieve the objective for a free democratic Cuba which would mean their return to the Island. Most of these Cubans are convinced that US leadership and active participation in this struggle are essential for success. Therefore, they can be expected to follow and support the US in any venture promising an early elimination of Castro."[46]

—"Cuba and Communism in the Hemisphere," National Security Council papers, May 4, 1961.

★★★

Fidel Castro's Cuba was a priority for the Kennedy administration and proved an unsolvable conundrum throughout the president's tenure. They sought to covertly remove the dictator from power without the overt use of military might, relying instead on ingenuity and creative action. One of the earliest was the use of the many Cuban exiles who'd organically formed anti-Castro groups in Miami upon their arrival. These Cubans were bonded by their common desire to stir trouble against Castro, though they all possessed varying visions of a future Cuba.

The US government's formal authorization to enter into a quest to remove Castro from power predated John F. Kennedy's presidency. On March 17, 1960, President Eisenhower approved a CIA-proposed plan compiled in a paper titled "A Program of Covert Action Against the Castro Regime."[47] Their plan, budgeted at a conservative $4.4 million, consisted of four phases:

a. Formation of a Cuban exile organization to attract Cuban loyalties, to direct opposition activities, and to provide cover for Agency operations.

b. A propaganda offensive in the name of the opposition.

c. Creation inside Cuba of a clandestine intelligence collection and action apparatus to be responsive to the direction of the exile organization.

d. Development outside Cuba of a small paramilitary force to be introduced into Cuba to organize, train and lead resistance groups.[48]

The Agency's plan, as outlined above, omitted entirely any mention of the US government's involvement. The use of Cuban exiles in place of American military forces would shield the US from culpability in the interference and overthrow of another government. The CIA document included plans for further masking the management of the assigned exiles: "Agency personnel in contact with Cuban exiles would be documented as representatives of a group of private American businessmen."[49]

The operation's administration level was hidden, which left the issue of the mercenaries themselves. The commandos couldn't appear as assets of the US military in any capacity, so they needed a cover agency. Enter the aforementioned FRD.

The Cuban Democratic Revolutionary Front, the collective comprised of the five anti-Castro groups, was founded on May 11, 1960 after a series of meetings in New York and Miami.[50] It used the guise of a creation of American businessmen, as proposed in the CIA document. The anti-Castro members of FRD's Brigade 2506 began paramilitary training in Panama in July 1960.

With the completion of the initial four organizational tasks, the next stages, as outlined in the Presidential briefing paper of August 1960, listed the next action against Cuba in three phases, all to be executed by the Cuban exiles:

> The initial phase of paramilitary operations envisages the development, support and guidance of dissident groups in three areas of Cuba: Pinar del Rio, Escambray, and Sierra Maestra. These groups will be organized for concerted guerrilla action against the regime. The second phase will be initiated by a combined sea-air assault by FRD forces on the Isle of Pines coordinated with general guerrilla activity on the main island of Cuba. This will establish a close-in staging base for future operations. The last phase will be air assault on the Havana area with the guerrilla forces in Cuba moving on the ground from these areas into the Havana area also.[51]

The expansion of the Cuba program had grown over the course of 1960 and into 1961.[52] In August 1960, an additional $10 million was allocated to it, and in December an additional $28.2 million was obtained by the Bureau of Budget and Planning. The establishment of a base in Guatemala helped expand the exile training under the direction of the US Army Special Forces. Additional sites in Nicaragua and New Orleans were forthcoming, and the JMWAVE station in Miami and the Homestead, Florida air base were both active.

However, the number of recruits only reached half of the expected quota by turn of the year, so recruiting teams were sent to Miami to bolster the numbers. The size of strike force personnel swelled from 644 in January 1961, to 1,443 in mid-April. Their ages ranged from a fifteen-year-old student with forged registration papers to a fifty-four-year-old World War II veteran paratrooper.[53]

In the midst of this complex operation, the US underwent an administration change as John F. Kennedy was sworn in as the 35th President on January 20, 1961. The Cuba project slowed with the personnel shift, though on April 17, the go-ahead was given for the planned strikes into Cuba. However, it turned out Castro was waiting for them.

Castro's intelligence had discovered the training facilities being set up by the US government. In the April debacle at the Bay of Pigs, eight of the attacking planes were shot down, and the remaining eight were damaged.[54] Invading troops from the shore of Girón Beach advanced directly into Castro's troops, numbering in the thousands. William "Rip" Robertson, a former World War II captain turned CIA agent, commanded the ship *LCI Barbara J* into battle, disembarking on Red Beach. All told, more than 1,100 of these attacking exiles were captured and held hostage by the Castro regime. Within three days, the invasion that had been planned for a year was decidedly over.

The US's limited participation beyond planning and preparation came under criticism. Many believed the US's distance from the project led to an absence of support that was missing in Brigade 2506's crucial moments. Dr. Enrique Llaca, one of those captured and ransomed, said, "We were told there would be air cover. Not officially. But it might as well have been official. We all knew the United States had a hand in the matter. We were transported to the training area in United States planes. We were trained by Americans. Our weapons and planes were American. What else could our conclusion be? We are not morons. No one wanted to commit suicide."[55]

Another point of contention in the handling of the project was the shift in level of commitment after the administration change. John F. Kennedy wasn't as engaged with the project as the previous administration had been. After some internal debate, the administration decided to proceed with the plans, but there was a prevailing sense that this wasn't JFK's passion project as it had been Eisenhower's. On April 24, however, White House Press Secretary Pierre Sallinger read a statement in which President Kennedy accepted "full responsibility for the events of the past few days."[56]

Acceptance of that responsibility was eventually passed along from the White House to the CIA, where on June 28, 1961, President Kennedy announced to the press he was considering making changes to the Agency. Two days later, Arthur Schlesinger, Jr., Special Assistant to the President, presented Kennedy with a scathing memo highly critical of the CIA's role in the Bay of Pigs. In it, he stated the CIA "has about used up its quota. Its margin for future error is practically non-existent. One more CIA debacle will shake faith considerably in US policy, at home as well as abroad."[57] It went on to suggest unprofessionalism in the Agency's handing of previous successes, citing "a gross and repeated CIA failing has been its occasional readiness to succumb to the temptation of favorable publicity." Over the course of a year, CIA director Allen Dulles, Air Force General and Deputy Director C.P. Cabell, and Deputy Director of Plans Richard Bissell, Jr., all the top echelon of the of the CIA, retired.[58] During his first year in office, President Kennedy had given both the CIA and Cuban exile groups reasonable cause to feel betrayed.

Both Morales brothers had missed serving in the Bay of Pigs invasion. Pucho was installed in the strike force team, but he suffered an appendicitis attack while in Santo Domingo before the deployment of the team. He was flown from the island for surgery in the States, while Ricardo was recruited by a unit separate from 2506. His role in the ongoing actions against Cuba came in Joaquin Sanjenis's CIA-sponsored side project called Operation 40—an elite specialized unit created parallel to Brigade 2506—and would continue for years after the Bay of Pigs invasion.

★★★

There has been a fair amount written about Operation 40, with varying accounts as to its purpose, its actual use, and the level of the CIA's involvement in its operation. The team has been covered in the pages of books, articles, and testimony. Far more scant, however, is the mention of Operation 40 in any official declassified CIA documents, outside of a couple of casual mentions to an entity referenced by third parties. Its organizer and lead recruiter, Joaquin Sanjenis (sometimes Luis Sanjenis, Jose Sanjenis Perdomo, Sam Jenis, and AMOT-2), another defecting Castro officer, first came to the US seeking asylum in February 1960.[59] He was serving a post in the Ministry of the Treasury when he split from Castro's regime. He became an asset for the CIA and compiled a squad consisting of specialized mercenaries during the assembly of Brigade 2506.

Sanjenis screened all potential Operation 40 candidates whose paperwork was funneled to him from local recruitment stations. An Agency memo regarding the relocation of a recruitment office in Miami dated April 6, 1961, directed personnel to channel incoming applications to "AMOT-2's office for checking."[60] Sanjenis had provided the Agency with the initial information on Ricardo Morales, confirming the exile's arrival in Miami but the FRD's inability to locate him.

Morales and Pucho were eventually found by Sanjenis when he came across their names on a signup sheet at a church on SW 27th Avenue.[61] Operation 40 was designed as an intelligence unit, initially tasked with preparing files on the recruited Cuban exiles to weed out potential Castro operatives. Then, after the planned Bay of Pigs offensive on Cuban soil to depose Castro, Operation 40 was to infiltrate Cuban government offices, secure all documentation for examination, and function as temporary administration while the official reorganization was underway.[62]

After restructuring Cuba's administration, the unit was slated to take on a secondary function. They still needed to obtain classified information not found on paper in government offices, which would then necessitate the interrogation of officials. For some of the more dangerous Castro officers, Operation 40 would need to enforce a more permanent solution. Frank Sturgis, the gringo Operation 40 agent who would later serve as a Watergate burglar, later stated, "[Operation 40] would, upon orders, naturally, assassinate either members of the military or the political parties of the foreign country that you were going to infiltrate, and, if necessary, some of your own members who were suspected of being foreign agents. We were concentrating strictly in Cuba at that particular time."[63]

The Virginia-born Sturgis first met Fidel Castro in 1957,[64] and he then moved to Cuba to train under him, eventually rising to become Director of Security for the Cuban Air Force.[65] He soon began supplying the CIA and FBI with intelligence, then defected to the US on June 30, 1959 after Joaquin Sanjenis tipped him off that Raul Castro had gotten word he was providing information. Sturgis became one of the very few American-born operatives in the CIA's Cuban initiative.

Up in Washington, the Kennedy administration sat with egg on their face after the Bay of Pigs debacle that only seemed to embolden Fidel Castro and add to the myth of the unflappable dictator. The White House continued to devise plans over the next year that would appear in the administration's reports. Throughout the planning and revision process, one fact remained consistent—direct involvement of the US military was off the table. Therefore, the use of more indirect and covert penetration was required.

A November 30, 1961 memo from President Kennedy laid the foundation for his anti-Castro effort, titled "Operation Mongoose." The memorandum stated, "We will use our available assets to go ahead with the discussed project in order to help Cuba overthrow the communist regime."[66] The use of the Cuban exiles was part of the proposed planning, further ensuring that US forces would not be visible in the effort. Its objective, as explicitly stated by US Air Force Gen. Edward Lansdale, was "to help the Cubans overthrow the Communist regime from within Cuba and institute a new government with which the United States can live in peace."[67]

Over the next few months, a host of tactics were created to incite overthrow from the inside, including a propaganda machine to both encourage Cuban revolt while demoralizing Castro. One such tactic, outlined in a January 30, 1962 memorandum, called for a massive air drop of leaflets that placed a bounty for the delivery or assassination of various members of Castro's regime.[68] The list would serve to create dissension, and the last line of the price list would strike a blow to Castro's ego:

a. Informer—$20,000
b. Cell Leader—$40,000
c. Block Leader—$45,000
d. Department Head—$57,000
e. Foreign Communist—$97,000
f. Government Officials—$100,000
g. Castro—.02 cents[69]

After months of strategizing methods to keep US troops off Cuban soil, the administration finally broached the topic of direct US military involvement. If the administration was to initiate an offensive on Cuba, they needed a justification. The extent they were willing to go is most evident in an April 12 memo to Gen. Lansdale from the Joint Chiefs:

> We could develop a Communist Cuban terror campaign in the Miami area, in other Florida cities and even in Washington. The terror campaign could be pointed at Cuban refugees seeking haven in the United States. We could sink a boatload of Cubans enroute to Florida (real or simulated). We could foster attempts on lives of Cuban refugees in the United States even to the extent of wounding in instances to be widely publicized. Exploding a few plastic bombs in carefully chosen spots, the arrest of a Cuban agent and the release of prepared documents substantiating Cuban involvement also would be helpful in projecting the idea of an irresponsible government.[70]

While none of that came to pass, the US did use the CIA-trained exiles in Operation 40 for strategic strikes on Cuban assets. After the stain of the Bay of Pigs, Operation 40 continued to operate under the radar. Sources close to Sanjenis were quoted in a 1975 *New York Times* piece saying after the Bay of Pigs, Sanjenis "expanded his activities here with 'full backing of the CIA.'"[71]

★★★

On June 7, 1963, Ricardo Morales and nine other operatives boarded two seventeen-foot speedboats from the Operation 40 Florida base and headed for the shores of Matanzas, Cuba.[72] At five a.m. the following morning, they disembarked on the Cuban shore and proceeded to set up camp and review their plans for three days before setting out and striking their target.

The Arechabala Corporation Refinery was a multi-million dollar facility standing two miles east of the group's setup on the Bay of Cardenas. The operatives maintained radio contact with the JMWAVE base, staying abreast of intercepted radio transmissions from Cuba regarding security and policing of the waters. The oil tanks of the refinery were in the crosshairs of Morales and the other demolition experts burrowed in the sands of the Matanzas shoreline.

On the third day, the group became self-conscious about having stayed in the same location, and they coordinated with the Florida base for a move. They packed up under cover of night, boarded the two boats, and headed to Cayo Blanco, a mile and a half off the coast of Varadero Beach and northeast of their target in Cardenas. At dawn, they got within a hundred meters of the Cayo shoreline when their first sign of trouble appeared—a massive 110-foot naval frigate chopped through the waters behind the two boats. Morales and the team were undoubtedly spotted. Manolo Oraza, the Operation 40 officer leading the small team, made the call to plow forward. They cranked the speedboats for the coast, confident they'd outrun the ship. The frigate would bottom out if it approached Cayo Blanco's shallow shoreline, so it couldn't pursue much farther anyway.

The Florida base had not provided any intel about naval ships on the route that day nor any days prior. It seemed like a sneak attack, like the Cuban navy was lying in wait for the exiles. But fate makes for far less entertaining fare. Nothing was coming over the radio because the naval frigate wasn't patrolling, nor did it have any intelligence on their mission. Unbeknownst to the invading forces, it just so happened another event, a very unofficial one, had occurred on the same morning as the planned raid.

Fidel Castro wanted to go fishing.

The dictator had directed his navy to the waters off Varadero Beach at sunrise where the biting was to his standards, when the ship came upon the two boats. They gave chase, but the speedboats kept far ahead.

Once ashore, the exile group sent one man up a pine tree to serve as lookout while the others hunkered down and reviewed their plans. Whoever had just discovered them would order a sweep of the shorelines and land masses off the coast. Operation 40 needed to hit the target that night.

"The frigate is back!" It was the lookout atop the tree, shouting down to the troop. The ship had approached within a hundred fifty meters, close enough that Morales could read the *Las Villas No. 57* printed on the side. They crouched and watched as four heavily armed men left the ship, loaded into a small motorboat, and sped toward the shoreline. The exile brigade instinctively raised their weapons and set their scopes on the approaching soldiers, but halted, deciding to wait for the men to come ashore rather than allow their gunfire to give away their position.

The exiles slipped back into the brush on the shoreline, out of sight from the frigate, and watched the four Cuban soldiers come ashore. The exiles allowed the approaching men to come into the thicket and then leapt out, shouting to drop their weapons.

The Cuban soldiers hit the ground, but one of them fired off two rounds from his submachine gun. The exiles returned fire, striking and killing two of the soldiers, and capturing the other two. There was no doubt that the troops on the ship had heard the exchange of gunfire and would launch reinforcements. The exiles would be sitting ducks for an approaching armada and air assault if they stayed.

They bound the Cuban soldiers' hands, boarded the speedboats with their prisoners, and sped the hell out of Cayo. The plan was to outrun the frigate, hit the refinery in broad daylight, and take to the water again, back to the Florida base with their two prisoners.

Oraza's boat sped through water too shallow and ground to a halt, bottoming out as the battleship closed in on them. The exiles' second boat circled back to Oraza's when it was obvious he couldn't maneuver the motor to free it. Morales and the others jumped out and began pushing the boat as Oraza wriggled the motor, though to no avail. The water began to pop around the struggling exiles as the Cuban soldiers began firing four-inch shells at them. Mud clogged the churning pump on Oraza's boat, and the engine growled and began to flame.

The ship was gaining. They wouldn't keep missing for long. The Operation 40 agents returned fire while still trying to rock the boat free. Evangelio Rufin was hit in the back in the chaotic exchange and fell into the water.

Fuck the boats. The team helped Rufin to his feet, grabbed the two hostages, and stomped through the shallow water to the shoreline of the Cayo.

The frigate couldn't move any closer to shore, and the mercenaries dodged gunfire, landing in the swampy channels in the Cayo brush. They followed a path to a canal and slowed when they came upon an eighteen-foot boat, where an old man was fishing. He froze, fear in his eyes, thinking the Castro militia had come upon him in the swamp. The exiles explained that they needed help getting away from the navy and whatever forces had been dispatched. Castro's men likely saw the hostages and wouldn't turn away with men of their own held captive.

"I don't have enough gasoline," the fisherman said. One of the soldiers placed a rifle against his stomach, which was sufficient to facilitate his help. The twelve men boarded the boat, which lowered its top edge nearly to the waterline. The fisherman crept along, trying to keep the vessel from taking on too much water over the top. A mosquito landing on one of the soldiers would've sent the boat under.

The operatives shot each other looks when they heard planes buzzing overhead, no doubt Castro's Air Force searching for them. They took cover under a sail they unfurled and pulled over themselves. The old man followed the canal out to sea and reported the frigate was no longer in the open water. They continued to listen for planes as the boat crept along, eventually coming upon a thirty-six foot fishing boat marked *Cardenas Fishing Cooperative*. The old man stopped beside the larger boat and asked for gasoline, but the captain was no doubt preoccupied by the sight of a dozen soldiers crawling out from under a tarp. He forgot the gasoline request.

"I've wanted to get away from this island a long time," he confessed to the exiles. "I will go with you to Florida."

They had their ride. They all loaded into the fishing boat and made it to the Florida Keys on June 12 without incident. The US Coast Guard responded and took everyone into custody, while an ambulance carted Rufin to the hospital. Morales and the rest of the Operation 40 crew were released, but the two hostages and fisherman were detained.

New York Times sources close to Sanjenis reported that by the mid-1960s, his Operation 40 was going full throttle, working with a budget of about $2 million a year. It also had logistical support in the form of a private plane for members traveling between south Florida and several South American countries.

"It was like a small secret army," one Cuban recalled to *The New York Times*.[73] Morales would serve that secret army for a few more years, with his final mission into Cuba involving the involuntary commandeering of a military helicopter without Operation 40 knowledge. He directed the pilot from an air base in Cuba to fly him to a designated spot, likely with a gun at his ribcage or at least the mention of one.

As the chopper neared the location, Ricardo directed the pilot to lower it closer to the ground, as he needed to hit a small target from directly above. Lower still, steadied and hovering, Morales opened the side door and leaned out, dropping his parcel on its mark. Bingo.

Before closing the door, Morales pulled out a camera and snapped a photo of the dozen roses lying perfectly centered on Raul Morales Despau's grave.

★★★

If the Bay of Pigs debacle wasn't confirmation that US intervention in Cuba was slipping from Kennedy's priority list, the events of October 1962 were. The peak of Cold War fears of nuclear annihilation came in the staredown between President Kennedy and Soviet Premier Nikita Khrushchev over the placement of Russian nuclear armaments in Cuba. After a warning to Khrushchev from Kennedy, the White House received confirmation via surveillance photos of military build-up in Cuba. The pictures, taken by US aircraft on October 14, showed the construction of bases housing medium-range and intermediate-range ballistic nuclear missiles in Cuba.[74]

So began the collision course between two global superpowers with the capability to shred the planet, as the Joint Chiefs of Staff supported both an air strike to destroy the missiles and a subsequent US invasion of Cuba. A more diplomatic approach touted by some in the administration called for continued warnings to the USSR and further monitoring of the military build-up. Kennedy landed between the two options and ordered a naval quarantine of Cuba on October 22, cutting off incoming supplies and weaponry in the seas surrounding the island. Khrushchev responded by calling the quarantine an "act of aggression" and stated the Soviet ships would proceed past the blockade, potentially setting up a cataclysmic game of chicken.[75] That, combined with continued surveillance photos indicating the Russian missile launching points nearing completion, slid the DEFCON number up to 2, signaling a highly elevated global threat.

Fear gripped Americans as nuclear holocaust preparation became part of their lives, from "duck and cover" drills in schools, wherein children hid under their desks, to the construction of fallout shelters in public buildings. President Kennedy was posed with a lose-lose situation, risking destructive military action in the short term to limit growth of communist might in the long term.

Ultimately, the two leaders lowered their sabers, with each side offering a concession. Khrushchev agreed to dismantle Cuban missiles if Kennedy pledged to not take military action against Russia's outpost in the Caribbean and to remove American missiles from Turkey. Each disarmament was a win for both nations, given the proximity of Cuba to the US and Turkey to Russia.

The resultant agreement to go hands-off on Cuba turned down the heat on the escalating threat haunting Americans daily, keeping the US out of a globally catastrophic exchange with the Soviets. The US would privately violate that oath in its continued use of covert Operation 40 deployments, like the Arechabala Refinery raid foiled by outdoorsman Fidel Castro. But the US's overarching message suggesting the end of overt engagement with Cuba was heard loud and clear by the exile community in the US. They saw it as a broken promise, plain and simple.

John F. Kennedy's assassination on November 23, 1963 devastated and frightened a nation captivated by the young president's charisma and inspiring messaging. The question of Cuba remained, and President Lyndon B. Johnson sought broader action with the implementation of the Organization of American States (OAS) embargo on Cuba.[76] Yet the Johnson administration didn't shy from more active, targeted measures on the ground. The Joint Chiefs of Staff recommended to Johnson actions "involving the employment of covert assets to conduct interdependent operations, including the covert collection of intelligence, propaganda actions, economic denial actions, and externally mounted sabotage operations against Cuba."[77] The exiled Cuban operatives were not out of work just yet.

Operation 40 continued to service the CIA, though not solely in Cuban-related conflicts. Ricardo Morales was tapped to be part of an even more select group of nineteen Operation 40 members who would become contracted agents of the CIA for a specialized, high-risk assignment.

Chapter Three Belgians in the Congo (1964)

Cuba wasn't the only crisis in which the CIA had become embroiled in the early 60s. The perceived threat of communism and its spread was the hot-button issue of the American political landscape, and the Belgian Congo had become a contested area after winning its independence from Belgium in June 1960. The installation of new Congolese Prime Minister Patrice Lumumba was of particular concern, as US intelligence had identified him as a communist. As predicted, Lumumba turned to Russia for military and financial assistance to prevent the West from becoming involved.[78] The United States was globally touting the call against the spread of communism, and therefore would be expected to lead the charge in situations where it posed a significant threat.

As in the case of Cuba, the US government became involved clandestinely in the Congo, seeking for the removal of Lumumba while itself remaining vaporous. Congolese opposition forces assassinated Lumumba in January 1961, beginning political jockeying and conflict that would continue for years. The subsequent military-controlled government under Congolese Army Chief of Staff Joseph Mobutu was intended to serve as an interim body. It began to receive US operational funding, and this supply wouldn't cease for years.

A special contingency fund was established under the Kennedy administration on June 21, 1961 to further support the stability of the Congo.[79] The fledgling government's requests for financial assistance continued, substantiated by threats of involvement by rival communist governments, mutiny attempts within Mobutu's Congolese army, and the outbreak of rebel violence. Now committed, the US continued to support the effort lest they lose the African country to Soviet control. More critical was control of the Congo's uranium—a vital component in nuclear weaponry. The prospect of the enemy's unmonitored mining of the resource was on the minds of those in the White House.

Rebel factions, some united politically and others tribally, were splintering off throughout the country. In August 1964, the province of Stanleyville fell to rebel forces, this particular band calling themselves "Simbas," the Swahili word for lions. Simba rebel forces, receiving support from the Soviets and China, had taken Stanleyville and held several hundred Westerners hostage in the US consulate building in the city.

A troop of three thousand Belgian and Congolese soldiers, as well as mercenaries from Rhodesia and South Africa, were coordinated for a Stanleyville raid and retrieval of the captives.[80] This mission was titled Operation Flagpole. A group of nineteen soldiers, not included on paper as part of the aforementioned collective, would emerge from this mission as the MVPs.

★★★

Morales sat for an interview with polygrapher Victor White on February 10, 1964.[81] White's findings would be added to the comprehensive file on Ricardo before his addition to the CIA payroll as a contract agent at the promised rate of $200 per month.[82] The payment was to be deposited in a savings account in Miami, set up by agents in Magda's name.[83] Morales was one of a subset of Operation 40 assets recruited for a special deployment, about which he was told very little. The handful of mercenaries were told only that they'd be going overseas to continue the fight against communism, and that was likely all they needed to agree.

The month prior, Morales was first approached by Agency case officer Kenneth Sakovich to serve on a paramilitary team being assembled.[84] In late February, the CIA sought operational clearance for Morales to serve as radio operator and leader for paramilitary infiltration.

Morales was given a more extensive psychological interview with intellectual tests on June 3, the results of which made him a strong candidate for the CIA operation.

"Mr. Morales seems to be fairly understanding of people," the report stated, "and he tries to put himself in the place of others to understand their views. But he is not just a good arbitrator, for his is a forceful personality capable of exerting a good deal of influence on those around him. Mr. Morales is a complex person."[85]

The assessment concluded, "Mr. Morales impresses us as an above average man for his job, compared to other assessed Cubans."

In addition to these assessments, Morales was in training for a new mission which at first seemed like just another Operation 40 jaunt into Cuba. However, the addition of the new psychological interviews and polygraphing seemed to indicate otherwise. Additionally, his return to a secret training camp, now for an extended period of nine months, also suggested something more complex was afoot.

Morales and the other eighteen mercenaries selected for Operation Flagpole continued their training at two CIA training camps under military cover, codenamed ISOMETRIC and MKCOSMOS. Morales received extensive training in demolition and explosives, including the use of C4, a malleable, claylike explosive that can be wrapped around objects to be detonated when affixed to a blasting cap. He was taught to use complex weaponry like the .57mm recoilless rifle which was more like a small, shoulder-mounted cannon than a gun.

The CIA was arming the exiles with training beyond what traditional rank and file soldiers might receive. By the end of the nine months, Morales and his cohorts had ample instruction and practice in mapping, patrol, raids, jumps, communications, demolition, counterinsurgency, clandestine movement, covert actions, survival, and psychological warfare. Morales would later say of those nine months, "I received the best training available."[86]

William "Rip" Robertson was to command the operation for which the select group of exiles had been chosen. Robertson was one of two US commanders who plowed forward without US air support into the Bay of Pigs conflict, disembarking on Red Beach and fighting beside his Cuban soldiers. Robertson had earned the loyalty and respect of the exiles, and he was one of the reasons Morales committed to the project when initially recruited.

In September, after those nine months of specialized training, Morales and his team were loaded into a military transport plane with blacked-out windows.[87] The squad transferred flights multiple times over a three-day period, each time flying blind in a transport with obstructed windows. Finally, in the final half hour of the trek, Robertson unveiled a map of the Congo, and the team knew their destination.

The map was marked with color-coded zones indicating which sections of the country were still controlled by the Congolese government and which had fallen under rebel control. The larger mission was to stabilize the government and keep it from the hands of communist interests. Robertson's Cubans would be attached to a larger unit called 5 Commando Brigade, or "The Wild Geese," as they were dubbed and immortalized in the 1978 film. The brigade was commanded by Maj. Mike Hoare, a former British officer and soldier of fortune.[88]

The Wild Geese had their sights set on Stanleyville, the city under Simba control since August, and they were specifically tasked with freeing the Western diplomats held hostage in the consulate. The exiles were first recruited back in January to help secure the Congo's contested region, but that changed once Americans' lives hung in the balance. Time was of the essence—the Simba rebels had already executed 137 Congolese captives accused of being European sympathizers.[89]

The combat between the Congolese army and Simba rebels presented a savagery like nothing the civilized world had seen. The Wild Geese, fighting beside the Congolese army, would witness their torture of the men and women they encountered. Further, the Simbas captured parts of Stanleyville using unusual forms of black magic. A few hunkered Americans described watching their own capture from a window in the consulate building as a bare chested witch doctor walked down the street below chanting and waving palm branches. The 1,500 Congolese army troops who'd formed a blockade in front of the consulate dropped their weapons in fear and ran, leaving the building exposed to a group of three hundred Simbas with spears and bows.[90] The soon-to-be hostages at the window watched in awe as the army withered before the witch doctor's voodoo. The Simbas proceeded to take the occupants hostage, adding to the total hostage count, which was already in the thousands.

The deployment of Rip's Operation 40 Cubans introduced them to a brand of violence and disregard for human life they weren't expecting: a pack of cannibalistic Sima rebels who would rape, burn, impale, dismember, and disembowel.[91] Morales was particularly affected by the carnage; images of the savage slaughter he encountered were permanently burned in his head. Yet he remained fully committed to the mission.

During the battalion's advance through the jungles toward Stanleyville, a nearly thousand-mile trek in Jeeps with mounted machine guns, they came across a small village destroyed by the Simbas. Mutilated bodies lay in the open before burned shacks and terrified Congolese civilians, many still hiding under debris and in the underbrush. As the 5 Commando team marched through the area, the sight of a wide-eyed little Congolese girl, five or six years old, caught Morales's eye. She stood alone, her family perhaps dead. Who knew what she'd just seen?

Morales was struck—the girl's face was blank. She wasn't crying, her face bore no fear. Rather she watched with curiosity as the white people with guns walked through. Morales's partners watched as he broke from the men and walked to her, saying something to her in French. He knelt, and she climbed on his back, wrapping her arms around his neck, and they rejoined Rip and the Cubans.

"Okay," Morales said. "Let's go."

The mercenaries laughed initially, but the laughter morphed in a comic disbelief as their partner carried her throughout the day. Where her family was and who she'd left behind was not of consequence.

"She was safer with me," Morales later said.

The girl stayed with the Operation 40 crew. They fed her, tucked her away as safely as possible when sleeping, and Morales continued to transport her on his back all day as they advanced. One day as he and the passenger on his back caught up to the team, one of the other Cuban mercenaries pointed over at him.

"Esta el mono," he said. In English—"Here's the monkey." With that insignificant joshing of soldiers in combat, Morales's lifelong handle was born. Only his closest circle and those with him in the Congo knew the origin.

★★★

Morales's innate battle skills were intertwined with a recalcitrance that made his service in Rip's brigade memorable for the team. He had a photographic memory and spoke English, Spanish, and French, which factored into his high-priority status for recruitment.[92] But Morales's oversized presence was tough to deal with at times. One of his common amusements was waking up the troop in the middle of the night by detonating a couple of hand grenades, undoubtedly for his edification alone.[93] Morales was removed from the operation when case officer Alexander Ratwick terminated him for a security violation. Morales sought information about the operation, "going so far as contacting wives of agents committed on Operations."[94] The memo concluded with the officer's judgment that Morales was "not recommended for re-use."

During a future deposition, Morales told a slightly different version of events.

"We got in a brawl with the CO, the case officer" he said. "The whole team."[95]

Regardless of which version happened, Morales remained on the team. Agency officer Bruce Cheever advised the Chief to "disregard previous cancellation" as Morales was "being utilized by [the] Special Operations Division."[96]

Joaquin Sanjenis's conflicts with other complex leadership personalities proved to be a challenge for the CIA. Back in June of 1961, the Agency had to get involved in disputes between Sanjenis and Jose Miro Cardona, the first Prime Minister under Castro who'd defected and joined the efforts against Cuba.[97] Miro and Manuel Antonio de

Varona, also a former Cuban Prime Minister now defected, began a smear campaign against Sanjenis. In addition to managing an international campaign, the CIA had to handle these squabbles in the Miami JMWAVE station and sift through allegations as significant as possible misappropriation of FRD funds and as petty as Sanjenis being accused of "bragging" about CIA support. The WAVE station suggested sending Senjenis away on an "unofficial mission" to Louisiana for a cooling-off period and the ancillary benefit of setting up "independent anti-Castro assets throughout Louisiana."[98]

The flurry of memos hitting CIA desks about reassignments, cancellations, and violations regarding the Cuban exiles was evidence that the US military was not dealing with the obedient automatons they may have been used to. This was a concession the US government made in order to yet again keep its participation in a violent campaign invisible.

Not long after the exiles' deployment to the Congo, the troop uncovered a curious detail during a bombing raid on the rebels. When the CIA operatives and rebel guerrilla soldiers began cursing each other out in Spanish, the exiles realized Cuba had joined the fight.

Castro's army was there.

The Cuban dictator had aligned with the rebel forces and lent troops to help the Soviet-sponsored overthrow of the Congo. And while Castro was only there in spirit, Che Guevara was there in the flesh. He'd resigned his ministerial position in Cuba, forfeiting his citizenship, and he threw in with the guerrillas, boots on the ground. When The Wild Geese discovered Castro's Cuban army was present, a new fire was ignited under their asses.

Morales had been in the Congo since September, chopping his way through the sweltering jungle for nearly two months when, finally, on November 26, Rip Robertson told the team they would reach Stanleyville that day. Morales deposited his young traveling companion in the care of a Congolese army troop on their way back to base. The Wild Geese were likely on the precipice of heavy combat in Stanleyville, and the girl would be in mortal danger if she stayed with them. The coalition of Belgian and Congolese soldiers and The Wild

Geese was slated to converge on the city, destroy the Simbas, and free the hostages.

★★★

Ten-year-old David McAllister had added another shell casing to his little collection.[99] There were more on this day, for some reason, and the promise of hunting so many had him excited. Guns were scary, sure, but this improvised Easter egg hunt kept thoughts like that at bay.

Young David and his four-year-old sister Ruthie had been held for three months at a mission compound guarded by fiery Simbas. They shot their weapons skyward that morning, agitated, shouting at each other and at the hostages—twenty-five missionaries kept eight kilometers outside Stanleyville in their mission house. These captives weren't diplomats, businessmen, or CIA employees holed up in the consulate, rather they were missionaries, members of the non-denominational Unevangelized Fields Mission (UFM), stationed in the Congo to spread the word of Jesus Christ to the impoverished.[100] Fourteen of the twenty-five captives were children, like David and Ruthie.

Tensions were high as the Simbas accused the missionaries of using a radio in the mission house to call the planes flying overhead. Of course, none of the missionaries, mostly Americans, knew anything about the planes nor believed that a transistor radio could contact the armed forces. But they were scared; their captors were wild, unpredictable. Suddenly, the adult hostages heard a directive come over the radio.

"Men, women, and children have no scruples; kill them all."[101]

The Simbas gathered the missionaries from around the compound and led them all into the house. Ruthie whispered to her father, Paul McAllister, standing beside her.

"Daddy, are they going to kill us now?"[102]

Once inside, the Simbas separated them. The men were led out to the front yard while the women and children were told to sit. Furious Simbas began smashing up the house and shooting holes in the walls. Bullets flew everywhere, injuring two of the hostages inside.

Then gunshots came from outside, followed by Paul McAllister's cry, "You've killed my best friend!"[103] Beside him lay Hector McMillan, shot dead. McAllister then took a round and dropped to the ground, too. He played dead next to his friend. It saved his life.

★★★

Morales looked up as another plane flew overhead. Rip's Cubans had watched the air traffic that day as they drove the final stretch into Stanleyville, and they knew they were late to the party. When the Cuban exiles blazed into the center of town, they encountered no gunfire and no screaming. Uniformed groups of soldiers were moving about the town, leading the hostages freed from the consulate. It was done—no one had waited for The Wild Geese. The overhead planes were indeed part of the offensive that had deposited teams of Belgian paratroopers into the town. The mission had been accomplished, and the hostages were freed. There stood the Cuban Wild Geese, their vehicles stopped, watching the cleanup and gathering of the hostages. For Rip's team, this was an empty climax to the two-month mission, not to mention the nine months of training prior.

Amid the busy scene, a tall, thin American man bounded down the street, hopping from one group of soldiers to another, pleading for their help. The man, Al Larson, had just been freed from his captors outside Stanleyville.[104] He explained to the mercenaries that he was the chief of the UFM, and a group of his missionaries were still being held by Simbas at the mission house located eight kilometers from where they stood. He asked the soldiers to come with him to check on them.

The Belgians and Congolese army immediately said no, but Rip heard Larson's story, walked to his Cubans, and conferred in Spanish. He returned to Larson.

"We'll do it," he said.

Robertson ordered his men and Larson into the two Jeeps with mounted machine guns. They ventured out of Stanleyville into the most dense stretch of gunfire yet—a five-mile barrage of nonstop assault. They blasted their way through anything that moved.

Morales was operating the mounted machine gun in the rear when he felt a burn rip through his back, just beside his spine. He winced in pain, knowing he'd been hit, but he gripped the gun and kept shooting. If he took his eyes off the rebel gunmen and ceased to fire on them, the path would be blocked and the battalion would be put at risk. He was the only one hit on that harrowing ride; the Simbas obviously didn't prioritize marksmanship training as high as witch doctor spells.

Morales kept at it for the last couple of miles, standing and firing, warm blood streaming down his back into the crack of his ass.

Simbas had fired on the mission house and then inexplicably abandoned the hostages inside. Some missionaries had taken to the surrounding woods to hide from the possibility of returning Simbas. They peeked out when they heard the Jeeps ride into the compound. They didn't recognize the nondescript green fatigues with no markings that the soldiers were wearing, but they were obviously safe—Al Larson, the mission chief, was in one of the Jeeps.

Within fifteen minutes, all the living missionaries were loaded onto the vehicles, and they were told to tuck their heads down between their knees because they would likely encounter more gunfire on their way to the airport. Once it began, hot shell casings were bouncing all over the Jeep. Four-year-old Ruthie climbed onto the lap of burly Juan Tamayo who took the red bandana off his head—he wore it to distinguish himself from the Simbas as he was the only black Cuban in the brigade—and draped it over hers to protect her from the casings. Her older brother David wasted no time in crawling around the Jeep collecting his prizes.

Miraculously, or more likely due to the ineptitude of the rebels, no one was hit on the way out. They arrived at the airport where a plane was waiting to take the missionaries out of Africa. Without much conversation—everyone was shell-shocked from the events of the past few hours—the missionaries parted from their saviors.

The majority of Rip's Wild Geese went back to the US on December 5, but Morales and a wounded soldier named Alberto Perez Martinez stayed behind.[105] The squad couldn't wait for Martinez's date of discharge, December 8. Morales, his thirst for mission never satiated, volunteered to stay and look after his compatriot while nursing his own bullet wound. A CIA memo dated December 1 sought authorization to leave him with Perez, stating "Morales is an intelligent English-speaker who should cause no security threat. His minor wound all but healed."[106]

The two CIA operatives returned to the States on a December 11 flight into New York's Kennedy Airport, though Morales wouldn't stay for long.[107] The war against the communists was not over—not in the Congo, and certainly not beyond its borders. Morales reenlisted for continued service in the Congo, which was granted no doubt in part due to his high operational status in the Agency. A December 1964 CIA fitness evaluation reported that "Morales showed surprising leadership capability...he is definitely recommended for special ops in a leadership capacity."[108]

On December 15, he signed an Agency agreement stating he "wouldn't divulge, publish, or reveal by work, conduct or other means, any intelligence information" related to his operations.[109] His pay was increased to $370 per month while in the Congo and $270 while in the US.[110]

★★★

Morales's tenure as a CIA operative fighting communist-supported Congo rebels would last until August 26, 1965. The African country would court instability for decades, and communism was certainly not a dead issue. Congolese General Mobutu secured power from opposing forces and eventually renamed the country the Republic of Zaire to shed its history of contention. He ruled for decades amid corruption and exploitation. Che Guevara even bailed after his failed efforts supporting the rebels, fleeing the Congo for Tanzania, and eventually landing in a safe house outside Prague.[111]

While Operation 40 remained intact after the offensives in Cuba and the Congo, the group's focus changed. One Cuban source who was approached by Sanjenis to join in 1962 refused the offer. This source remained close to federal agencies, stating that Operation 40's mission had morphed into "domestic snooping, plain and simple."[112] He explained the group pivoted from focusing on Castro's Cuba to America's Cubans.

"As far as I know they haven't discovered a single Castro spy here," he said, "but they sure made many detailed reports, including gossip, about personal lives of all prominent Cubans…usurping the functions of the FBI."[113]

By 1970, Sanjenis's operation had reportedly shrunk to a handful of men with nothing much to do except update existing files on Cubans in the US. Sanjenis retired from the CIA in 1972 when friends say the Agency presented him with a secret medal for his service. The documentation of the Cubans under surveillance was filed in Washington after the closure of his office.[114]

Sanjenis's fate after Operation 40 is a little more mysterious, tinged with the brand of outré that serves as fuel for today's Internet conspiracy theorists. A 1975 *New York Times* article about Cuban exiles serving the CIA stated Sanjenis Perdomo died in 1974.[115] Some more recent blogs, wikis, and message board posts theorize that he was the doorman at the Dakota on the night Mark David Chapman killed John Lennon in 1980.[116] The more aggressive entries posit that Sanjenis was complicit in the assassination, serving the CIA in a plot to eliminate the musician.

With the termination of the exiles' service for the Agency, 1960s South Florida saw an influx of unemployed young men, bellies full of fire. The Cuban demographic had disproportionately grown in Miami, especially in Little Havana. Morales was now left in the US to fend for himself, as were the other Cuban operatives with their formal ties to the CIA cut. The men were highly skilled, though their specific skillset learned at the behest of the CIA and Special Forces left few mainstream opportunities.

In August 1965, Morales returned to Miami for his longest period of uninterrupted time with Magda and their two boys, Raul and Rick, Jr. The demolition expert had lost none of his desire to act out against Cuba, however, and he had a few hundred other CIA-trained operatives to work beside.

PART TWO
RICHARD

Chapter Four The Hottest Spot North of Havana (1966)

Miami's Little Havana section measures just over ten square miles, bordered to the north and east by the Miami River, the west by 37th Avenue, and the south by US-1.[117] Its dense concentration of Cuban residents and rich culture traces back to 1962 when the *Miami News* building was converted into the Freedom Tower.[118]

The narrow seventeen-story Spanish Renaissance-style monolith with ornate cupola and spire piercing the sky is located downtown on Biscayne Boulevard. The newspaper tenant vacated the property in 1957, and the building sat empty for five years until the passage of the Migration and Refugee Assistance Act.[119] That legislation provided monetary assistance to refugees, particularly those fleeing from Cold War-era communist countries. It also extended the terms of the Fair Share Refugee Act, allowing nearly twenty thousand refugees to enter the US under the Attorney General's parole authority from 1960–1965.[120]

The former *Miami News* tower was repurposed as an assistance hub for the throngs of Cuban refugees. Its Cuban Assistance Center helped thousands of new residents transition into society. The settling of many Cuban refugees near the Center in areas like Riverside and Shenandoah rapidly reformed the population and culture of the mostly Jewish district. Little Havana was born.

For the refugees, leaving Havana behind also meant leaving an environment with a personality and style uniquely its own. It wasn't a fair trade, or even a trade at all—the new Little Havana hadn't yet developed any identity to offer. Two-story square apartment buildings of cinder block were separated by overgrown, empty lots. The neglected stretches of vegetation were havens for the lizards, snakes, and frogs soon to be evicted by the new arrivals. Mosquitos in astounding number danced in the humidity. Freedom came at an inglorious price.

Tens of thousands of refugees rapidly gave this characterless city a new flavor, opening bodegas, cafés, and stores. After a few years, the Grand Union supermarket on 14th Street was well stocked with Cuban food, and if a specialty ingredient wasn't on a shelf there, it would be at the corner bodega. The *bolita* man went door to door collecting for the illegal Cuban lottery, and the café at 12th and Flagler offered a street-side order of *café con leche* and became the central hangout for locals. *La Cubanisma* radio WQBA 1140 AM played out of car windows, in bakeries, and on transistor radios atop tables hosting games of dominos in the park. Just like that, between the Miami River and 37th Avenue, Cuba was in everything one tasted, heard, and saw.

Many of the refugees in Little Havana shared family ties from back home, so an informal network sprung up and made assimilation easier for many. That network was convenient for the hundreds of CIA-trained exiles returning to their new home. Eventually, Little Havana was filled with residents that either knew each other's families from Cuba or fought beside each other for the CIA. The latter group wasn't ready to forfeit that battle just because the US seemingly had.

In the first half of the '60s, parallel to the US government's covert campaign against Cuba, small anti-Castro activist groups had formed throughout the burgeoning Cuban community. Members were loosely interwoven throughout the different groups, many serving several cabals at once. The activities and reach of the individual groups varied—some were more violent than others, some were active in Miami alone, and others were acting out against perceived pro-Cuban targets in cities across the US.

The groups kicked up the intensity of their actions after the Kennedy administration's failures. Flyers with anti-communist doctrine were commonly distributed, and explosive components became a hot commodity. In short time, bombs were going off all around the city. The ease with which Miami turned to tinder was precipitated by a few factors.

Many members of Miami's anti-Castro groups had served Brigade 2506 and/or Operation 40 and were therefore knowledgeable clandestine operators in the business of explosives. The Little Havana groups weren't replicating the structure of social activist organizations, but rather that of the paramilitary strike forces they'd served. That, coupled with the top-tier training they'd received, presented groups with a deep roster of highly qualified volunteers with violent ambition.

Morales later testified to the size of the underground operation, saying, "Oh, there were so many groups at the time that we [would] reload practice hand grenades, and there were about three or four bomb factories going on in Miami, and we were giving a helping hand to whatever group [wanted] to get and assemble bombs."[121]

The growing supply of materials was another factor. C4 plastic explosives, blasting caps, and other components for bombs had become widely available due to the proliferation of groups and their CIA-connected members.

"Miami was a powder keg," Morales said. "There were pounds and pounds of C4 and dynamite and blasting caps."[122]

The groups, though separate, were all part of the same overarching mission—the crippling of Castro's Cuba and the snipping off of any tentacles that reached into the US. Therefore, supplies were often willingly shared between groups. Publicity for bombings and the resultant credit for them was important to each group, so in that way competition did exist, but the singular mission was most important in the early years of the anti-Castro groups. One could often find explosives free of charge in Little Havana's network. "In terms of money," Morales continued, "it cost nothing. Anyone could, you know—'You got any C4?' 'Yes, I've got fifty pounds.' 'Okay. Let me have ten pounds.'"[123]

The final element to the perfect storm in Miami was the unpreparedness of local law enforcement. In 1960, the Public Safety Department of Dade County (PSD) consisted of 623 sworn officers. They were responsible for both policing the city streets and carrying out law enforcement operations at the Port of Miami and Miami

International Airport.[124] This new refugee population, partnered with a new brand of politically motivated crime, presented the PSD with an unexpected task. The shell-shocked department was taken by surprise with the addition of an entirely foreign culture being dropped into the city.

This provided the anti-Castro groups fertile ground in which to grow their operations. The earliest incarnations included the aforementioned FRD, comprised of the heads of five exile groups, whose military branch provided the CIA its Brigade 2506 soldiers. The most explosive growth, however, came after the return of the mercenaries.

Dr. Orlando Bosch, a Cuban pediatrician turned overzealous anti-Castro militant, ran MIRR (Insurrectional Movement of Revolutionary Recovery, translated) which organized raids into Cuba and conducted bombings of Cuban assets in the US.[125] Bosch said he was approached by Evelio Duque of the ECA (Anti-Communist Cuban Army, translated) who proposed a merger, indicating his group might be getting CIA backing.[126] Together they presented a plan to the Agency, but it didn't advance.

Some groups were wise enough to use propaganda effectively, and possibly honestly, in their campaign. Bombing group Commandos L issued a brochure outlining how the local law enforcement's seizure of their weapons and explosives was enabling Castro to remain in power. They itemized losses from seven separate raids beginning in 1963, telling residents of Little Havana that US authorities had dealt a blow to the war against Castro by taking $52,512 in arms meant for use by the exiles.[127]

Federal officials seemed to confirm the success of this messaging, and the community expressed supportive sentiment for the exile mission. When asked about police efforts in Little Havana, one official told *The Miami Herald* that "public sympathy and empathy for the Cuban exile cause is such that it would be difficult in obtaining a conviction."[128]

The anti-Castro paramilitary group Alpha 66, whose founder Antonio Veciana was an intelligence asset for the US Army, became one of the most active groups. They bought guns and boats, and they recruited and trained commandos for their numerous raids on Cuba.[129] While organized groups like Alpha 66 and others had sizable membership consisting of competent operatives, ragtag bands of young Cubans eager for action also developed.

★★★

On May 24, 1966, Ricardo and Magda Morales welcomed their third child, Sylvia, into the world. Ricardo had been back from the Congo since his August 1965 separation from the CIA and found himself parking cars at the Luau Restaurant and the Americana Hotel on Miami Beach. For the time being, he was finished with the CIA, though he knew he was not done with the mission. He foresaw no immediate jaunts away from Miami, but his thirst for adventure offered no guarantees. Despite his inbred operational restlessness, or maybe because of it, he established himself in the city on a more permanent basis.

Morales was well acquainted with the exile community and knew most of the players personally. Little Havana simmered with a palpable sense of impending action as the area was overrun with young men who saw themselves as commandos despite their taking orders at the cafe or parking cars at the resort. They'd switch hats at the drop of a dime when a mission presented itself.

Morales's moonlighting for the bombers kept him out of the house often and at erratic times. Magda had taken a third-shift job as a switchboard operator and front desk clerk at the Shelbourne Hotel, the deco style mainstay in Miami Beach. She alternated shifts with her mother Emelia, who worked there as a housekeeper and would watch the children while the other was working. The whole family was in the expanding hospitality business, and nearly every available dime went to Catholic school for the children.

The Morales kids were surrounded by plenty of family in Miami. On the Morales side, *Tia* Yolanda and *Tio* Antonio had two girls, Lynette and Annette, while Pucho and his second wife Dania lived with Pucho's son Rolando from his previous marriage.

Ricardo's older brother Pucho was regarded as an upstanding man of character by all who knew him. He'd served Brigade 2506 and emerged respected by fellow exiles and refugees in the community. He was an introvert in a sea of less disciplined mercenaries and was dubbed "The Mute" by friends. Pucho didn't continue actions against Cuba or bomb any establishments once coming to the US and completing his service for the CIA. He assimilated rather quickly, a man with no agenda, going to work to support his family and not running afoul of the law.

On the other side of the family, Magda's brother Hector Cornillot lived nearby with his wife Joanne and their four kids. Unlike Pucho, Hector was a hellion possessing that tendency toward action still alive in many of the CIA exiles. Like Ricardo, he couldn't refuse an anti-Castro group's invitiation to participate. The brothers-in-law shared a similar ambition in Cuba, and they committed their lives in the US to the same mission.

★★★

Hector Cornillot was first arrested in Havana as a teenager with his father, a seasoned revolutionary, after a raid on their home by Batista's police wherein a cache of weapons was found. Senior Hector was a member of a formal anti-Batista group, Unión Insurreccional Revolucionaria, and though his son was not, young Hector still gravitated toward action.

A high school teacher of his named Clarijo had made a profound impact on him on the day Batista strong-armed control of Cuba from President Prío in March of 1952. As the tanks rolled through the streets toward the presidential palace, Clarijo told the class, "You shouldn't accept that type of government, and it is your duty to do something about it."[130] It made an impression on Hector, and it turned out many students across the city felt similarly, too.

University of Havana students had organized anti-government groups and began clashing with police. Hector and some friends from high school connected with the college students they knew from the neighborhood and began acting out alongside them.

"Our only objective was to idealize what Cuba could be under a democratic, capitalistic government without dictatorship and without corruption," Cornillot said.[131] Students espousing a similar idealistic doctrine organized and gathered at the school while police waited for them to approach. Students perched in trees along the campus began firing guns at the cops as all hell broke loose.

When Hector and his father were arrested at home, they were taken to the police station and knocked around by the officers. Then they were thrown into a holding cell with thirty other suspected insurgents from all walks of life—ministers, doctors, lawyers—all told they'd be charged with conspiring to kill Batista. After being held for a month, Hector, Jr. was released as a minor. His father and the others would eventually be released after some fighting by lawyers working on their behalf.

After his release from jail at age seventeen, Hector joined a training camp of 150 men opened by former president Prío in Santo Domingo, Dominican Republic. They prepared for a joint invasion of Batista's Cuba with another revolutionary named Fidel Castro, who was preparing his own group in Mexico. Despite their plans, the impatient Castro pressed on without Prío's group and carved his place in history.

After arriving in the US, Hector was approached by a revolutionary group called 30th of November.[132] This group, formed in 1961, sought rebels with experience in warfare, and Hector worked with them seeking sponsors, gathering arms, and planning invasions into Cuba. The CIA, after having failed with their earlier efforts in Cuba, continued their recruitment of willing mercenaries, and in 1966 Hector and a handful of the 30th of November members were approached. They accepted the offer of training with the expectation they'd carry out missions into Cuba yet again.

But the Agency quickly discovered these exiles were not as easily controlled as the earliest crop of mercenaries five years ago. The wide-eyed optimism of those early exiles had disappeared by the time Hector Cornillot, Eladio Armando Ruiz, and the other 30th of November guys were approached by the CIA. They completed training, for which they thanked the Agency, and made it clear they would not be answerable to them during their missions into Cuba. For years they'd been planning to enact their own operations, not the Agency's. The group was openly opposed to following CIA directives.

"We were not going to trust the CIA once we were on the field," Cornillot says. "And they didn't want anybody doing things individually."[133] After training, the CIA detached the group from the operation.

The US government's track record in Cuba was etched in the minds of those who'd first signed up for the fight, once willing to lay down their lives for what they believed was a verbal contract with government. The pain of that abandoned promise didn't wane easily and really never did for so many Cubans.

"I have nothing but disrespect for the CIA and the government intelligence agencies," Cornillot said. "I think they are not truthful people. I don't think they are good for the nation; they are a bunch of sellouts. Betrayals at every step."[134]

★★★

Nautical crane operator Horace Barron was loading cargo onto the 180-foot British ship *Oro Verde* at the Miami city docks when he noticed something below the waterline at the boat's hull. Barron didn't think anything of it, and the crew kept loading the ship. After a few hours of casual glances at what looked like a balloon floating just below the surface, however, Barron called a stevedore over to look.

"I couldn't figure it out," Barron said.[135] It seemed tethered to the ship somehow, as it bobbed in that same spot the entire time. They decided to call the Coast Guard, and at 11:28 a.m., they responded and took one look.

"Call the bomb squad," the officer said.

Capt. Tom Brodie of the bomb squad responded with his team, took a look from the pier, and then slid off his shirt and shoes. He dove in the water and retrieved the balloon, in actuality a condom, as well as the cigar box that clung to the hull, held in place with magnets. He deactivated the bomb, separated the condom from the box, and came to the surface for further examination of the makeshift device.

What sat before him and the other deputies was a very sophisticated explosive compared to what they'd been seeing in the city. An ampule sat inside the condom, a round glass container filled, in this instance, with acid. When the rubber was palmed and squeezed, the pellet would crack, releasing the acid that would eat at a detonating cord connected to the cigar box. Inside sat a destructive chain reaction masterminded by some demented Rube Goldberg.

In time, the acid would fray the cord, triggering a spring that would cause a small hammer to strike the primer of a blasting cap, which would then detonate the cord and two pounds of Pentolite. This military-grade explosive more powerful than TNT was molded inside the cigar box on the hull. If detonated as placed, it would have penetrated the steel and blasted a two-foot hole in the hull below the waterline. But it hadn't.

Since returning from the Congo, Morales worked with nearly any group that asked for his assistance. His pedigree in Operation 40 allowed him to float through the anti-Castro community with known credentials, and the fact that he was an expert craftsman with explosives added to his draw.

Morales testified to building a Pentolite bomb for an anti-Castro group to blow up Rodriguez Market on West 29th Street in Hialeah.[136] The proprietor, Julio Rodriguez, had been the subject of a previous vandalism attack due to his political stance.[137] Miami detective Ted Semanski said Rodriguez had views about the Cuban government which were not popular in the area.

The sanctions placed on Cuba by the Kennedy administration via the 1962 trade embargo did not reassure the exile groups that Cuba wasn't receiving goods and support, indirectly or otherwise. Further, other countries failed to enact similar restrictions. The exiles felt they could impact this issue without the assistance or approval of the US government.

Mexico was one of the countries that exile groups notoriously targeted for their unrestrictive policy toward Castro's Cuba. In deposition, Morales claimed responsibility for the bombing of the Mexican Consulate's residence and office and the Mexican tourist office.[138] These attacks were affiliated with his brother-in-law Hector's group.

Morales described his time in the mid '60s in Miami as "running from one house to another, one organization to another...doing their little bombings."[139]

With so many groups cropping up, there was bound to be a gradient in the professionalism with which each operated. The amateurs, eager to make a quick name at the expense of thoroughness, gave the well-organized groups a bad name. Morales had little patience for those not as rigorously precise as he; the perfectionist in him was at odds with anyone who wasn't.

One of the groups he was working with was called ESA (Anti-Communist Secret Army, translated). They'd recently burned down the FORDC building on 1st Street after it hosted Castro sympathizers, which Morales described as "a nuisance."[140] When the ESA was recruited to assist in an attack on a freighter, they requested Ricardo's services. He was asked to construct the bomb to be used on a ship they said was delivering goods to Cuba. He accepted; commandos help commandos. One mission.

He went to work and eventually handed a cigar box containing the convoluted but fail-safe device to a young man named Alanis, who jumped in the water beside the *Oro Verde*.[141] The ship had arrived in Miami on Sunday and unloaded bananas at the dock of the Banana Supply Company on the Miami River. It would sit there until Tuesday morning before departing for the Miami city docks, just after Alanis climbed out of the river.

Investigators were stymied by the choice of ship targeted. While they'd recently seen Pentolite showing up in the Cuban exile bombing circles, this instance was odd because nothing about the ship should've interested the refugee bombers. Capt. Brodie confirmed with the operations manager that the vessel had no business with Cuba at all.[142] The *Oro Verde*, it turned out, was hauling bananas and cargo between Ecuador and Miami. That gaffe, coupled with Alanis's embarrassing oversight—he never crushed the pellet to activate the bomb—caused infighting between ESA and the group they'd assisted. Morales claimed that this led the ESA to cease partnerships with several groups.

He stated, "The alliance we [had] with two to four different groups was broken because there was no excuse why the time device…[was] not crushed, and that's the reason why the bomb was discovered, and the motivation we found out for attacking the freighter was unreasonable."

Despite the failures, the bomb was a notable creation and made for conversation in the police department, the press, and the exile community. Morales, who never met a stage he didn't like, later testified to its being "a masterpiece."

"It's part of the museum here," he joked.[143]

The *Oro Verde* mission may have failed, but the word on the bomb was out, and the Michelangelo of destruction was now in high demand.

Chapter Five

Left Turn

(1967)

On Thursday night, June 1, 1967, a bomb exploded inside Epicure food market on Alton Road. Though bombings were common in Little Havana, this incident was curious because it was the second that same day, and neither target was consistent with the groups' profile. Both locations, Epicure and a dry cleaning store on Collins Avenue, were free from suspicion regarding dealings with Cuba or pro-Castro communists. Epicure Gourmet Market was opened by brothers Eddie and Leonard Thal back in 1945, and Rand's Dry Cleaners was a family business run by Jack Rand and his son James.[144] This was a departure from the modus operandi of the political bombings frustrating law enforcement in Miami.

Closer examination would yield a commonality—one that did not escape local law enforcement. Though nothing about Epicure drew any comparison to Rand's, the food market's neighbor did—Alfie's, a twenty-four-hour newsstand. The proprietor, Alfie Mart, was a suspected bookmaker and his small storefront was a hangout for gamblers. Though his location was unharmed, the proximity to Epicure was noteworthy when Rand's Dry Cleaners was thrown in the mix.

Jack "Chappie" Rand was a local bookie as well.[145] One could posit that the Epicure bomb was some kind of message for Alfie. The string of bombings in Miami was now extending beyond the anti-Cuba targets, and law enforcement began to identify a combustible dual track of explosives detonating in the city. *The Miami Herald* even began tracking the activity in what they called the "Bombing Box Score of 1967," keeping count of the detonations around the city in the calendar year.[146] Epicure and Rand's were numbers eight and nine.

Shortly after the night of the double bombing, Morales got a call at home from CIA trained Operation 40 compatriot and demolition expert Luis Posada Carriles, who was looking for a favor.[147] Since landing in Little Havana, he and Morales had been active in the same business, and he needed Morales to clean up an error he'd made—Epicure.

"The main target was Alfie's," Posada said when meeting with Morales. He'd errantly bombed the food market instead of the intended target next door. And now he needed to make good and hit Alfie's newsstand for his paying sponsor.

Posada was on his way out of the country. He'd recently been hired as an inspector for DISIP (Directorate of Intelligence and Prevention Services), Venezuela's governmental intelligence agency, and was in the process of packing up and heading to Caracas. But more than the imposition on his scheduled move was his need for Morales's expertise. Everyone on both sides of the law suspected the Epicure bomb was misplaced. The cops' antenna was up, and Alfie Mart's was too, no doubt.

In addition to the challenge of pulling off the job under this increased scrutiny, Posada's guy had some very specific instructions. Posada told Morales there was a mirrored partition in the rear of the store that was protecting a back room used for taking bets. Posada's guy needed the glass wall blown out but with no body count. The job was to expose the gaming operation without maiming anyone.

"You know," Morales told Posada, "this will require some recognizance from the inside."

"You'll be compensated," Posada assured his friend.

"Who's behind this?"

"Fellow I know. Frank Rosenthal."[148]

Morales had never heard of him, but money was money. He headed down to the newsstand and checked out the mirrored wall hiding the bookmaking operation in the back. He called Posada.

"Luis, the job can be done the way this fellow is requiring. But there's a lot of cops there. I would like to meet this guy and know who he is, who he works for, what his intentions are. Because this is a risky proposition now."[149]

In addition to checking out this sponsor, Morales also placed himself in line behind Posada, who was about to depart for Venezuela. With the middleman gone, Morales would be this Rosenthal guy's direct connection.

Posada brokered the meeting to happen at Fun Fair on the Causeway at 79th Street. Morales knew the area, having worked parking cars at Luau Restaurant across the street. It was familiar turf.

The sounds of Fun Fair amusement center danced through the lot and fused with the aromatic blend of grilled hamburgers, crispy pizza crust, and boiled hot dogs. Morales could see Luau from his vantage point as he met a well-dressed, thin man just over six feet, with slicked back sandy hair behind a well-receded hairline.

Morales and the man known to all as "Lefty" had a casual chat. He told Morales he was Jewish but connected with the Italian organized crime family in Chicago, known commonly as The Outfit.[150] He owned an operation called Rosenthal's Multiple Sports News Service, wherein he distributed gambling sheets to be sold at betting parlors. Bookies looking to operate independently without purchasing Rosenthal's sheets, which really meant working outside the scope of the Chicago mafia, would be sent a message. The disintegration of the mirrored wall protecting Alfie's renegade operation was a fine example.

Lefty and Morales connected on a personal level from that first meeting, with Rosenthal telling him about his upbringing in the city he loved, Chicago, where he was an usher in a theatre, and about his time in the US Army in Korea. Then it was down to business—Alfie's refused to buy his sheet.

"You were recommended very highly by Luis," Lefty said to Morales, agreeing he was the "right man to get a tricky job done."

Lefty explained there was a conflict with bookies in the city, and the purpose of the Alfie's hit was to dramatically drop the partition and not get anyone hurt. Morales listened and considered the job.

"Listen," he began, "the whole place is crowded with cops. It's obvious, according to the newspapers, they're expecting Alfie's to get hit."[151]

Rosenthal seemed nonplussed. He explained that he had an "understanding" with law enforcement who would be standing by, ready to go inside and make arrests for the activities going on behind the partition. Someone just had to get the thing down so police had a reason to respond to the location.

On July 16, 1967, just two weeks after the Epicure blast, Morales entered Alfie's newsstand and used the pay phone located beside the mirrored wall. He left, and a short time later the wall blasted apart. Morales had attached a C4 explosive to a time delay pencil in the booth.

Rosenthal paid Morales $1,000 for getting Alfie's attention. More importantly, however, Rosenthal had found the right guy to help his friends in Chicago tighten their grip on Miami's bookmaking business.[152]

★★★

Frank Rosenthal was born on Chicago's West Side on June 12, 1929, the son of a produce wholesaler.[153] As a young man, Rosenthal obsessed over studying the racing form at home and in school. Pre-stock market crash action like bookmaking was rampant in Chicago, so the forms weren't hard to come by.

Lefty's father owned horses, so he was often at the racetrack as a young teen, working the stables and studying the forms—an ideal existence for the young loner.

"The ponies are really my first love," Rosenthal wrote on his website years later. "I literally lived on the racetrack, worked in the stable area, owned and trained thoroughbreds, and experienced first hand the full cycle for a game that's generally referred to as the sport for Kings and Queens."[154]

He soon began betting with some friends who would cut school with him and head to the track. On one such day, he showed his partners just how finely tuned his acumen had become.

"We stayed for eight races, and I punched out seven winners," he said. "My pals thought I was the Messiah."[155] Anyone in the know would've known even the Messiah couldn't pick seven winners without the inside knowledge of the chicanery that was prevalent in the sport in those days.

Rosenthal's early exposure to the horses introduced him to sports wagering, but he learned just how vast that landscape was while visiting Chicago's Major League Baseball stadiums. He likened the bleachers at Wrigley Field and Comiskey Park to open-air casinos with constant action, housing a bunch of guys barking numbers at each other all day long. "There were about two hundred guys up there every game and they bet on everything. Every pitch. Every swing. Everything had a price."[156]

Action takers with pockets full of cash took the bets and set odds for all situations that occurred throughout the game. This high-speed, high stakes crash course in wagering mesmerized Rosenthal. That intrigue never left him throughout his life, as would be profiled by Robert DeNiro's portrayal of him under the fictional name Sam "Ace" Rothstein in the film *Casino*.

"You like something and you get into it," Rosenthal said. "I was studying all phases of gambling in my late teens."

Rosenthal's mentors were the guys on the street. In the days before gambling was openly and legally advertised, there weren't any books or websites with well-presented sharps from which to learn. You had to find those guys in the neighborhood.

Hymie the Ace was once such local. He taught the eager Rosenthal that if he was going to be serious about gambling, he had to treat it like a job. He should be immersed in it, and he should get up early to do it. Lefty abided, waking in the predawn hours to study the sports pages of forty newspapers from across the US, looking for tidbits in a team's local paper that hadn't yet made its way around the industry. With such nuggets of hidden information, he'd place his own bets and handicap odds for local bookmakers working for the Chicago crime syndicate. It was during this time Rosenthal met up and coming tough guy Anthony Spilotro.

"We were like this," Rosenthal said in a 1995 interview, crossing his two fingers. "Tony was a natural leader. He was not a 'dees' and 'dose' guy. He had good manners. We hit it off."[157]

Spilotro was connected, and he gravitated toward Rosenthal's skills in one of the syndicate's main industries. Their friendship allowed

Lefty to form ties with the Chicago gangsters before heading to Florida. Rosenthal's documented run-ins with law enforcement didn't start until he arrived in Miami, where he was first picked up for operating a gambling establishment on December 31, 1960.

In 1961, Rosenthal was called before a Senate hearing on gambling and organized crime, wherein he invoked his Fifth Amendment right against self-incrimination thirty-eight times, even when asked if he was left-handed because of his moniker.[158]

In 1963 he was convicted of "conspiracy to bribe athletes" in North Carolina after pleading no contest to the charge.[159] He'd allegedly "point shaved" a college basketball game, wherein players on one team were paid to win the game only by a certain window of points, allowing bettors and bookies to win their positions.

By the time he met Morales in 1967, Rosenthal was digging his hooks into Miami, and, by extension, the Chicago Outfit. Morales would soon learn their interests in the Sunshine State would extend beyond just gambling.

★★★

Ricardo began spending time with Lefty at Capra's Restaurant on Biscayne Boulevard, eventually joining his new business associate there nearly every night.[160] Rosenthal conducted a fair share of business in the Italian restaurant, and Morales was more than happy to watch Lefty work the room, sitting with different people and talking shop. The world of Italian organized crime, Cosa Nostra, was new to him.

"I used to go down to the places he was meeting with, you know, his so called organized crime friends," Morales said. "It was sort of fascinating. I never been exposed to that kind of situation."[161]

It was at one of those dinners at a restaurant on 79th street called The Place for Steak where Morales first met John Clarence Cook. The thirty-seven year old Cook was a master jewel thief, described by Rosenthal as the best in the country, and it turned out he had a problem.[162] He talked with Rosenthal about it, out of earshot from Morales. The next day, Lefty phoned Ricardo.

"John's kid is being harassed," he told Morales. He explained Cook's wife was very upset by this, as the teenager was being threatened by a grown man, and Cook wanted to send a message to this guy. Rosenthal was a little short on details, but he said Cook wanted the message to come in the form of a bomb—meaning this was a job for Morales. The only issue was they didn't yet have a verified address on the target, but one was to be provided shortly at a meeting scheduled for Fun Fair's parking lot, the same place Lefty had first met with Morales.

They pulled into the lot and Morales spotted Cook sitting alone in his Cadillac a few spots over. They sat in their two respective cars, no one making contact with each other, when another car entered the lot. Morales slunk down in his seat when he saw the driver—a Latino male he later testified to having recognized as a police officer named Zamora.[163]

The off duty cop walked to Cook's car and got in, never glancing in the direction of Lefty's vehicle. It was a puzzling scene. If it was a sting, cops would have swarmed the area, but a sting for what exactly? Maybe it was an undercover operation, with the officer wearing a wire and prompting Cook to tell him all about the impending bombing. Or maybe they'd bust them all right there when the right words were transmitted to a listening car. But after a short time, the police officer left, and Cook came over to Rosenthal's car without incident.

"I got the address," Cook said as he got in. He turned to Morales and spoke to him as he would a short order cook. "I want this thing done tonight."

"Well, what do you want?" Morales asked.

"Just throw something there—a hand grenade, a piece of explosive. I want an explosion at this fella's house."[164]

Morales charged him $500 up front because he'd need to purchase the materials. Cook paid him, and Morales left to perform what seemed an easy gig.

Morales headed back into Little Havana, and in no time he had a piece of C4, a safety fuse, and a blasting cap. That night, July 12, 1967, he went to the address provided and simply tossed the explosive onto the front lawn of the house, where it detonated and ripped the landscaping apart. Simple job, no one hurt. They should all be like this.

But Morales was not satisfied at all when he saw the headlines the next day. In fact, he was pissed.

He sought out Lefty and told him the headline—police officer Jerry Saslaw's home had been bombed the previous night with a little girl inside.[165] He was dismayed that he'd allegedly witnessed a police officer hand over the address of a fellow officer for nefarious purposes. Morales professed a value system that prevented him from doing harm to law enforcement. Further, he told Lefty the police would come down hard in arresting someone who'd harmed one of their own.

"You never told me who the intended target was," Morales said to Rosenthal. "If I had known it was a police officer involved I never would have done it."

Lefty told him not to worry. "It was an authorized hit."

Morales didn't know if that was true, but it was the second time he'd been told by Rosenthal that he had the power to steer the eyes of the law—the first being clearance for the Alfie's hit. Maybe the Saslaw cop was crooked; after all, he'd been harassing Cook's son terribly. Though it turned out there were yet more details Morales wasn't made privy to.

Cook's teenage son had been picked up by Miami PD Officer Bob Weiss for a minor violation that required a trip down to the juvenile detention center.[166] Cook told the police that he felt they were picking on his kid to get to him instead, as he was an entity well known to the authorities. A couple of years prior, two of Cook's Miami associates, Jack "Murph the Surf" and Allan Kuhn, had been arrested for the theft of the Star of India, then the world's biggest sapphire at 563 karats, and twenty-three other precious jewels from New York's Museum of Natural History.[167] Cook was trailed by the FBI during the investigation because of his ties to the men. In response, the well-known jewel thief rammed his car into the FBI trail car, landing himself in jail for eighty-five days. He saw his son's arrest as continued harassment, albeit two years later, and precipitated the symbolic bombing of a Miami cop's property. The real details of the story were not divulged to Morales;

instead, Cook presented the job for hire as if it were merely a response to the harassments his son was enduring.

Miami Herald Bombing Box Score entry #12: Officer Saslaw's property.

★★★

Though Cook was not tagged with any direct connection to the Star of India heist, aside from vehicular assault on the surveilling FBI agents, he was not entirely removed from it, given his connection to thieves Murph the Surf and Allan Kuhn. Another possible link to the crime lies in Herman "Hy" Gordon.

Gordon, described by the FBI as the nation's top jewelry fence, was used by the FBI as a go-between for the precious stone, and his efforts assisted in its safe return to the New York museum. The entire haul, estimated by museum bookkeepers at $400,000 ($3.7 million in today's money) was a sophisticated job. Murphy and Kuhn lowered themselves into the museum with rope, then used duct tape and a glass cutter to breach three glass cases, leaving not a single fingerprint in the process.[168] The heist made headlines and ignited the public's imagination.

Just before midnight on July 18, 1967, more than two years after the Star of India's safe return, Gordon was shot in the head near NE 10th Avenue and 87th Street, in what he described to detectives as a robbery by "two Latin males."[169] But Gordon still had $1,700 cash on him and his Cadillac was filled with rare vintage coins. It seemed less a robbery than a hit, and this is where more familiar names than mysterious Latinos come into play.

In Morales's deposition, he confessed to having gone down to the dark street with Rosenthal for a planned meeting between Rosenthal and Hy Gordon. In the course of the discussion, Gordon became aggressive toward Rosenthal, at which point Morales testified that he produced a .22 handgun and shot Gordon behind his ear to protect his partner.[170] Gordon lived to tell his robbery tale to police from his hospital bed the following day, but it ultimately yielded no leads or arrests.

It is unclear what, if any, connection John Clarence Cook had to the jewel fence's shooting, but Lefty's and Morales's presence at the assault is worth noting, especially because it occurred only five days after Rosenthal brokered the contract bombing job between Cook and Morales. Cook's possible distaste for Gordon's involvement in the museum heist's investigation that landed his two friends behind bars may have lingered. That, paired with a different but problematic theft deal—maybe a car full of rare coins—may have led to the hiring of the Cuban exile who got difficult and dangerous things done.

★★★

The payphone at a 7-Eleven store behind Lefty's housing development was the main avenue by which Lefty communicated with Morales. The month following the Officer Saslaw bomb and Hy Gordon shooting, Morales and Rosenthal had one such phone call.

"I want you to bomb John's house," Lefty said.[171]

John meant John Clarence Cook, the man who Lefty had once introduced as his friend, the man who'd paid Morales $500 for the Saslaw bomb. Morales asked for more details.

"There is going to be a Cadillac parked in front of the house, and there is a Donzi boat underneath a carport." Lefty wanted both hit, preferably detonating at the same time. Cook, though nowhere near as close to Morales as Lefty had become, was still a partner in their new circle. The only insight Rosenthal offered into the reasoning for the job was a vague animosity about a split between them, which would turn out to only be partially true, like most of the information being divulged to Morales.

Ricardo accepted the $1,000 job and headed out to the address Lefty provided. The house was on a cul-de-sac and backed up to a canal just off Biscayne Bay. The driveway and outside carport were easily accessible. The job could be done without harming anyone, which was another instruction from Lefty, similar to Morales's anti-communist bombings that targeted property and not people.

In order to ensure the simultaneous detonation of the two vehicles, Morales would construct the explosive using a prime cord. Also called a "det cord," this thin, waxy rope is unspooled to any length to allow sufficient distance from the blasting cap and explosive device.[172] The charge travels down the cord, which is combustible as well, to the blasting cap, detonating the cord and bomb.

At 3:45 a.m. on August 22, 1967, two bombs blasted the new sky blue Cadillac and red speedboat to smithereens, while also busting all the windows of the house wherein Cook, his wife Marianne, and their four children slept.[173] No one was injured, but Cook remained at the location as police and media appeared at the scene. He screamed that the Miami police, currently surrounding him on site, were responsible for the blast and the FBI had no doubt witnessed the act, since they were always surveilling his home.

"They blew up everything I own except my boat!" he proclaimed. Behind the home, sitting majestically unharmed and moored in the canal, was his prized twenty-six-foot cruiser named *Marianne,* after his equally prized, former Playboy bunny wife.

At three o'clock the following afternoon, Lefty called Morales and said now the *SS Marianne* had to go, too. He must've read Cook's quote in the papers.

Morales agreed to surveil the canal and get back to Rosenthal.

"I will have to swim to get over there," he said.

"I want the boat," Lefty reiterated, fending off any resistance to getting wet.

Morales pointed out how intense the police presence would be around Cook's house. Lefty once again told him that would be handled once Morales confirmed to Lefty when it would be done.

"Don't worry," he said. "You are going to have support from police officers that are friendly with us. They will secure the area for you."

Morales had reason to believe him. Besides the Alfie's bombing that sent waiting police into the gambling den, the "authorized" Saslaw job hadn't brought any heat down on them. Morales was growing increasingly more attuned to that aspect of Lefty's business.

One particular night at Capra's restaurant, he'd witnessed Rosenthal meeting with "the Italian guys," as Morales put it in a 1982 deposition. He testified that the topic of their discussion that night was a Miami police lieutenant.

> Q: Who was it he was talking about?
>
> A: Lt. Black
>
> Q: Charlie Black?
>
> A: Yes, sir.
>
> Q: ...Did you eventually obtain objective information that Black was, in fact, covering for Lefty?
>
> A: Yes.[174]

That night, August 23, 1967, Morales drove to a clearing up the canal from Cook's residence and jumped in the water. He swam very slowly so as not to make any disturbance on the water's surface. He carried five pounds of C4 and a timing pencil in a tied condom, tethered to a cord held between his clenched teeth.

He stopped at the *Marianne* and surveyed the area, watching for any activity in the surrounding homes. When the coast was clear, Morales dropped the device into the boat and then swam up the canal, into his car, and cleanly out of the area without spotting a single patrol car making the rounds. The boat blew apart.

Whether or not Lt. Black was actually involved in a plot with Rosenthal, someone had obviously cleared the decks for him to pull these jobs off, as particularly evidenced by the second Cook blast. Police presence would've been beefed up in the area regardless of whether or not Cook was a frequent target of law enforcement. Cook had drawn increased scrutiny after the bombing of Officer Saslaw in July, as stated by retired Miami Police Assistant Chief Phil Doherty in his book *The Miami Police Worksheet*.

Doherty wrote of the Saslaw bombing, "...suspicion pointed to Cook as the perpetrator or the contractor for that criminal job. The police activity around the Cook home and surrounding area increased fourfold."[175]

It was very unlikely that a bomber could've gotten that close to a high profile target after successive bombings in the same general area. It begs the question: how could this happen?

★★★

The Miami media distinguished the underworld bombings from the anti-Castro groups with use of the term "the bookie wars." All the incidents were lumped together in the *Herald*'s bombing box score, but there was a clear distinction between locales like the Cuban Representation in Exile office, Peace Center of Miami office, and the Cuban owned Piranha Boat Company in Hialeah, from Alfie's newsstand, Chappie Rand's dry cleaners, or the two Cook bombings.

Despite the bombings targeting gambling locations, the media-titled "bookie war" really hadn't been a war at all, or at least it was the most one-sided war ever fought. Local press was unaware that the bombings weren't between rival outfits, but rather were the mastermind of the Chicago boss. According to two FBI memos, a high-ranking informant reported the 1967 bookmaking violence in Miami was ordered by Sam Giancana, the reputed boss of the Chicago Outfit, to wrest control of his city.

"Regarding the other bombings," the memo states, "Mooney [Giancana's nickname] has ordered that all bookmakers in the Miami area be brought under control and emphasized this authority with the bombing of recalcitrants. Among these were 'Chappy' Rand, Irving 'Mickey' Zion and Alphie [sic] Mart, all Miami Beach and Miami bookmakers and all victims of bombing attacks. Informant said these orders specifically exclude the Italian bookmakers and gamblers."[176] Lefty, with his Chicago connection, was in a position to ensure this was done. An FBI memo cited the order to bomb Cook as also having come from mob boss Giancana over a payment that never reached Chicago.

"Informant advised that 'Mooney' ordered these last two bombings against Cook," it began, "and that Frank 'Lefty' Rosenthal, a Chicago and Miami gambler, received the contract. Informant advised that because of dissatisfaction against Cook [sic] involved his holding out on some $300,000 in rare coins which Cook had taken in a series of burglaries over the past several months."[177]

This calls to mind the stash of rare coins found in Hy Gordon's car after his shooting, and yet another possible connection to Cook and the impromptu fireworks show to which his neighborhood was treated. The puzzle pieces lock snugly in a picture that shows master thief Cook using jewel fence Gordon to move the stolen coins without sharing his cut with Chicago. It seemed Rosenthal had been sent south to assign certain organized crime interests to Chicago's jurisdiction.

Morales wasn't told of all the entanglements around his targets; he didn't need to know, and it was better for all involved that he didn't. But Rosenthal did indicate to Morales that he was connected to Chicago, and Morales's experience taking orders from political agencies no doubt allowed him to surmise the activities for which he was paid extended far beyond Lefty.

★★★

"Go by John's place and tell him that you were the one who bombed him."[178]

That was the directive from Lefty to Morales one afternoon. Morales's confession to the bombings would certainly be an effective inducement for Cook to come with him, as Morales was told to deliver Cook to him and his friend Tony. Rosenthal's guest had flown in from Chicago, and they were awaiting Morales and Cook in the last unit of a row of townhouses belonging to a kid Lefty described as his stockbroker. He had been telling Morales he was investing heavily in Lum's food chain, never expanding on why that commodity was so attractive.

Cook answered his door and invited Morales inside where he delivered his message nonchalantly, and told him Lefty was waiting for them. Cook left with Morales, undoubtedly not without a racing mind and a sweat-soaked shirt. Morales's confession, followed by the news that Tony was in town to meet with him, meant business.

Anyone connected to Chicago knew "Tony" was Anthony Spilotro, Lefty's old friend and feared enforcer from back home.[179] His flight to Miami meant official business from the Chicago Outfit. But if Cook was to be assassinated it would've happened already, not after Morales admitted to bombing him.

Upon arriving at the townhouse, Morales was asked to sit just outside the room where Spilotro and Rosenthal told Cook he was required to split a percentage of his proceeds with Chicago, reinforcing what Giancana iterated in the FBI memo. If he complied he'd be afforded the opportunity to continue his jewel theft operation in Las Vegas under their auspices. The Outfit would assist in making Cook aware of potential targets as well. They were proposing a partnership in Vegas—one of those offers one couldn't, and shouldn't, refuse.

★★★

Lefty had done about as much in Miami as he could and still remain under the radar. He was named a key witness in a Dade County grand jury probe, when in September detectives in the Sheriff's Intelligence Unit reported he'd cleaned out his place and left. His next move would cement him in organized crime history as he was assigned to Las Vegas to look after the Outfit's interests in the city, which would eventually encompass secretly running the Stardust, Hacienda, Marina, and Fremont casinos. Since Rosenthal had met Morales, the Cuban exile had served him well and kept him in the good graces of the Chicago bosses.

One must wonder if Lefty broached the subject of Morales joining him on his move west. Morales had proven himself a valuable asset and passed muster as far as reliability. Word could have easily gotten back to Chicago via Spilotro or Lefty himself, and Morales could've landed a valuable spot helping Rosenthal run the Vegas operation. Certainly there were jobs in the desert earmarked for men who got difficult and dangerous jobs done. Morales would've been a shoe-in, especially given how much information Rosenthal had confided in him.

He ostensibly wouldn't have done so if he didn't see a future of some kind with Ricardo.

How had Morales so quickly found himself wheeling and dealing in the Miami underworld, entrenched in the stuff of bookie wars and unpaid tributes for Chicago mafia bosses? Once Morales took a bombing job from his friend and fellow mercenary Luis Posada, he was instantly led off course, trading mission for money. It was uncharacteristic; Ricardo Morales was a soldier. And though at first glance the activities of the military might very much resemble those of the mafia, there is one glaring omission—passion. It was a trade Morales would not have made.

Less than year after starting with Lefty, Morales was off the hook as Rosenthal and Spilotro set out to keep Vegas an extension of the Outfit. Business was good out there, whether by design or the city's favorite commodity, luck. And as luck would have it, in 1969 the Lum's corporation, in which Lefty had been pouring investment money for a few years, purchased the new crown jewel of the Las Vegas Strip—Caesars Palace.[180]

Who knew?

The most valuable lesson Morales learned from Lefty was the manipulation of law enforcement. Unlike Lefty Rosenthal, Morales didn't have a lot of money or close connections to the Chicago Outfit to leverage with government agencies. But there did exist a currency even more important to law enforcement that he possessed—information.

And in the coming year, he'd have the opportunity to master this most valuable resource.

Chapter Six

Fingered (1968)

On February 21, 1968 at around 5:30 a.m., a blue Ford Mustang pulled into the second parking spot from the southeast corner of M Street in Washington, DC.[181] The two men inside had driven all night. They only stopped at a gas station once entering DC to pick up a street directory to confirm their exact location.

The passenger exited and walked along 16th Street with a bomb under his medium-length coat. He stopped before the building they both determined was the target—the Soviet embassy.

The man stopped at a first floor window beside the front door and took a Clorox bottle from under his coat. The bottle was filled with C4 explosive, with a fuse dangling from the top of the bottle. Placement was key—the bottle needed to tilt toward the window, with the fuse pointing out toward 16th Street so the force of the blast would shoot out the bottom and into the window.

The man in the Mustang fidgeted; his partner Soto had been gone far longer than expected, so he started the car and pulled out to check on him. Maybe there was an issue with building security or something. As he got to the intersection of M and 15th Streets, the Mustang was rocked by a massive blast from up ahead. He sped around the block to 16th and M and picked up his partner.

The next day, Hector Cornillot and Omar Soto were back in Miami. They hurried back via I-95 and were stopped by highway patrol in Georgia for speeding. The officer collected their names, confirmed the vehicle was on loan from their friend and registered owner Miguel Diaz, and they were released with a warning.

On February 23, the AIP News Agency and WFAB radio station received an anonymous letter:

> Cell Number Two of Cuban Power in Washington wishes to make known via this medium that the motive for this attack on the Soviet Embassy in that city is the fact that the Government they represent is not in accord with the wishes of the Russian people, which they have enslaved. We take this opportunity to inform the governments which trade with the communist government and puppet of Havana if they do not break relations with said government they will be judged by our anticommunist tribunals.
>
> —GERARDO TORRES CONTRERA.[182]

The name Cuban Power was becoming popular. Word on the street was that Dr. Orlando Bosch, organizer of the anti-Castro group MIRR, had folded that organization and was moving the leaders to a new group he would head, also named Cuban Power.[183] His and Hector Cornillot's groups were unrelated, aside from the name and their common cause of creating chaos in the name of anti-communism.

Cornillot's Cuban Power had been busy. Since the start of 1968, just seven weeks before the Soviet embassy bomb, they'd pulled off six bombings, three of them on one night:

> January 25: Servicos Especializados (Specialized Services) warehouse, Miami.
>
> January 25: Tiger's Garage, Miami (Cornillot claimed the owner was a communist).
>
> January 25: All Cargo Transport, Miami.
>
> February 1: Residence of Mexican Consul Rafael Reyes Spindola, Miami.

February 8: Residence of British Consul Francis J. Pelly, Miami.

February 21: Soviet embassy, Washington DC.[184]

Ricardo Morales, by then Miami's explosive expert for hire, was in the same business as his brother-in-law, though he did not assist in the high-profile Soviet embassy job.

Morales couldn't. He was in jail.

Servicos Especializados, located at 3526 W. Flagler St, was allegedly shipping food and medical supplies to Cuba and was therefore a prime target for anti-Castro groups in the city.[185] On the night of January 25, that same target was on the schedule of two separate individuals, each unaware of the other's plans.

Ricardo Morales arrived at the door of the establishment first. The streets were empty enough, so Morales slid an envelope through the mail slot on the front door. The envelope was filled with a putty-like C4 explosive, timing pencil, and J-1 blasting cap. Morales sauntered off, having chosen a timer that allowed an extended period to pass before detonation. He wanted it to happen late at night when the streets were mostly free of pedestrian traffic.

Shortly after he left, a second group arrived at the same location unaware that the business had been visited already. The new bombers placed their device in the doorway of Servicos Especializados—also a C4 explosive, though this one with just a thirty second fuse. The second team, comprised of Hector Cornillot and Omar Soto, took off and their bomb blew up the entranceway. As a result, Morales's recently delivered envelope was torn apart, splaying C4 putty all over and separating it from the blasting cap. Unfortunately, neither brother-in-law shared their caper with the other that day.

Emergency personnel responded and processed the scene. As they sifted through the detritus beyond the entranceway, no one noticed Morales's blasting cap sitting on the floor across the room. It was still connected to the timing pencil, still functioning, still counting down. Sargeant Leesburg of the Miami police was standing nearest to the blasting cap when it combusted, spraying him with shrapnel. Though the officer suffered injuries, the separation of the blasting cap and timing pencil from the C4 prevented more destruction, injury, and possibly deaths. Despite the destruction of Morales's device, what little remained of it would prove to be his downfall.

Fresh on the heels of the *Herald*'s bombing box score, the surge in both number and scope of political bombings was creating a real problem for law enforcement in Miami. Most constricting was their inability to penetrate a world imported from abroad, replete with its own culture, language, and history.

★★★

Law enforcement was conflating responsibility for Cuban Power bombings; they struggled to understand the underworld of anti-communist groups. Their puzzlement was endemic of the larger problem of trying to decipher the intricacies of the movement while simultaneously investigating previous crimes and preventing any on the horizon.

On January 22, 1968, Bosch's Cuban Power released a missive titled "Declarations of Cuban Power" in which it claimed responsibility for the bombing of a B-25 cargo plane at Miami International Airport on January 20.[186] This letter, one of seven recently released under the banner of Cuban Power, showed federal agencies a newfound pattern. The signatures varied and seemed to indicate two different operating cells.

An FBI memo dated March 28, 1968 highlighted the discovery:

"Of the seven documents issued anonymously in the name of Cuban Power, two documents were similar in typewriting and were signed with the name 'ERNESTO, General Delegate.' The first of these was a three-page document dated 1/22/68, setting forth the purposes and principles of Cuban Power and claiming credit for instant bombing. The second document was entitled 'Declarations of Cuban Power' and also claimed responsibility for the bombing of the B-25 cargo plane at Miami International Airport."[187]

The FBI would begin to see the name "Ernesto" attached to Cuban Power documents more frequently, while another signature, "Gerardo Torres Contrera," on others, as had been the case for the Washington, DC bombing. Another discernible pattern that suggested the possibility of two factions using the same name lay in their choice of targets. The "Ernesto" Cuban Power seemed to target vessels like planes and ships, while the "Contrera" brand was blowing up politically associated buildings such as the Soviet embassy, homes of two consuls, and the specialized services warehouse for which they'd already claimed responsibility.

That kind of labyrinth wasn't unique. The tentacles of the groups setting off bombs in Miami were beginning to have real reach and would continue to frustrate authorities for some time. The competency of each sect varied greatly too. Which groups should be taken seriously by agencies, and which were merely a few disorganized guys seeking to show their displeasure for *Fidelistas*, Castro supporters? Further, the second wave of emigration was underway, having started in 1965 after the Cuban Missle Crisis had paused.

★★★

One very big development for Morales was that he had a fourth child on the way at home, though not the home where his other children were.

Irmina Bouza, known as "Mimi" to friends, fit comfortably into Morales's rollercoaster world. She was secretary to Wendell Rollason, the director of the Inter-American Affairs Commission, a private organization assisting emigrating Cubans by acquiring visa waivers. She also worked at the *Miami Herald* where she would eventually become an editor.

Mimi's childhood in Cuba, like Morales's, was tied to the Batista regime. Though they lived well, they knew Castro's overthrow of the government would be their demise. Mimi was able to first move herself, followed by a total of around twenty family members and friends out of Cuba.[188]

Mimi first started working at the *Miami Herald* as a switchboard operator, though her more productive work, according to the CIA, was going on under the radar as a courier and contact for Cuban Power.[189] She maintained critical documents for the group and was a dutiful administrative assistant to the underground group of bombers, doing everything from carting C4 explosives in the trunk of her Pontiac convertible to managing finances, as she was once stopped with Ricardo Morales's bank book. That account, held at Riverside Bank in Miami, contained a receipt for rent on an apartment at 951 SW 1st Ave that was used as a safe house for Cuban Power. In a memo from the CIA deputy director to the FBI, Mimi is called "one of the most active members within Cuban Power."

Statuesque and slender at 5'9," Mimi had been working closely with Morales within the organization when their business association morphed into something else. Morales had begun seeing Mimi while still married to Magda, and she became pregnant in the summer of 1967. His children with Magda were now seven, four, and the newest, Sylvia, was just one.

Morales swung by his older sister Yolanda's for one of his periodic visits with her and his adoring young nieces, Lynette and Annette. Yolanda's husband, Antonio, was an editor at the *Miami Herald* and frequently worked ungodly hours. Morales figured Yolanda and the girls would be alone, and he walked in knowing he had to tell his sister what was to come. He'd moved out of his home with Magda and their three children and was staying with expectant Mimi at her NW 5th Street apartment. There was no easy way to drop that casually in the middle of a conversation, but Morales, ever the rascal, would try.

Yolanda, fourteen years older than Ricardo, was usually the one to offer counsel.[190] Ricardo opened up more easily to her than anyone else, often to her disdain. And he was usually more truthful with Yolanda than to his associates on the street. Yolanda wanted it straight, and she gave it back in the same fashion.

"What the fuck do you think you are doing!" was the immediate reaction from Yolanda, and it didn't get any better, or quieter, from there. "*Dios mio*...what am I going to tell people?"[191]

"Everything will work out," Ricardo said, trying to shrug it off. He sat at the kitchen table, back to the wall as always, and picked at his favorite dessert made by Yolanda, *natilla*. He was then treated to hearing a list of all divorces in the family and of anyone they'd ever known, and the resultant catastrophic effect they had.

"*Esto es en colmo,*" Yolanda muttered loudly to herself, but more to him.

The final straw, the ultimate sin. Ricardo should disappear from the face of the earth from shame now. If the drama quotient hadn't been raised enough, she invoked the ultimate.

"You're going to kill mama!"

Ricardo eventually moved on from Yolanda's and confessed to his mother when he next visited her. It was more civil than his sister's display, but the recipe didn't reduce the measurement of drama. Ines turned her face down, her face tragic, and lit a cigarette. She smoked in silence then thanked God that Raul wasn't alive to see this. One cigarette after another, with not much more to say. Cuban mothers of a certain era were known to employ guilt as quickly as a nation would enact a trade embargo.

Morales's world was chaos. It was impossible for him to proceed any other way, and his family was growing accustomed to dreading what was to come next. But flowing just beneath the worry was also an admiration for what Ricardo and Pucho had done in Cuba and for America. Ricardo's nephew Rolando, Pucho's boy, was sixteen at the time.

"To me, Ricardo and my dad were Gods here on earth," he said.[192] But as with all grand ambition, grand consequence dances beside her. Everyone was also aware of that.

Then came the phone call that Ricardo had been arrested for the January 25 bombing of Servicos Especializados.

★★★

Investigators at the Servicos Especializados explosion were fastidious in their collection of potential evidence. They found a folded corner of an envelope, torn by the blast, which just happened to contain evidence against Morales.

That piece of envelope underwent a process that, in 1968, was worthy of some explanation to the public. *The Miami Herald* reported that the corner of envelope "was subjected to a process developed by Robert Worsham of the Metro Crime Laboratory which utilizes traces of body chemicals left on surfaces to bring out fingerprints."[193] A lifted print was then sent to Joe Musial in the fingerprint division, who manually compared it to the department's file of Cuban exiles, each having been fingerprinted when emigrating.

Had Hector and Omar not chosen the same location, Morales's device would have detonated and destroyed the envelope, and thus, Morales's fingerprint. When questioned about the incident years later during a deposition, he lamented as much.

"No respect at all for the professionals."[194]

At 6:15 a.m. on February 14, Morales was placed under arrest.[195] His bond hearing was set for the next day, and Magda attended with their three children. She was questioned by Assistant State Attorney Al Sepe wherein she testified about his travels to Cuba and the Congo. Bail was set at $25,000, a fortune for him in 1968, and he was thus remanded into custody of the city of Miami again.

While in jail, Morales had plenty of time to mull over the events that had led to that point. Every day was an aggregation of the sunrises and sunsets before, and there was plenty that Castro, G-2, Lefty, and the CIA were whispering in his ear. Lefty's crafty use of law enforcement was fresh in his mind, as was the federal agencies' dependence on new intelligence. Morales observed that the four arresting officers were *gringos*. The head of the city's intelligence unit and his three sergeants were all white guys who probably didn't understand the motives behind the guys they were chasing. Though they could lock up criminals, any real penetration would be impossible for them.

Morales hadn't seen much success at the federal level either. There was plenty in the press about "terrorist bombings" and the *tres letras*, or "three letters"—the exiles' name for the CIA, FBI, IRS, DEA, etc. The government had certainly gotten comfortable with the concept of anti-Castro offensives. But the fact that the tactics being employed were taught by the Agency itself and being carried out by their contract soldiers was not getting as much ink.

It took Morales two weeks to post bond. Just before he did, he missed the birth of his fourth child when Mimi gave birth to Roberto at Mt. Sinai Hospital in Miami Beach. Morales was able to see the baby boy within days of his birth, though his lifestyle would keep him out of the home as much as he would be in it. His family with Magda now saw even less of him, as the first three children were sharing him with daytime work, nighttime bombings, his new family, and now, jail.

On April 3, Morales arranged a meeting with Officer Mario Jimenez of the Dade County Criminal Intelligence Division.[196] He'd brokered the meeting through a common acquaintance and Cuban Power member Francisco Rodriguez Tamayo, who'd been in a Cuban prison with Jimenez. The meeting at Tamayo's house lasted for over two and a half hours and was audio recorded from a location four blocks away.

"I'm going to tell you something the FBI is crazy to find out," Morales told Jimenez. He went on to relay that the Soviet embassy bombing was carried out by his brother-in-law Hector, Omar Soto, and a friend of Soto's named Miguel. Morales said he'd gotten all the details right from the source after his release on bond and subsequent meetings with Hector.

Did the fact that he was informing on his wife's brother make his account more believable or less so? It likely crossed the investigators' minds and obviously crossed Ricardo's. Morales, ever the raconteur, removed the question of his motivation from the equation as only he could.

"Cornillot is a megalomanic," he explained earnestly. "He's extremely disappointed that I was arrested for the January 25 bombing and not himself. He desires publicity as a fearless revolutionary and leader of the Cuban Power organization."[197]

Jimenez was finding out what everyone around Morales already knew—he was irresistible. He radiated charm, sarcasm, and overall likability despite an underlying sense of danger in his eyes. He was magnetic.

Cops are skeptical of anyone trying to save their ass by offering up the head of another, but Morales's story had a couple of points of credibility. Firstly, he had the airtight alibi of being in jail when the bombing occurred, so there was no chance he was shirking his involvement in the Soviet bombing. Despite not being there, it was believable that he would have gotten wind of the plan, being he was active in Cuban Power with his brother-in-law.

Plus, he'd added one very specific, verifiable detail in his story. He'd said Hector was pulled over in a Mustang on I-95 in Georgia while driving back. Since the stop had happened on the interstate, it was likely the Georgia State Police did it, and they'd have a record on file. Officer Jimenez brought the findings back to his partner, Officer Cesar Camacho, and they went to work.

Meanwhile, Morales and his attorney got busy with their defense plan should the Servicos Especializados bombing case go to trial. They hatched a twofold plan to create doubt in the juror's minds. The fact that Morales's fingerprint was on the envelope that held the bomb did not necessarily indicate he was there. Hector Cornillot was the bomber, they would posit—the brother-in-law of the defendant who, obviously, had access to his home. Hector having grabbed an envelope because he either ran out or never had them was not implausible.

Further cementing that theory would be the imminent arrest of Hector Cornillot for the bombing of the Soviet embassy in Washington. They felt his highly publicized arrest plus the borrowed envelope defense would give them a shot.

Officers Jimenez and Camacho worked the Mustang angle handed to them by Morales. They found that on April 1, two days before Morales's interview with Ofc. Jimenez, Dade Country Crime Laboratory officers observed three individuals handing out Cuban Power leaflets on Biscayne Boulevard in Miami.[198] They were observed entering a blue Mustang with the license plate number 1-99226, registered under a Miguel Diaz. The officers on scene pulled them over and noted the occupants as Diaz along with Omar Soto.

Jimenez and Camacho could now link the blue Mustang to the "Miguel" from Morales's interview, as well as Omar Soto, who Morales also implicated. The leaflets in their hands tied them to Cuban Power, and thus, to Hector Cornillot. Everything fit.

Satiating local police might keep them off his tail for a while, but Morales knew the *tres letras* had eyes on him by that point. The Monkey was known throughout the exile world, and it was impossible for federal agents not to focus their crosshairs on him. He'd need to make the first move.

On April 25, 1968, Morales called the FBI field office where he made contact with Special Agent Joseph C. Ball.[199] Morales told Ball he needed to speak with him, and an in person meeting was arranged wherein Morales explained Cuban Power was in fact two groups. He shared what he'd told Dade County about Cornillot, and reported that Dr. Orlando Bosch, who was very much on the FBI's radar at that point, had reached out to Morales through a friend for a meeting. He knew Morales was a relative and working associate of Cornillot's and wanted his assistance on combining both factions of Cuban Power into one.

Nothing Morales ever did was without strategy. He had his hand on the biggest chess piece on the board, but he couldn't let on that there was a larger plan at work—an employment, of sorts, of the US government for his own use. As justification for his call to the feds, Morales said he was angry with Bosch for being disingenuous in his motives with the Cuban exile community.

"My belief in what was going on was the biggest phony scheme that can be put over on the Cuban exiles here," he said. "And my belief [is] that he did not represent the true feelings of the Cuban people, and my belief [is] that the actions that were going on only helps communist Cuba."[200]

If Agent Ball was skeptical, as he likely was, it didn't matter much. Sitting before him was one of the most prolific men in the anti-Castro exile movement, with an endless string of contacts and knowledge of who was responsible for the bombs detonating in Miami. And now that the violence was spreading throughout the country in Washington,

New York, and California, obtaining credible information and having ongoing access to it was essential.

Morales would serve up the appetizer and whet the government's appetite for what might come after. He said he'd outline the two organizations for them and deliver *both* Cuban Power groups to them by next penetrating Bosch's. Within six months, Morales would become a paid contract agent for the FBI, and all charges stemming from the Servicos Especializados bombing were dropped.

Chapter Seven Dr. Bomber (1968)

Morales confirmed for authorities that Cornillot's Cuban Power was not to be confused with Dr. Orlando Bosch's bombing network of the same name. The duplication was a simple error of two factions operating independently without knowledge of the other. Cornillot's Cuban Power was using the signature "Gerardo Torres Contrera," which Morales knew to be a fictitious name made up by his brother-in-law, and he therefore assumed Bosch was doing the same with his "Ernesto" signature.

The bookish-looking forty-two-year-old pediatrician with his trademark pencil-thin mustache and Coke-bottle glasses would've likely avoided suspicion for anything nefarious if gauged by appearance alone. He looked like the kid in class who you'd want to do your homework and the adult who you'd want to do your taxes.

Orlando Bosch Avila was born in Potrerillo, Cuba, outside Havana. He got his medical degree from the University of Havana where he was a classmate of Fidel Castro.[201] They were close enough to call each other "brother" and shared long nights smoking cigars and philosophizing at all-night cafés. The doctor completed his medical program in the US, doing his internship in Toledo and his pediatric residency in Memphis. He then returned to Cuba to assist his friend in the overthrow of Batista, becoming a chief in Castro's 26th of July Movement.[202]

After Castro assumed the reins, Bosch became disillusioned and left Cuba in July of 1960. From Miami, Bosch encouraged the defection of other Castro revolutionaries. In response, four officers and over one hundred soldiers of the 26th of July Movement took to the Las Villas mountains in August of 1960 and formed what would become

Bosch's first anti-Castro group, MIRR. The military leadership of the group was headed by former rebel army officer Victor Paneque, and Dr. Bosch became the general coordinator.[203]

Bosch's initial responsibility in MIRR was to arrange strikes against Cuba with other groups and secure financing for them. Donations came initially from a Chicago-based exile, Paulino A. Sierra, who allegedly put together cash from gambling interests in the city.[204]

As the FBI learned more about MIRR's formation and Miami-based operation, they investigated the funding of the organization, and in March 1964 they placed a thirty day mail check on the group. They intercepted communications from the group to wealthy Cuban exiles who were threatened if they didn't make large financial donations to MIRR. Dr. Bosch was implicated in the extortion attempts but was acquitted at trial.

MIRR spread its wings after the CIA rejected their proposal for a joint effort in conducting strikes in Cuba. The anti-Castro group then began flying missions on its own. Bosch said that through his association with Frank Sturgis, the former Operation 40 soldier of fortune and CIA operative, they pulled off eleven air strikes over Cuba.

Bosch's unfocused ambition got ahead of him occasionally, obscuring details that should likely have been considered in the planning phase. The House Select Committee on Assassinations of the 95th Congress wrote "his efforts at times have been described as 'bumbling' but he has also been termed 'single-mindedly' and 'morally committed.'"[205] His 1964 arrest for towing a radio-controlled torpedo through the streets of Miami during rush hour traffic stands as an example of such haste.[206]

Another qualifier might be his 1966 arrest in Naples, Florida at a police roadblock on US-41.[207] Authorities were looking for an escaped convict, but instead found six 100 pound surplus aerial practice bombs stuffed with dynamite in the backseat of Bosch's beat up Caddy. To his credit, his honesty with police must've been refreshing when he told them he was headed up the west coast of Florida "to a secret base where there was a boat we could use to bomb Castro." It's worth noting that Bosch's chosen car for this transport of contraband in his backseat was a convertible. He was given a three year suspended sentence by a Naples court.

Some gaffes were more costly for the MIRR in an economic sense, such as the time Bosch spent $3,000 of borrowed money on a boat, six hundred pounds of explosives, and a .30-caliber machine gun for a mission.[208] The boat sprung a leak and sank near the Bahamas with all purchased provisions in it.

Reports were coming in to the FBI that members of MIRR were tiring of Bosch. Confidential informant and MIRR member Orlando Rego Borrego told the FBI that "Bosch has become a fanatical egomaniac, to the point where most of the members of the MIRR are becoming uneasy under his leadership."[209] On October 29, 1965, Borrego gave a statement that members also began to question the money trail under Bosch's direction, stating "…it had been established now that the Bosch clique has not been making an accounting for funds received or disbursed…"[210]

Later that year, Borrego would report that Bosch's resources were depleting, stating, "He has no commandos or frogmen operating anywhere, and he has no known supplies or equipment outside the Miami area."[211] Considering the group's souring reputation, Bosch began to abandon the MIRR name in favor of his new Cuban Power moniker which, perhaps coincidentally, had been carrying out significant missions elsewhere with much publicity.

Though described as scattered, no one could deny Bosch's savvy or smarts. His meetings with Morales to consolidate the two groups would serve a couple of purposes; he sought to piggyback the press of Cornillot's Cuban Power for increased coverage and grow his own dwindling membership and resources through acquisition, like any good CEO would.

★★★

Morales laid out an infiltration strategy to Agent Ball and said it wouldn't take long for him to find Bosch. He was becoming more present in Little Havana and was widely recognized as the former leader of MIRR, though his Cuban Power brand was gaining traction. Morales set out to engineer a chance encounter with the doctor, which he outlined in his extensive trial deposition regarding the renewed relationship between the men.

Morales testified that on April 25 he was driving in the southwest section of Miami and noticed Bosch in the passenger seat of a black Ford Flacon driven by Andrés Jorge Gonzalez-Gonzalez, a known associate and member of Bosch's group.[212] Morales and Bosch exchanged waves and pulled over at 1st Street between 7th and 8th Avenues. The men got out and Gonzalez-Gonzalez, known on the street as "Bombillo," translated "Lightbulb," headed across the street to a warehouse.[213] Bosch and Morales then discussed the recent Cuban Power statement bearing the trademark signature of Ernesto. Bosch bluffed, saying that Ernesto and the leaders of the organization based in Cuba had arrived here with a "suitcase loaded with money" and they intended to base Cuban Power out of the US.

Morales watched the salesman emerge in the charismatic and gregarious Bosch and cut him off, Ricardo's bullshit meter flashing wildly.

"Listen," Morales began, "I have been in revolutions for a long time, and you can't fool me about some people coming from Cuba. Through my own research and my own study of the document, I believe that you are the one behind that document. You are the one signing with Ernesto's name."[214]

Bosch then realized he was speaking to not only a fellow revolutionary, but one who'd undergone the same CIA training as he had. Morales and him were equals; Bosch too realized he was standing across from someone who would shoot holes in any posturing.

"Yes," Bosch confessed, shrugging. "You know how those things work in this business." Bosch asked if the FBI had contacted Morales about the signature, suspecting they might be on to him. "Did they mention my name?"

Morales told him they had; the FBI had a short-list of three possible "Ernesto's," and Bosch was one of them. It was only a matter of time, he said, before they eliminated the other two.

Before parting, Bosch asked if Morales was willing to assist in furnishing equipment, which Morales knew to mean explosives. He gave Morales his new phone number and told him all contact with him was to be made through his girlfriend, Aimee Miranda. They went their separate ways and didn't meet again until June 12.

Bosch's Cuban Power made more headlines between the two meetings. On May 4, British shipping vessel *Granwood* was en route from Miami to Mobile, AL when an explosion rocked the vessel.[215] It was determined the explosion had originated on the outside of the ship. Leaflets were soon distributed wherein Bosch's Cuban Power, through "Ernesto," claimed responsibility.

Later that month on May 30, the Japanese freighter *Asaka Maru* suffered an explosion while at port in Tampa, several days after it docked at Dodge Island in Miami.[216] Local news media received a letter of responsibility for that as well, also signed by "Ernesto, General Delegate, Cuban Power." Two days later, the Japanese freighter *Mikagesu Maru* was victimized while docked at Pier 40 in Galveston, TX.[217] Similar to the other ships, the explosive device was determined to have been placed on the outside of the vessel, six to eight feet above the water line.

Mikagesu Maru's previous port? Dodge Island, Miami.

On June 12, the FBI issued a memo from Lt. Commander Williams of the US Coast Guard Base in Miami: "As a result of the fact that three foreign ships have experienced explosions after having been in the port facilities at Dodge Island, Miami, Florida, [Commander Williams] has instituted a complete tightening of all Coast Guard security in and about the Dodge Island facilities."[218]

A curious discovery regarding the *Granwood* bombing was its cargo—large rolls of newsprint. There was nothing heading to or from Cuba, and an FBI report cited a British agent as having said "the vessel doesn't trade with Cuba and had no reason to believe [the] explosion [was caused by anything] other than internal ship problems."[219]

What they hadn't taken into account was the bomber's carelessness. Morales told Agent Ball that he turned in Bosch because the doctor was running the "biggest phony scheme that can be put over on the

Cuban exiles" in his choice of targets. Morales said, "None of the ships that were bombed [by Bosch] nor the companies that owned those ships have been making any kind of trade with Cuba."[220] Morales's claim that Dr. Bosch was in it for the publicity and not the interests of the exiles was corroborated by the earlier statement from the British agent. Haphazard missions rushed for personal glory caused shoddy work, and that irritated Morales.

Morales's June 12 meeting with Bosch happened by chance after Ricardo ran into Aimee Miranda at a restaurant. Morales told her that he wanted to meet with the doctor again, and she promised to relay the message when she saw him later. Within an hour, Bosch walked into the restaurant and sat alone with Morales.

He was unhappy that the press coverage for the *Granwood* bombing hadn't been bigger, and he stated the FBI was breathing down his neck because they knew he was Ernesto. Bosch then admitted to sending a telegram to England, challenging their statement that the bombing was a mechanical error. He wanted to prove that the *Granwood* bombing was intentional.[221] Morales relished the moment—the guy he was feeding to the feds was so miffed by not getting credit in the press that he'd rather admit to having blundered his choice of target than let anyone think the blast was caused by a mechanical accident.

"I need more explosive equipment," Bosch continued, "and some underwater equipment."[222]

He said he was trying to secure a rebreather, a diving tank that recycles the diver's oxygen rather than expelling it, preventing bubbles on the water's surface. It allows one to stay submerged for periods of time without detection. Bosch had put Bombillo on that task.

Morales contacted Bosch and invited him to his apartment, where he arrived with Bombillo in tow. To Bosch's delight, Morales unveiled a rebreather and harnessed it onto Bombillo, then gave a full tutorial on its use. Morales was passing muster, and Bosch could hardly hold his cards to his chest. The Monkey seemed to be all he'd been built up to be.

"I need one hundred pounds of gelatin dynamite," Bosch said.[223]

★★★

Agent Joe Ball opened his trunk in the parking lot of the Howard Johnson on 27th Avenue and Morales looked down at a box marked "DuPont Company."[224] It was July 2, about three weeks after Bosch's request for more firepower. The FBI was proving to be reliable, having obtained the rebreather for Morales and now this parcel sitting in Ball's trunk.

Morales inspected the box, bypassing the printed warnings and looking for something more specific. He found it.

"There," he said, pointing at the "D" on the box. "Okay, we're good."

Morales wanted confirmation he would be giving Bosch a dummy load of explosives.

"It's legitimate," Ball said. "We got it directly from the DuPont Company in Birmingham." Morales knew what to look for, having worked with both dummy and real dynamite in his CIA training. He transferred the box to his trunk and headed off to his apartment where he was slated to meet Bosch.

There were two cars parked in front of Morales's apartment when he got there: a white '64 Ford that he recognized as Bosch's wife's car, and a green '62 Oldsmobile driven by a man with sideburns who Morales didn't recognize. Ricardo waved to Bosch who exited the Ford and joined him, and the man in the Olds came out behind them.

"Morales," Bosch said, "this is Tony Prieto. So, you have the dynamite?"[225]

Morales led Bosch to his car as Prieto opened the trunk of his green Olds.

"Is it dangerous?" Prieto asked upon joining Morales and Bosch. "Will it explode if we drop it on the floor?"

Morales picked up the box and threw it on the ground at his feet.

Prieto, satisfied with the answer, put the box in his trunk and drove off, leaving Bosch to talk with Morales. The doctor said he had a few more bombings planned, but would first hold a press conference announcing himself as Ernesto's delegate. He was lapping up the attention from his most recent string of bombings and sought to thrust himself into the spotlight as the face of the organization.

The two spoke again on August 5 when Bosch related a recent failure they'd had with the dynamite Morales procured. Apparently, the target ship arrived at all of its ports without incident, and Morales asked what Bosch made of that. He took the blame.

"We chained the bombs to the propeller rods," Bosch said. "They'd been loosened and caught by propellers." More than likely they were chained just fine; the chain was simply securing a dummy load.

Morales anticipated Bosch making a bigger deal about the dynamite's failure, maybe even beginning to doubt Ricardo, but he hadn't. The doctor had a more pressing issue.

"I must show up as the delegate for Ernesto and claim credit for everything going on here."

On August 8, 1968, there was an explosion aboard the ship *Caribbean Venture* while docked in Miami, which surprised Morales.[226] Had there been actual dynamite mixed in the FBI's shipment of dummy devices? There was a chance another group was responsible for that hit, but it seemed unlikely given Bosch's recent modus operandi and desperation to create more headlines. That was confirmed when he next spoke with Bosch.

"You should feel very proud that the dynamite you furnished was used on the *Caribbean Venture* job," Bosch said. Morales was perplexed.[227]

Bosch went on to order more dynamite from Morales, two hundred pounds more, as well as C4. Morales knew Agent Ball could procure the dummy dynamite from DuPont, but he wasn't sure about C4.

"No," Morales said. "Forget about C4, forget about Pentolite and TNT. Only dynamite is available."

Bosch accepted that but said he was concerned about how Morales's dynamite had failed in other jobs. Regardless, however, Bosch reiterated his thirst for more dynamite, as he'd need to produce hits so he could call the press conference and be named the delegate for Ernesto. Morales found it remarkable that Bosch's egotistical appetite was blinding him to what was really happening there. The FBI ruse was proving easier than Morales had anticipated.

But what about the *Caribbean Venture*? Bosch had just credited Morales with having produced the explosives. This gnawed at Morales.

"I'm surprised you need more equipment already. How much did you use on the *Caribbean Venture*?"

Bosch explained he'd used Morales's supply as well as some additional dynamite he'd procured from a mining company. There was no way for him know only half his supply had actually detonated.

Morales contacted the FBI and arranged for another pickup of dummy dynamite. A string of pickups from the FBI and drops to Bosch and his associates would continue through the summer. As the drops became more frequent, Ricardo met more members of Bosch's crew. He was slowly being ingratiated into the group and was now known to individuals like Bombillo, Tony Prieto, El Iseno, and Bobby Balan.[228] Either Morales had won Bosch's trust or the doctor was completely preoccupied by his Ernesto antics. Morales was exposed to multiple locations they used for drops and their system of frequently switching vehicles. Cuban Power was obviously comfortable with Morales due to his reliability, reputation, or both.

Bosch rang Morales at home in early September.

"Listen, Morales, the equipment is no good." Morales then left for Bosch's house after leaving a message for Agent Ball reporting where he was going and why.

Morales entered Bosch's and discussed the dummy bombs. Bosch was becoming increasingly edgy over the misfires and was frustrated when his visitor got there. Morales suggested water damage again.

"Maybe the timing devices are leaking water into the canister," he said.

"No. Those bombs are waterproof. We drill little holes and pump air into them, then we submerge them in a water tank to see if air bubbles come out. They are foolproof."

Morales needed to stay in control and keep the operation going despite the repeated failures. He asked how much dynamite was left from the load, and Bosch said about a case.

"Well, listen, let's go out and test it. I can tell you if it's phony or not."

Morales had to broach the subject of possibly having unwittingly given Bosch a phony load. Bosch was a former CIA mercenary, so bullshitting him with mechanical jargon wouldn't work. He'd already refuted the water damage defense by drilling the outer layer of the canisters to ensure they floated and would resist water. Bosch said everything was stored at Aimee's, so they went there first.

Aimee had been managing a cache of weaponry for Cuban Power in her apartment. Morales saw a couple of boxes of M1 rifle grenades loaded with C4, soap boxes filled with Pentolite, a military grade explosive, and dynamite. They grabbed a stick of dynamite from the remainder of Morales's load and drove to a canal behind Miami International Airport. Morales placed a blasting cap on the dynamite, lit the fuse, and retreated. They watched as the blasting cap popped without triggering the dynamite.

"What is your opinion?" Bosch asked.

"This is phony dynamite."

It was reasonable to think Morales, and by proxy, Bosch, had been ripped off. They stood in the silence of the moment for a bit, each man formulating a very different plan.

"Well, let's go see the source," Bosch said.

Morales was put on the spot. They both stood in the Florida marsh with confirmation that the lauded Monkey Morales's supply was bullshit. And now Bosch wanted to meet the fictitious street source of the dynamite.

They went to an apartment where Morales had previously mentioned his source lived. Fortunately, no one answered the random bell Morales chose to ring. They agreed to return at a later date.

★★★

On September 15 at around 8:00 p.m., Morales was getting dressed to go out for a quiet Sunday dinner when Bosch showed up at his apartment.[229] They still hadn't revisited the fake source of the dummy dynamite, and Morales hadn't reached out to him in the past five days.

"I need you," Bosch said. "Do you have tools—screwdrivers? Pliers?"

Morales did and was instructed to grab them and go with Bosch. They got in his car and began driving in circles, turning the lights off and on, employing elusive practices.

"We are clear," he finally said. "There is no FBI surveillance. They are giving us a free hand."

What that free hand was for, Morales still wasn't certain. Wherever they were headed clearly needed to be outside the prying eyes of *tres letras*.

They pulled into the driveway of Aimee's apartment building where Morales saw Tony Prieto and Bobby Balan standing in the darkness. Morales noted that they wore all black. That, coupled with the fact that Bosch hadn't mentioned the reason for the rushed meeting, began to move Morales's internal gauge past caution and toward a state of preparedness. Morales and Bosch exited the car and went into the apartment, followed by Prieto and Balan, where Aimee met them. They led Morales into the kitchen and to a large .57mm recoilless shoulder mount rifle on the floor.

"The trigger housing is not working," Bosch said. "Can you fix her up?"

Morales had been roused from his home and brought to Aimee's artillery bunker to perform a repair on the cannon sitting on a kitchen floor. Bosch hadn't called in advance, and for some reason two of Bosch's men were needed to supervise.

"I'm going to try," Morales replied.

He went to work on the weapon while the others all helped. After three hours of pulling the weapon apart, Morales identified the culprit.

"It's the spring that goes into the cocking rod," he said. "I can go up to Hialeah tomorrow and get a new spring."

"No, no," Bosch said. "It has to be tonight."

There was obviously a mission at hand, and Morales had been pulled into it. He turned back to the weapon. The cocking system was defective, and without the spring, a manual load of artillery was the only way to arm the rifle.

"The only way you can fix this thing for tonight is for a single shot."

Bosch nodded. "Well, let's try and do it that way."

There was an additional problem—the long range weapon had no scope. What proceeded was a spellbinding clinic on guerrilla improvisation. Using adhesive tape, a wire clothes hanger, and a piece of string, Morales fashioned a makeshift scope atop the weapon that was outfitted and sighted with the same mechanics of a mounted scope.

"What kind of ammunition do you have for this?" Morales asked him. Bosch directed Balan to hand Ricardo a green TNT shell. Morales examined it and discreetly scratched at the paint with his thumbnail. As he suspected, it revealed a blue surface under the green paint—a discovery he kept to himself.

While Morales had been working on the weapon, Bosch continued to muse about Cuban Power's success, the most recent of which occurred in Puerto Rico when the Spanish vessel *Coromito* was bombed.[230] "Ernesto" had sent a press release to radio stations WQBA and WFAB claiming responsibility for the job. By that point, Ernesto's name was followed by "mythical head of Cuban Power" on FBI memos.[231] The ruse was wearing off, if it had ever been effective in the first place, and Bosch continued to remark that his imminent reveal had to appear on press releases claiming responsibility for new bombings, ensuring media coverage. His frenzy of activity on the seas was anchored to his desperation to stand before his community in an official position of authority.

They were done with the gun, but it was clear their night was just beginning, and Morales was hesitant to try and break away. It was obvious Bosch had designed the night to carry out this way, and Morales was about to be made an accomplice in whatever was about to happen.

★★★

With the gun now assembled, Balan and Prieto were dispatched to swap cars while Morales walked outside with Bosch, where a '64 Dodge Dart sat waiting for them. Morales hoped the FBI had been staking them out, though it was unlikely. Bosch had engineered this impromptu visit without contacting him in advance; there was no chance for him to have called Agents Ball and Davis to notify them he'd be out with Bosch and his crew.

As they drove, Bosch told Morales the rifle was being used that night, and he wanted him to stay with them. At around midnight they picked up a man introduced to Morales as Paulino Gutierrez, who Bosch told, "everything is set for tonight."[232] He then suggested a pit stop.

"Let's go out and get something for dinner."

Bosch drove Paulino and Morales to Rancho Luna Restaurant on 8th Street in the southwest district. Bosch enjoyed a full meal while Morales and Paulino each sipped a beer, and Bosch and Paulino talked Cuban Power business. Paulino said his son Jorge, a partner in a radio and TV advertising agency, had been working on the next press release, and Bosch said the Cuban paper *Replica* would be running a story the following morning saying Ernesto was going to appoint Dr. Bosch as the head of Cuban Power.[233]

Morales figured the men were so engrossed in business talk that he could slip away for a bathroom trip and hit the pay phone to call one of the agents. He excused himself and slid out, but Paulino said he'd go too and walked to the men's room with him. No phone call.

They left the restaurant and drove to MacArthur Causeway, a two-way stretch of road with nothing but water on each side that connected downtown Miami and Miami Beach.

"There it is," Bosch said, pointing out the window to a huge ship sitting in the harbor. It was the *Polanica,* the Polish cargo ship, lit up in the night with its search lights pointed down into the water. Morales noticed Coast Guard patrol boats in front of the ship—evidence of the increased security in Miami's ports promised by the Coast Guard. The recoilless rifle, with a range of up to several thousand yards, now made sense to Morales. Swimming up to the hull of any ship in Miami and sticking some dynamite on it was now impossible, even with the rebreather.

They kept on and passed Prieto, who was parked on the other side of the Causeway in a light green '57 Chevy. Bobby Balan was nearby, holding a fishing line off the causeway into the water.

"There they are," Bosch said. "That car belongs to a mechanic friend of Bobby's." His guys had done yet another switch while the three of them were at the restaurant. Prieto and Balan had the recoilless rifle in the trunk and were awaiting instruction to fire the weapon then dump it over the guard rail into the water.

Bosch, Morales, and Paulino made a U-turn and went back to the Miami side where they parked by the Miami Herald building, allowing them a clear view of not only the harbor, but also any cars entering and exiting the Causeway.

"Morales," Bosch said. "How is it going to sound?"

"Boom, zip, boom," Morales said. Bosch nodded and the three men settled in and waited, with Bosch eventually going into the backseat to sleep.

At 2:45 a.m., a boom reverberated through the area, and the three men popped upright.[234]

"That's it!" Bosch yelled, roused from slumber, howling and laughing. "Let's go!" Paulino pulled out and they were off.

Bosch was electric on the ride back, rambling about calling the newspapers and radio stations personally the following morning to tell them about the attack. He also said he was praying that some of the Poles on board were killed by the blast.

But it was very unlikely that any Polish sailors were harmed, much less killed. The blue paint beneath the green artillery shell was a remarkably fortuitous discovery.

★★★

Special Agent Benjamin Grogan secured the Edwards Model 75 pocket tape recorder on Ricardo's body as agents William Dowling and Lawrence Coutre looked on. Morales had been contacted earlier that day by Dr. Bosch, requesting Morales meet him at his home that night, September 26.[235] Morales reported this to the FBI who decided they'd better start getting Morales's dealings with Bosch on tape. They had the entire story of the *Polanica* bombing from Morales's reporting, and they sought to corroborate that with recorded evidence that Bosch had masterminded the attack.

The recorder's on/off switch was snaked through Ricardo's pants and secured in his front pocket where he could turn it on when he got to Bosch's. He headed to NW 48th Place and got everything he'd expected to and more on tape number one. It didn't take long for Bosch to discuss the *Polanica* shelling and others.

> Bosch: [FBI translation] "We have hit very hard. One ship, and another ship, and another ship, and another ship—and the explosion, and the hit there, and the hit here. I believe that we have worked intelligently. We have developed this matter intelligently."[236]

Bosch went on to admit he'd exaggerated his retelling of the *Polanica* hit to the press.

> Bosch: [FBI translation] "I told the people many things and there were two cars with those people riding around and there were two companions on the beach with a walkie-talkie and two at the Miami Herald with another walkie-talkie...the cannon was fired and the Coast Guard responded with machine guns. Morales, what did we win with the other war?"
>
> Morales: [Translated] "Propaganda."[237]

Bosch was a master at that. This fabricated version of the story was a far cry from the actual hit.

Bosch's brand of propaganda came with a flair of theatre as well. In the long-anticipated press conference announcing the transfer of power, a hooded figure appeared, his face covered, and announced himself as Ernesto. He then declared Orlando Bosch was the new public representative of Cuban Power.

What Bosch never discussed, and might not have even realized, was the lack of damage suffered by the *Polanica*. Artillery sold on the black market is often not what is advertised, and Morales noticed the shell's green paint wasn't exactly military grade. The blue underneath revealed the ammunition to be a practice shell. An actual shell fired from the .57mm recoilless would penetrate steel, but the most damage a practice round would do is make a dent and splinter into fragments. Though Morales still felt it necessary to try and notify the FBI that a Cuban Power mission was underway, he knew no significant damage would befall the night's target.

A wired Morales next met with Bosch and associates on September 30, 1968, and again on October 1. He caught more discussion about the *Polanica* shelling and the Cuban Power organization on tape, netting more members in the FBI's web. At one particular meeting at Bosch new headquarters in the Jose Martí Building, Cuban Power member Bombillo Gonzalez and Morales were recorded after stepping into a back office for a private conversation. Gonzalez related concerns over the amount of attention the organization was getting from the feds, having himself been interviewed by agents after the Russian embassy bombing.

Morales broached the subject of Bosch's possible arrest, and Gonzalez indicated Cubans in cities across the US were prepared to take action if it happened.

> Morales: [FBI translation] "Do you believe that they intend to apprehend Orlando?"[238]
>
> Gonzalez: [FBI translation] "I do not think so. They are very such afraid of the reaction...they are going to come out for him afterwards in Miami. For they know who Orlando is. Los Angeles, New York, New Jersey, Miami. They will paralyze it. The wise guys and the crazy ones will go out and place bombs...if they arrest Orlando, the wise guys are going to place

> bombs here—bang! bang!—[they are] going to come out because of sympathy, because it will be stirred up."
>
> Morales: [FBI translation] "The people support you one day, they support you two days, then they forget you."
>
> Gonzalez: [FBI translation] "To the people, it is necessary to give them a piece of bread in one hand, and a cudgel in the other."

Bombillo then suggested if the Cubans in Miami were to take action, given their strength in number, it would be crippling. He thought the FBI knew that and therefore wouldn't arrest Cuban Power members.

> Gonzalez: [FBI translation] "We are going to paralyze Miami—the hotels, the tourism is starting up now, brother."[239]
>
> Morales: [FBI translation] "With tourism coming up now, if Miami is paralyzed by a protest because of the arrest of Orlando, just imagine."
>
> Gonzalez: [FBI translation] "Why do you think that they are following us so closely there? In order not to permit us to do anything. They do not want to pick us up."
>
> Morales: [FBI translation] "That's right. That would call attention and things like that."

Within days of the FBI turning over four cassette tapes with translated transcriptions, a grand jury returned a sealed indictment on Thursday, October 10.

Early Friday morning, October 11, in a coordinated effort across the city, thirty-six FBI agents arrested Dr. Orlando Bosch and eight members of Cuban Power, including Bobby Balan, Bombillo, Paulino, and Aimee.[240] Bosch was charged with the most counts—five—and had bond set at $50,000. In addition to the charge of attacking the freighter, Bosch received three counts of sending threatening cablegrams to Gen. Francisco Franco of Spain, President Gustavo Diaz Ordaz of Mexico, and Prime Minister Harold Wilson of Great Britain. Western Union confirmed Bosch had sent the cables signed "Ernesto."

Cubans around the country didn't react as Bombillo had predicted, nor was there any widespread labor action in Miami. Revolutionaries, Cubans understood, were in the business of fighting.

On November 16, 1968, Orlando Bosch, head of one of the highest profile international terror organizations, was convicted and sentenced to ten years in prison. It was a huge win for the FBI. Bosch had never served time for any crime he'd been charged with despite his encounters with nearly every branch of law enforcement. Furthermore, the successful capture and prosecution of a prominent anti-Castro bombing group organizer indicated that the politically motivated violence in Miami could be effectively combatted with reliable information from an operative on the inside. It was a service that Ricardo Morales would turn onto an occupation.

Chapter Eight
Blood in the Streets (1968)

While Morales was preoccupied with Bosch's Cuban Power case, Hector Cornillot and his group kept busy with bombing targets they believed to be pro-Cuba. Cornillot's group determined Canada was being too gracious to the Castro regime, and on October 18, 1968, the group bombed an Air Canada office in Miami Beach.[241] Morales had pointed the FBI in Hector's direction after clarifying the issue of the dual Cuban Power factions, and by doing so, implicated him in its crimes as a result. Hector Cornillot was already in their crosshairs when Air Canada happened.

Morales's intel about the two Cuban Power groups was the first of many instances wherein he used information to replace his trapped foot with that of another exile. His brother-in-law understood the bond between mercenaries living in the collective service of a singular mission. Other organized crime syndicates would impose a death sentence on an informant simply to protect their own personal gains. It's all crime for gain, for greed, with no mission statements attached.

The US government's initial plans to target Cuba had ready participants in the Miami exile groups. The aggression in the exiled mercenaries didn't have to be ignited via some military indoctrination process—they were being sent to defeat the regime that had destroyed their families. It was personal. The exiles' propulsive mission was an eventual return to a Cuba they knew was possible, one they'd seen a glimmer of before—*el gran sueño,* to them, the "grand dream."

Because of that shared passion for a singular goal, there was a working reciprocal code among the Cuban mercenaries even after the US abandoned its plans in Cuba. "Ratting" didn't exist. The sacrifice of *one* allowed the mission to continue for the others. "One mission" seemed to be their governing principle, and a barrage of information kept the government scurrying as the bombings continued. Those that went to jail because of another exile's information did so to keep the informants operating. They didn't make up bullshit leads, as agencies would quickly tire of that game and label their organizations as unreliable. Rather, the win-win scenario was to keep the mission going, while feeding occasional raw meat to the *tres letras*.

The exile community didn't disrespect law enforcement; they were not the enemy. Though the US government was not beyond reproach—many exiles felt the plan to combat Castro was discarded too quickly—the exiles understood that the federal agents were working men and women. In the defense's deposition of FBI agent Bernardo Perez, the agent indicated he remembered first interacting with Hector Cornillot when just seeing him around the community. They nodded to each other, not knowing who the other one was.

> Q: I mean, do you nod at everybody on the street that you pass by?
>
> A: He is Cuban and I am a Latin, and people—Latins—tend to be very friendly. There is no animosity. We have a job, and he feels we have a job, and you don't get uptight about it.[242]

This mindset contributed to Morales's distaste for the Cook job, wherein he was unwittingly hired to bomb Officer Jerry Saslaw's property. His anger upon learning the target's identity was rooted in that unwritten contract with law enforcement. Morales was sincere in his declaration that he wouldn't have accepted the job had he known he would be bombing a cop—that's a mafia thing. Not a Cuban thing.

Hector Cornillot was arrested and charged with unlawful throwing, placing, and discharging of a bomb.[243] The thought of going to prison for decades wasn't daunting to Hector. He was the son of a revolutionary, first arrested in 1958 by US officials at age seventeen while trying to sail back to Cuba with his father to join the fight against Batista. In his current case, he advised his public defender Steven Mechanic not to even speak in his defense. Furthermore, Cornillot told the jury, "If the charge is being a revolutionary, then I am guilty."[244] On May 5, 1972, the jury took that to heart and Hector Cornillot was convicted and sentenced to thirty years.[245]

He stood stoic when the jury returned after only an hour and read the verdict. He felt nothing. No revenge, no anger. It was the next stage of his life.

"The medals of a revolutionary are prison and death," he said.[246] He harbored no animosity toward Morales on a personal or professional level, even though he was divorcing his sister for another woman and tossing him in prison. "I loved Ricardo," he said. "I don't blame him."[247]

Hector would embrace the revolutionary lifestyle and make his time in prison work for him. He educated himself, wrote letters to the courts for the other inmates, and read incoming mail for those who couldn't read. He spearheaded a prison program called Reality Therapy, which focused on overcoming obstacles and moving forward.

"Willpower is a muscle you have to exercise with short-term, easily achievable goals," he says of the program. "I did that in prison. It worked. I had a big following of prisoners that quit smoking. It was healthy for them."[248] One short-term goal Hector would accomplish, which might've served as a testament to the program's effectiveness for inmates, was escaping from federal prison years later in 1976.[249] At age thirteen, young Rick walked into his Aunt Vivian's house rather surprised but also elated to see his *Tío* Hector sitting on the couch watching TV. He greeted his uncle excitedly and asked why he wasn't in jail anymore.

"Eh, I got tired of it," he said. "So I left."

With the arrests and convictions of both Cornillot and Bosch, the government had dealt a significant blow to both Cuban Power groups. It did not go unnoticed that Morales was the catalyst in both instances. This was only the opening act in the Morales-FBI production.

Morales had been receiving small payments from Agents Ball and Davis since the Bosch investigation began. He was paid a few hundred bucks each month to recoup expenses once the FBI certified the reliability of his information. After the Bosch verdict, Morales took on a larger role with them by providing a steady flow of information.

At the rate of $700 per month, Morales became a paid informant for the FBI, feeding them information and providing much needed clarity on the who's who in Little Havana.[250] Agents Ball and Davis remained Ricardo's handlers, frequently meeting at the Howard Johnson's and talking all things that go boom in the Miami night.

The benefits of this relationship worked both ways. It was becoming known in Little Havana that, in addition to having been a contract agent for the CIA, Morales had added the FBI to his list of contacts. Depending on his predilections, he could steer the attention of authorities either toward or from certain members of the community. After having contributed to the arrest and conviction of his own brother-in-law, it seemed no one was safe. Let alone Morales.

Word had made its way back to Ricardo and his FBI handlers that a price was put on his head after the Bosch conviction. He didn't think Bosch initiated it—he was too savvy a mercenary—but someone with money had to be behind it, provided the rumor was true. The veracity of the rumor didn't matter; he was in as much danger as if it were fact.

Morales didn't take any additional precautions. He went about his business in the open, carousing the same places he always had, somewhat emboldened by the reputation he was building. He'd been a target before, whether during his defection from G-2 or the missions for Operation 40. If anyone had a gene for fearlessness, it was him.

The confidence with which Morales operated in the face of danger could've been interpreted as careless by a lesser operative. But Morales believed his cunning would always result in a win when pitted against the ineptitude of others. He assumed anyone foolish enough to pick up a contract on The Monkey was probably in the latter group and would be easily foiled.

★★★

Atomico became a legend in Little Havana. His nickname, translated "Atomic," was uttered in the community for years with a dubious reverence. His real name was Julio Aton Costanzo, and before garnering his nickname he was busy recruiting exiles for one mission or another, though most never came to fruition. Before coming to the US, Costanzo was an officer in the rebel army in Cuba, and he was in charge of exterminating political enemies.[251] The Directorate General of the Spanish Ministry of Government reported "several violent deaths are attributed to him and he is considered to be mentally unbalanced."[252]

In 1965, Costanzo broke into the Miami anti-Castro groups by recruiting Cuban exiles for a commando team being formed by rebel soldier Odelio Garcia Derizanzo and Gerald Patrick Hemming, an American adventurer and soldier of fortune.[253] Miami was full of young unemployed refugees, which made assembling a list of recruits easy. By offering pay of fifty dollars a day, they hired forty-nine exiles and eleven Americans, training and readying them for battle in the Dominican Republic. The team was to fight General Antonio Imbert Barrera's loyalist army in his battle against rebel forces. However, Hemming's past efforts staging anti-Castro missions out of Miami and the Florida Keys had consistently been aborted, and he was viewed as unreliable.[254] Morales's friend Luis Posada, who'd introduced him to Lefty Rosenthal, stated to the FBI that although Costanzo and Hemming were "constantly involved in plans for revolutionary activity, the plans never materialize and it appears highly unlikely this plan will ever be put into force."[255] It wasn't.

By 1968, Aton Costanzo was released from prison after sixty days for planning yet another aborted raid, this time of Haiti.[256] As he reintegrated in the community, word began trickling in to Morales that Costanzo was asking around about him, inquiring as to what car he drove, where he lived, and what places he frequented. Then, as Morales testified at deposition, he got confirmation of what he'd suspected.

"He picked up a contract on my life right after the Orlando Bosch trial in 1968."[257]

Morales, never one to sit back and allow circumstance to dictate, went on the offensive. He later testified to having seen Costanzo in his neighborhood on the night of November 22. Morales immediately grabbed a couple of associates and a .45 caliber M3 submachine gun with silencer.[258] Morales got in one vehicle, driven by a man identified only as Gonzalez, while his associate Aguedo got in a second vehicle designated as the "clean car." Also referred to as a crash car, this second car's function is to follow the main car in a mission and block the road behind the primary activity. With the road obstructed, the primary car is afforded a clean getaway. If the situation gets particularly dicey, like a police pursuit, the secondary car is to crash into the pursuing vehicle, thus its alternate label.

Morales directed Gonzalez to circle the blocks surrounding his and Mimi's NW 5th Street apartment. A little after 8:30 p.m., they turned onto SW 7th Ave and encountered Costanzo walking alone. Gonzalez slowed the car, and Morales raised the machine gun out the window and drilled seventeen rounds into the fellow exile.[259] The two cars sped off without detection as emergency personnel responded and rushed Costanzo to the hospital.

Ricardo's decision to shoot Aton Costanzo was, in his words, a "him or me" situation. Morales's kills in the Congo were casualties of war; violence was part of the trade. Any hesitation, any thought spent deliberating the morality of a bullet fired would land one in a body bag. It seemed that reflex transferred from the jungle to the streets.

Morales was precise in his stateside bombing missions and always kept civilians safe from any collateral damage. He'd stressed the importance of that to Lefty Rosenthal during their partnership, and Rosenthal was of a similar mindset. Morales had only shot jewel fence Hy Gordon out of instinct when he went for Lefty. Morales didn't do contract hits on people. He fired on instinct, when it was necessary, and he had a keen sixth sense about people in his world and the complicated situations in which they found themselves.

In Aton Costanzo, Morales saw more than a neighborhood guy telling the community he was picking up the contract on The Monkey. Costanzo's reported instability, coupled with his desperation to make a legitimate name for himself after all the false starts with Hemming, signaled this was a guy who was willing to take a shot at someone like Morales. In doing so, Costanzo would've made a more substantial name for himself in the exile world.

The events of November 22, 1968 produced a new nickname for Costanzo when the people of Little Havana read in the newspapers he'd been shot seventeen times—and lived. Aton Costanzo, known as Atomico from that day forward, was alive and talking from his hospital bed. In short time, the exile was back on the streets of Miami, passing residents who looked at him like a figure from folklore, both mystical and ghoulish.

Atomico's younger brother, Avelino, told the press that the shooting was done by Castro's G-2 in their attempts to eliminate the top revolutionaries in Miami.[260] As spectacular as that story would've been, rife with international intrigue elevating Costanzo so high that Fidel Castro was gunning for him specifically, it wasn't an accurate portrayal of Atomico's status.

Though he was contacted the Miami police force a few hours later, Morales was not arrested for the attempted murder of Aton Costanzo, nor would he ever be. Costanzo refused to press charges due to either mercenary code or fear. It was not a secret who'd done this to him—he'd seen Morales firing at him. Furthermore, Costanzo's partners who'd visited him in the hospital were spinning quite a yarn to support the grand theory that Castro had a hand in the assassination attempt. Francisco "Pancho" Varona, an exile in Costanzo's circle, was emphatic in convincing him that Joaquin Sanjenis and someone named "Enrique the American" had been acting on Castro's orders and sent Morales to do the job.[261] Ultimately, Avelino Costanzo publicly stated he felt Varona and his sponsors were attempting to use his brother Aton for self-serving propaganda, and that talk faded.

Residents of Little Havana were growing accustomed to the continued exile activity and the increasingly outrageous characters in the violent opera playing out in their streets. Youngsters playing stickball on SW 7th Ave stepped over Atomico's bloodstain for years, rounding it as they headed for third. To the older residents, it was a monument, of sorts, to the mysterious war being fought on behalf of all who still dreamed of a return to the Cuba in their collective imagination. Both Morales and Atomico would now separately receive awestruck stares as they passed by residents of Little Havana, for very different reasons.

The sentiment—"How the hell is he still walking around here?"—was the same for both men.

★★★

Morales shook off the inconvenience of failing to assassinate his would-be killer and continued his work with Ball and Davis. The FBI continued to pay his $700 monthly fee in exchange for answers to any questions they had in the course of their investigations in South Florida. As far as sources went, Ricardo Morales was a dream come true for the feds.

But he was a tough nut. He continued to carry his fully automatic .9mm Browning, his favorite weapon, despite not having a license to do so. It was registered with ATF, given its ability to fire automatic, but he'd never been given a permit from Dade County to carry it concealed. Agent Davis had been getting complaints from the State Attorney's office about it and advised Morales to stop.[262]

"You could be arrested for that," Davis said. He told his informant there was no shortage of people looking to embarrass the Bureau, and they'd pounce on an opportunity like this. He recommended Ricardo keep the pistol in the trunk of his car instead. Morales thanked him for the advice and continued to carry it anyway. George Davis had a piece on him at all times and didn't have a bounty placed on his head in Little Havana. 'Nuff said.

Though the feds had benefited from Morales illuminating the shadowy Cuban bombing network, local law enforcement was still feeling around with their hands and bumping into shit.

Chapter Nine Diaz in Dade (1972)

Morales found himself surrounded by dozens of patrolmen in the Public Safety Department building. It wasn't exactly unfamiliar turf, though the same couldn't be said for the circumstances under which he was there.

By the early '70s, Little Havana had fully bloomed into an active enclave for Cubans of all ages, redolent with the aroma of *cafecito* and the uptempo sounds of salsa music from storefront speakers. Tobacco wafted around the tables where the clacking of dominos punctuated the animated chatter of the old men. The ladies shopped on the *Calle Ocho* while the side streets were alive with stickball-playing children. Little Havana was a fully grown community now, forever tattooed on the peninsula stretching out from the bottom of the US.

After having fallen behind for years, the police departments in Miami sought to catch up by hiring Spanish-speaking recruits. Miami Police Chief Bernard Garmire explained the initiative and said Cubans were hesitant to participate due to the abusive policing they'd experienced in Cuba.[263] The department had been running ads on Cuban radio while also using their most direct asset—the few Cuban and Puerto Rican officers—to farm applications.

"Other things being equal," Chief Garmire said of the recruitment process, "the man who speaks Spanish is getting preference."[264] The language gap was having an effect on the department's ability to police their community.

That afternoon in the PSD building, Morales and Sgt. Vincent Oller met to address an unlikely partnership recently brokered by the FBI.

Morales was to begin assisting the police department in their quest to understand and penetrate Cuban exile groups and their networks.

Agent George Davis first broached the subject with Morales, asking him to get the younger Latino officers up to speed with what was going on in the streets. The police department had finally hired a sizable number of Spanish-speaking officers, but more than a decade of growth in the Cuban refugee community was behind them. As Davis and Ball continued to mine Morales for his seemingly endless stream of information, they saw an opportunity to also assist local law enforcement by sharing their prized tool. Davis told Morales to introduce the new officers to the streets of Miami that he knew.

"Assist," Davis had told him. "Assist these new Spanish-speaking officers with getting into the nitty-gritty of the Cuban community."[265]

Morales knew that meant driving around with them and spotlighting areas and people he felt to be of interest. Though the Bureau gave him freedom to use his discretion, the Dade PSD was interested in specific targets, and Morales was instructed to focus on them.

The intent of the FBI and police department was to have Morales explain the intricate web of players and activities that had formed over the previous dozen years in South Miami. Local police had open cases on people they didn't know much about, and Morales had the knowledge to connect the dots. He would submit reports to the FBI detailing the specific activities he was conducting with the local officers.

In addition to regular pay from the FBI, Morales was collecting sporadic payments from the Bureau of Narcotics and Dangerous Drugs (BNDD), the precursor to today's DEA, on a case-by-case basis when information he'd provided had proven useful.

His reputation made him an asset beyond the traditional agency-informant relationship. PSD Bomb Squad Capt. Tom Brodie had Morales come to headquarters and give a seminar about bombs to officers. Experts teach, right?

After the seminar, Brodie introduced Morales to Sgt. Oller of the Organized Crime Bureau. Oller had been active in the recruitment of the department's new officers, and that summer afternoon in the cafeteria, Oller would point out one of his rising stars and hook him up with Ricardo.[266]

Twenty-three year old Officer Raul Diaz was ten years younger than Morales. He had been active in Miami law enforcement since his 1967 internship for the Miami Beach Police while still in college. Upon graduation, Diaz joined the larger Dade PSD in 1971 and advanced quickly due to his time and efforts working with Miami Beach before.[267] He was soon detached from uniform detail and placed in Oller's Organized Crime Bureau, working a special project with Customs.

Shortly after the introduction in the cafeteria, Oller stopped at Diaz's desk in the OCB.

"From now on you're working with Morales," he said.

Diaz was working on a case for the US Customs Task Force. It was an extension of the famous French Connection case—the sprawling, decades-long operation that investigated the funneling of heroin from Indochina to Turkey, France, and into the Unites States.[268] In this instance, a group of Cubans in New York had moved down to Miami to receive and distribute heroin from France. Ricardo had previously provided information on one of those Cubans.

Morales and Diaz hit it off from jump street. Diaz was a dedicated, street-smart worker, and Morales saw a lot of himself in the young cop. Within a short time, they found they were bound by more than the assignment. One day while driving around, Morales found himself repeating Diaz's name, racking his brain to remember where he'd heard it before.

"Oh," he finally said, remembering. "Raul Diaz Galup. He was a teacher of mine from back home."

"Gym class?"

Diaz asked if Morales went to La Salle Catholic School. He had; Diaz's father had been his teacher. They later discovered their lives further intersected while discussing bombing cases in Miami. Morales recounted his adventures with John Clarence Cook, confessing to having been responsible for the bombing of his Cadillac and the boat named after his pretty wife.

"Marianne," Diaz said.

"You know her?" Morales asked, and Diaz revealed that his mother had been her seamstress and had missed the bombing by only a few hours that night.

And like that, Morales had met his new partner's parents.

★★★

The fit, young officer with TV star looks was poised to ascend the ranks of Miami's law enforcement community. He had only been in the US since 1961. At age thirteen, Raul Diaz and his younger brother were put on a plane bound for the US from Cuba as part of Operation Pedro Pan, a program enacted by the US government in 1960 after Castro's seizure of power.[269] Under the agreement, children between ages four and sixteen were permitted safe entry into the US from Cuba with a special visa waiver. Without a Cuban embassy in the US, the Catholic Charities of Miami served as a de facto processing agent, helping children into the country and caring for many who had no family here. More than fourteen thousand unaccompanied children emigrated in the program's brief two years.

Upon arriving, the Diaz boys spent their time living between Miami and Miami Beach. In 1964, Diaz landed in a gang—more a band of Cuban youth protecting each other than a traditional criminal street gang—and became the group's president. Diaz was driving his crew to New York City in 1967 when he was told two of the members were transporting several hundreds of hits of LSD. Diaz was furious because this risked the group's safety, especially if they were caught with drugs on the road. He turned around, went back to Miami, and fired eleven of his best friends in the gang.

Other than the purging of those members, that trip inspired something more significant in Diaz's life when he switched his college major from accounting to criminology. He began his internship with the Miami Beach Police Department that same year while still serving as the president of Miami's largest youth gang. That precarious position actually added great value to his time with the department.

Diaz had met the officers in the narcotics department, and he approached one with a problem he was having with a couple of street guys selling drugs to members of his gang. The department seized upon that rare opportunity, and Diaz was sent on the first undercover buy of his career—a twenty-five dollar purchase of one ounce of pot. After that, he set up a deal for two pounds which resulted in several arrests and five-year sentences. The eighteen-year-old Diaz had a major narcotics bust under his belt before graduating college.

Upon graduation, Diaz joined the Dade Public Safety Department, eschewing a career in Miami Beach for the larger PSD, which he figured would offer more opportunity for advancement.

After only five months in Dade PSD, Diaz moved out of uniform and into a US Customs task force in Sgt. Oller's Organized Crime Bureau. Diaz's work, with help from Morales on the French Connection offshoot, contributed to his transfer to the Narcotics Bureau. After completing more undercover busts there, he transitioned again to the Counter-Terrorism Unit.

Diaz and Morales's effective teamwork on local investigations was crucial to the BNDD. The federal agency would land successful prosecutions against Manuel Penabaz and six others for trafficking six kilos of cocaine, Orlando Lamadrid and four other defendants for moving seven kilos, and Elpidio Hernandez for trafficking.[270]

One constant in Diaz's journey up the ladder had been Morales's presence in his life, both professionally and personally. Aside from his collaborating with Morales on cases, Diaz was drawn to his key informant's personality. One particularly remarkable trait was Morales's seemingly impenetrable memory. Diaz even tested him while patrolling the streets by reading off more than thirty license plate numbers of cars they passed and jotting them on a pad as he did. A few hours later, Diaz pulled out the pad and asked Morales to recite them from memory, which he did successfully. Well, he missed one.

They began spending time together outside of work as well. Morales showed up for Saturday breakfast at the Diaz home every week. During one such breakfast with The Monkey, Diaz and his wife

Thania were jousting over some household issue, to which Thania lamented to herself, "Til death due us part."

Ricardo didn't look up from his newspaper. "That can be arranged," he deadpanned.[271] The mischievous duo was becoming a team.

★★★

When the Cuban community first began forming in Miami, enterprising publishers saw the need for news tailored to its residents. Jose Acosta was one such early publisher, starting two papers called *Patria* and *Cuba Libre* from his home with a run of two thousand copies per edition.[272] Underground Cuban news was distributed beside propagandist literature from the exile groups, handed out on street corners with cultivated messages aligning with the opinions of the publisher. It was an influential source for op-ed coverage of the topics important to a community that trusted so little of what the establishment had to say.

Cuban news grew as the '70s approached, with Max Lesnick Menendez's publication *Replica* benefitting. Lesnick started *Replica* in 1967 in his garage with a one hundred dollar investment.[273] He'd been a law school student beside Fidel Castro at the University of Havana, but he broke from the revolutionary regime and went to the US in 1961. Early weekly editions of *Replica* ran just eight pages, and they were written almost entirely by Lesnick. It changed to magazine format and expanded to forty pages in 1970 and sold for ten cents an issue. By 1972, the publication run was fifty thousand copies per issue, each exceeding a hundred pages, with twenty thousand copies distributed in Miami alone.

In early 1973, amid Morales's growing notoriety, he found himself in a feud with the publisher Lesnick, whose newspaper was controversial in the exile community due to its perceived soft stance on Castro and Cuba. Morales outright called him a *Fidelista,* and he was not alone in that opinion, evidenced by the eleven bombings suffered by the *Replica* offices. But the wily and adaptable Morales had refined his tactics for going on the offensive.

Replica had made a splash when it featured a sensational interview conducted with author José Pardo Llada, a friend of Castro's who'd documented his rise to power. Shortly after the controversial piece, the staff writer who'd conducted the interview was arrested in Miami and charged with federal drug crimes. His name was Manuel Penabaz, and he was convicted through intelligence that Morales provided to the BNDD.

Morales observed Penabaz's conviction resulted in embarrassment for the publication and a decrease in circulation. On February 29, 1973, Lesnick showed up at the FBI's Miami office and outlined what he claimed was ongoing harassment from Morales and his cronies.[274] He alleged incidents ranging from Ricardo giving him the evil eye in public to his car being rammed on the road. He also claimed that Morales was shaking down Cuban businesses and extorting money from them. When pressed for specifics, Lesnick could offer none, but he did offer substantiation from a powerful source.

Lesnick stated that an influential Miami city commissioner had directed him to go to the FBI with the complaints about Morales. The commissioner then met with Agent Davis independently and aired his own list of complaints about The Monkey, claiming that Morales tried to discredit him in the Cuban community before reelection and sicced the IRS on him which had resulted in a ten month investigation into the politician's finances.[275] Morales had become a significant thorn in the politician's side, who then confirmed to Davis that he had, in fact, sent Lesnick his way when learning of his issues with Morales. Having The Monkey out of the picture would've made his and Lesnick's lives much easier.

The commissioner's desire to help Lesnick may have also fueled by an additional detail. Morales's current girlfriend, Pilar, had dated the politician for three years prior to her leaving and taking up with Ricardo.[276] Suggesting that as the sole source of any grudge would seem sophomoric, but it may have served as an accelerant.

A month after Lesnick's contact with the FBI, the Miami Police received an anonymous typewritten letter about Morales. Identical copies were also sent to the publication *Diario de Las Americas* and the

US Secret Service. The letter, printed in both Spanish and English, was a one-page diatribe about Morales and, curiously enough, Luis Tornes, the publisher of *Replica*'s competing Cuban publication, *Impacto*:

> By this means we want to unmask a dangerous group of spies and delinquents which acting under the direction of a man named Ricardo Morales Navarrete, is operating in the US working for the international communism. Such a man, known by the rabble under the alias 'The Monkey', is a member of the G-2 who pretends to be a Cuban exile, even to collaborate with the FBI...why Mr. Ricardo Morales, who machine gunned in a public place a man named Aton Constanzo [sp] in front of numerous witnesses, has not been processed and convicted for murder?
>
> Why Mr. Luis Tornes, who committed the robbery and assault perpetrated in the jeweler's shop El Topacio, has not either paid for his crime?
>
> These actions, and many others whose enumeration would be endless, in spite of have been committed in public, and properly denounced, have not received the slightest attention on the part of the authorities. It has been simple negligence in the fulfillment of duty, or it is true what Mr. Morales Navarrete publicly brags about of receiving protection from Mr. Davis, public official of the FBI.[277]

Naturally, Lesnick was suspected, and he was called into the FBI's Miami office by Agent Davis for an interview. Lesnick arrived with *New York Times* reporter George Volsky, introduced as his interpreter, though an FBI report of the interview indicates Lesnick's English was no worse than Volsky's.[278] In the interview, Lesnick denied being responsible for the letters.

In the end, it was the FBI's official opinion that the letters were a "vicious attempt to discredit Morales and Davis" due to the successful 1968 prosecution of Orlando Bosch. The memo stated Bosch "is alleged to be a frequent visitor at *Replica*" since he was paroled on December 16, 1972.[279] Lesnick and the city commissioner were undoubtedly frustrated by The Monkey having slipped away.

★★★

Just seventeen days after Eladio Armando Ruiz was cleared of a murder charge, he stepped out of his car and into the balmy, NW 7th Street night while his nephew stayed behind the wheel. The sprawling apartment complex into which they'd pulled consisted of several three-story buildings with an open area parking lot in the middle. Apartment doors faced outward, motel style. Ricardo Morales watched from his second floor apartment window as his guest crossed the lot to the steps that led up to his unit. Morales noticed he adjusted a chain in his waistband that had a padlock dangling from the end.

The web that drew Ruiz to Morales's place that night is an example of the turbulence of the exile community in Little Havana. Those living on the fringe of the scene often found themselves in convoluted entanglements.

Long before ascending those steps to Morales's door, Ruiz was a local exile with a checkered past. He had several narcotics arrests and was implicated in a series of supermarket robberies in the mid-1960s with a partner named German Lamazares.[280] They were partners in crime, operating a car dealership together in Hialeah while engaging in illegal pursuits on the side. One afternoon in February of '73, upon a spontaneous search through one of the cars' glove compartments, Ruiz came upon some curious papers on which his name appeared throughout in German's handwriting. It took only seconds to see these were reports Lamazares had written and was going to turn in to the BNDD.[281]

Unbeknownst to Ruiz, his business partner was an informant for not only him, but also Ruben Monzon of the BNDD.[282] Ruiz put the papers back and, upon returning to the car lot, suggested to Lamazares that they grab some lunch. German Lamazares was never seen alive again.

Ofc. Raul Diaz, recently transferred to the narcotics section of the Organized Crime Bureau, spoke with Morales about the disappearance. His department, as well as Metro Homicide and the BNDD, began collecting information on the case. The disappearance of an informant was a priority issue. Morales told Diaz he'd known German and his wife Nancy from various gatherings and establishments in the Cuban community since the '60s. Their relationship was purely social, though—he didn't have any business dealings with German.

Nancy Lamazares was ever-present in the circles in which her husband operated, and she was known to everyone in the South Florida underworld and the cops who hunted them. Diaz first met her in 1972 when she was present at German's arrest by Diaz on cocaine possession charges. In April 1973, two months after German went missing, Nancy approached Diaz and told him she could take him to see her husband. Diaz contacted his team and she led them to a marshy area near the Doral Country Club, where they were soon standing over what was left of German Lamazares's dead body.[283]

Nancy had been having an affair with Eladio Ruiz's girlfriend Silvia. During a drunken bedroom confession, Silvia said she not only knew where German's corpse was, but also who killed him—her boyfriend Eladio.[284] Armed with this information, plus Nancy and Silvia's commitment to assist in the prosecution, Eladio Ruiz was arrested for German Lamazares's murder. Ofc. Diaz's investigation was also helped by his top informant, Morales. In a conversation with Ricardo, Ruiz himself confessed to killing Lamazares after finding the BNDD reports.[285] Imagine Raul Diaz's luck hitting the Monkey jackpot without even trying—an ex-wife walks in with a dead body, and his best informant hands him the killer.

Morales gave Diaz a formal affidavit stating that Ruiz told him he'd killed Lamazares. Eladio Ruiz was arrested, and the State Attorney's office almost immediately gave the discovery file to Ruiz's attorney—far too soon for Diaz's liking. In that file sat Morales's confidential affidavit revealing him as the source. Ruiz's attorneys no doubt saw it, and he was soon out on bond.

The following month, on the night of May 25, the ever-cautious Morales was parking his car near Pilar's apartment when he casually noticed headlights coming down the block in his side view mirror.[286] They crept down the street, slowing near his car, maybe looking for parking, but maybe looking for more. Once Morales was parked, he looked back to the side view mirror and saw the approaching car had killed its headlights. It was now beside him, and a gunshot rang out as Ricardo felt the slug hit his head.

He slunk down for cover as his mercenary instincts kicked in. A barrage was likely to follow, and his open door was lighting the car's interior. He reached up and unscrewed the light bulb so he could make an escape in darkness.[287]

No shots followed. Morales rolled out onto the sidewalk, pulled his trusted Browning, and crawled to the corner, leaving a slug-trail of crimson in his wake. He caught up to the car at the corner and saw Ruiz in the driver's seat, wearing a wig. Morales fired off a bunch of rounds as the car sped off, not sure if he'd made contact with anything. He then went into the nearest building and called Agent George Davis to report the incident, requesting an ambulance and uniformed police response.

"I'm not coming out until I see blue lights," he told Davis.[288] Paramedics responded and took him to Jackson Memorial Hospital where the self-sufficient mercenary informed the doctors he'd already removed the subcutaneous bullet while waiting for the ambulance.[289] The shot was incredibly fortuitous—had he or the gunman been off by a centimeter, the bullet would've penetrated his skull. He could feel the .25mm slug just under the surface of his skin while holding his head, and he pushed it back out the hole through which it entered. At the hospital he was treated and released to Raul Diaz, who'd been called by Agent Davis, and was placed in a Holiday Inn on Biscayne Boulevard, awaiting placement in a safe house from the FBI.

★★★

Raul Diaz ran into Nancy Lamazares at The Forge.[290] He was at the famous upscale Miami Beach restaurant on official business, checking on an undercover operation. He left the establishment with the widow, on very unofficial business, and they continued the evening at Sunny's Lounge. The last stop of the impromptu encounter was at Diaz's apartment—an encounter that would continue for months.

The PSD took particular interest in their relationship because Diaz was involved in the investigation of Nancy's husband's murder. Investigators prodded for details that would suggest impropriety, but Nancy wasn't an informant, nor was she suspected of any crime. A cop dating the widow of the subject whose case he was investigating wasn't necessarily violating any rules, morality notwithstanding.

Eladio Ruiz's day in court would come. Morales had provided the affidavit alleging Ruiz told him about the murder. Further, Silvia's testimony was validated by her showing police the actual body after Ruiz's confession to her. Prosecutors didn't have much more than that, but they likely wouldn't need it. Eladio's girl could put him away for life.

But at the last minute, in a dramatic turn of events par for the course in the Cuban exile circus of Miami, Silvia told the court she'd lied about Eladio's role in German Lamazares's death at Nancy's direction.[291] And on July 16, County Court Judge Arthur Maginnis dismissed the murder charge against Ruiz, who walked from the courtroom a free man.

★★★

Back at the apartment complex on NW 7th St, Morales moved from his front window when Ruiz began to ascend the stairs toward his door. He'd called Morales at 2:15 that afternoon of August 2, not yet three months from having shot Ricardo in his car, and said they should sit down and "make peace." They made a date for later that day at Ricardo's place. Morales's potential willingness to form an alliance with the fellow exile went out the window when he saw Ruiz messing with the chain around his belt line and his nephew down in the car, who placed a shotgun on the passenger seat.

Inside the apartment, Morales grabbed his fully automatic .9mm Browning pistol, silencer attached, and opened his door.[292] Before Ruiz could even knock, Morales fired seven rounds into his body at close range, dropping him right on the doorstep. Prepared as he might have been to handle the nephew in the car, he didn't get the opportunity. The second shooter peeled out of the lot without providing the backup promised. Morales ran from the scene, and within hours the police sought him for questioning. A witness living across the street placed him at the scene, seeing him run from the building after shooting Ruiz.

Investigators found a .22 caliber automatic handgun near Ruiz's body, which they confirmed was not the handgun used in the shooting and therefore was likely dropped by Ruiz. He'd approached the door with his gun drawn.

The following day Morales arrived at police headquarters with two attorneys, Albert Carricarte and Miguel Suarez, and they spoke with Homicide Det. Sgt. Eugene McCracken.[293] A lengthy interrogation followed wherein Morales turned over his handgun for inspection. The caliber matched, but an investigator in the case noted, "Half the Cubans in the rackets carry 9-millimeter automatics. It is a very popular model with them."[294]

In deposition, Morales later said he denied involvement in Ruiz's murder during this interrogation at the advice of his attorneys. Investigators didn't buy it and, without a more likely lead, he was arrested by McCracken and charged with first degree murder. The charges stood only as long as it took for Miguel Suarez to question the witness's eyesight.

When Raul Diaz was canvassing the site for witnesses and came upon the man across the street, the detective noticed he was wearing glasses.[295] In the man's recounting of events, he said he saw Morales kill Ruiz from his bathroom window while he was showering, ostensibly without eyeglasses. Diaz passed the info on to Agent George Davis who then told Suarez, handing their prized informant's attorney the singular weapon with which to slay the credibility of the sole witness. And, since that was the only piece of evidence against Morales, the charge against the incredibly valuable asset to federal and local law enforcement agencies was summarily dropped. The department returned Ricardo's handgun.

Shortly thereafter, Diaz and fellow officer Art Castro picked up Morales to head to the practice range and shoot targets, as they'd occasionally do together. While at the range, Morales told the two cops that his girlfriend Pilar had obtained reliable intel that there was a hit being planned on Ricardo.[296] She told him that her ex, the Miami city commissioner who had tried, along with publisher Max Lesnick, to have Morales jammed up with the FBI, was behind a plot to kill him. He was to be summoned to a meeting at a restaurant, where a confrontation would ensue. Morales would be goaded into pulling his pistol, giving a waiting gunman full justification to shoot him. It was a tricky proposition for the commissioner and his crew—Ricardo could beat them to the draw and pick off one or all of them first. But it seemed a risk they were willing to take to eliminate Morales.

This was Ricardo's new reality. He had, in fact, been invited to a local restaurant for a meeting shortly after getting this intel. Diaz and Castro felt this was a credible threat, but Morales shrugged it off. They then loaded their Brownings for practice and started shooting. All except Morales, whose gun wouldn't fire. He racked it again, steadied it on the target, and tried to no avail. The men unloaded it and found nothing wrong with the clip or the ammunition, but upon further inspection they found the firing pin had been cut. No firing pin, no projectile. Ricardo's gun had, in essence, been rendered ineffective and would be useless if he were to try to use it in self-defense, perhaps at an impromptu restaurant meeting he'd been summoned to.

Morales hadn't fired his gun since he turned it over to police during the Eladio Ruiz homicide investigation, and he certainly didn't cut the firing pin himself. It had to have happened while the gun was in police custody, and no one but an officer in the building would've had access to evidence. Morales and Diaz knew the city commissioner in question was best friends with a sergeant in the police department, who Morales testified to seeing give John Clarence Cook the address of Ofc. Saslaw before Morales bombed his lawn.[297] Everything in Morales's world seemed connected.

Never one to back down from some devilish fun, Ricardo kept his appointment at the restaurant anyway. Upon entering, he greeted the owner and then described how he'd found the firing pin was cut and made sure it was fixed before coming there. He showed it for emphasis, pulling it right out in front of everyone, and he didn't have a problem that night.

★★★

Rick's first exposure to the consequences of the revolutionary didn't come from his father, but rather from his *Tio* Hector.

Magda pulled her car onto US-27, the long, lonely stretch of road that brought her family to see her brother on Sundays. The prison in Belle Glade was located in Central Florida, near Lake Okeechobee, in the heart of the Everglades. It allowed inmates to sit outside at picnic tables with their families on designated days, and Magda would bring her parents and the kids with home-cooked dishes prepared by her mom. The visits themselves were uneventful—the grown ups talked while the kids fidgeted, dreading the long drive home.

The picnic setting, the trees, and overall casual atmosphere didn't feel like jail to ten-year-old Rick. It seemed everyone there was having spirited discussions in Spanish, making Rick wonder if it was a Cubans-only place. Those outings to see *Tio* felt like gatherings back in Little Havana, though the Belle Glade locale was actually prettier. It might've been a family get-together in the park, but Hector wouldn't be leaving with them.

While Magda was more realistic about her brother's situation, *Abuela* would repeatedly say her son was unjustly incarcerated. He didn't do anything wrong, she'd proclaim when the conversation arose.

"The family never considered it a crime," Rick says in reflection. "He was a political prisoner because it was a continuation of the battle."

But back then it was all confusing to young Rick. He knew his uncle and father had both been arrested for doing something with bombs, but for some reason one was in jail and the other was not. Why couldn't his father get *Tio* Hector the same freedom he had, especially since *Abuela* was always saying *Tio* hadn't done anything wrong?

The void left by his father's absence was beginning to widen in Rick. Time with his father was growing increasingly sparse, and it wasn't enough to see him occasionally after irregular absences. While visiting his uncle helped, *Tio* was still locked up, and occasional Sunday visits weren't going to cut it in the male role model department. Had his father been imprisoned like *Tio* Hector, he could at least visit him every week. But there was no real relationship there, and Rick was heading into those years of his life where having one might be greatly beneficial.

★★★

Luis Posada's foray into Venezuela that had opened the door for Morales to work with Lefty Rosenthal in 1967 had proven fruitful. Posada had climbed the ranks of Venezuela's intelligence bureau, DISIP, to become a senior officer.

Morales's duties for the BNDD involved travel as well. In January of 1972, he'd been granted a travel permit by the US Immigration and Naturalization Office to facilitate South American investigations for the Bureau. One assignment allowed him to reconnect with Luis Posada in Caracas, Venezuela. In the course of their conversation, Ricardo stated he was employed by the FBI and confessed to the murder of Eladio Ruiz. After his meeting, Posada contacted the CIA station in Caracas and reported the conversation. The resultant interagency memo referenced Posada, codenamed CIFENCE-4 in CIA documents, as "a Station asset…acting in his cover capacity."[298] The latter term, coupled with the Agency contact itself, suggests Posada was placed in Venezuela's DISIP intelligence agency as a CIA assignment.

As was often the case, The Monkey had effortlessly manifested chaos. That singular conversation tied three federal agencies—the FBI, CIA, and BNDD—into a knot around Morales. Memos began to circulate between the agencies in an attempt to confirm a potential triple-agent situation. A CIA memo dated 11/8/72 stated BNDD was aware that their informant was working with the two other agencies, with Morales stating he'd been invited by the CIA to visit Caracas, Venezuela from October 10–11 and spend a few days there.[299]

As November approached, Morales was due to testify in one of BNDD's cases. The drug bureau prevented the other agencies from contacting their informant, feeling the meddling might spook Morales. The BNDD stated they did not intend to confer with the FBI as to how their asset was to be handled; they intended to continue to utilize Morales as they had in the past.[300] The BNDD further froze out the CIA by stating it was their understanding "when two or more US government agencies have an interest in the same individual that [the CIA's] role...was merely to advise the interested parties of the situation and it would be left to the discretion of those US government agencies how the matter should be resolved."[301] The FBI also weighed in, stating they expected to be contacted by the BNDD to negotiate how their shared source was to be handled. The possessive BNDD responded by telling the CIA it had no intention to contact the FBI and would handle the situation "in their own way."[302]

While in Caracas for that October 10-11 stay, Morales also met with Orlando Garcia Vasquez who was stationed in DISIP as Special Assessor in the Ministry of Foreign Relations. Morales later testified in deposition that he was dispatched specifically to reconnect with Garcia Vasquez, a former CIA asset.[303] Posada and Garcia Vasquez were high-ranking intelligence officials that played a critical role for the US government. Venezuela's location at the northern tip of South America made it the gateway in and out of the continent.

By 1974, Ricardo Morales would be a permanent resident of Venezuela courtesy of a citizenship request written by Venezuelan President Carlos Andrés Pérez himself.[304]

Chapter Ten D.I.S.I.P.-pearing Act (1974)

The CIA described Orlando Garcia Vasquez as a "bright, aggressive rogue who is ruthless when necessary," going so far as to document his reputation as that of a political thug, murderer, con man, and pathological liar.[305] He'd served the governments of Cuba, Costa Rica, and the US after becoming a naturalized citizen in May 1945. He was described by sources as "a pro, one of the CIA's best intelligence operatives from the early '60s." By the time Morales connected with him in 1972, Garcia Vasquez was a Division Chief in Venezuela's DISIP, adding a fourth country to his services.[306]

Morales began putting his US-issued clearance for unlimited re-entry into the US to use. Throughout 1973, he began making more frequent trips to Caracas, creating sources and forging relationships there in preparation for his next assignment—holding rank in DISIP with Posada and Garcia Vasquez.

The issue of Morales's citizenship might've become an issue had his presence in Venezuela not been so important to influential people and organizations there and in the US. After he was made a naturalized citizen of Venezuela, Ricardo Morales was appointed Coordinator of Counterintelligence for the Caribbean in the Foreign Ministry Division of DISIP. Conveniently, though not coincidentally, that position was directly under the supervision of Garcia Vasquez. Morales soon led his own division as the Commissar of Intelligence for DISIP's Division 54, stationed at Caracas airport.[307] Morales now ran governmental intelligence from the largest airport in Venezuela and the closest airport on the continent in proximity to the United States.

The installation of the Cuban-born Posada, Morales, and Garcia Vasquez to high posts in national intelligence for a country in which they were not born and hadn't grown up was unusual. The one commonality, of course, was that they all had been highly valuable CIA assets. Morales later admitted to the cooperative, perhaps even downplaying it.

"We have what we called cooperation among friendly services," he said in regard to his contact with the CIA and FBI during his placement in DISIP. "So there was information exchanged."[308]

The US had a vested interest in keeping a hand in what was happening in Caracas. Amid growing political chaos in Latin America, Venezuela had a very stable democracy. Recent growth and low levels of economic inequality made it one of the richest nations in the region.[309] Morales's primary task in his $40,000 a year position in DISIP was tracking and uncovering plans of opposition forces. Specifically, Morales said, "The Russians, the Czechoslovakians, the Cubans."[310]

But his time in Venezuela would soon become a complicated game that involved four federal agencies and extended across four countries and two continents.

★★★

Morales still occasionally traveled back to the US during his time with DISIP. It was in his best interest to maintain his stateside contacts; he viewed DISIP and Venezuela not as a replacement for his US activities but rather as an extension of the overall mission. On July 2, 1974, during one such return to help Diaz with local cases and visit his four children, he was driving a rented Impala Custom when at the intersection of W. Flagler St and Milan Dairy Rd there was a thundering blast from under the car that crumpled the passenger side floorboard and shattered the windows. The flash of flame in the cabin told Morales this wasn't from outside. A hailstorm of pellets showered Ricardo as he instinctively hit the gas and kept driving, his car blasted and all but destroyed. He knew at once he'd been car bombed, and the job likely wasn't completed just yet.

Ricardo feared those responsible might've been tailing him to ensure he was killed, but the car died after seventy-five yards. Morales got out and surveyed the area, and then he called Raul Diaz from a pay phone to report what had just happened. He stood to the side with the growing group of gawking onlookers and waited on responders.

Police and press were soon buzzing around the scene as Morales wandered inside the tape and into the impromptu spotlight that found him, albeit after being nearly decimated. That seemed a fair trade—if it's gonna happen anyway, better to have an audience to spread the myth.

"They want to get rid of me," Morales told *Miami Herald* reporter Frank Greve at the scene. "I thought there might be someone in a car behind me waiting to finish me off, so I turned the corner and drove on a little."[311] This was the second assassination attempt on Morales's life in the past year. The Monkey knew he was working his way into more unbelievable headlines.

Newspapers, specifically *Replica,* were one plausible reason for the mangled car sitting in plain view of a growing crowd. It hadn't been long since the letter from *Replica* publisher Max Lesnick failed to discredit Morales, and only a year ago had the city commissioner's thugs failed to goad Morales into a fight with a missing firing pin on his gun. Was this yet another offensive launched by that team? Morales could envision them sitting around plotting in the *Replica* offices, Orlando Bosch's feet up on Lesnick's desk.

Enter the second possible theory regarding the car bomb.

While Morales was busy first establishing himself in Venezuela, Dr. Orlando Bosch had been paroled after serving four of his ten-year sentence. He returned to the streets unrepentant and admittedly unchanged by his time behind bars, as he told a reporter upon his release.

"I am the same man who entered an American jail a few years ago for battling for the just cause of the Cuban people. Jail has not changed me. I want to say in all humility without considering myself as a chosen one or a prophet. I have a mission which I will fulfill. I do not plan to violate American laws, but nobody will make me bend. I repeat, I am the same."[312] The outlet that landed the exclusive first interview with Bosch was Lesnick's *Replica*.

From the start of his parole, the FBI kept tabs on the bomber. A Bureau report from April 27, 1973 stated that confidential informant MM T-3, "who was well informed concerning Cuban exile activity in Miami," confirmed that Bosch was almost a daily visitor to Lesnick's offices.[313] The report tracking Bosch's movements also stated that on April 13, 1973, another confidential informant acquainted with many Cuban exile leaders confirmed that Bosch was working with publisher Max Lesnick and others to form a new group to be known as Social Martino. Informant MM T-4 said "one of the immediate goals of this group is to kill Ricardo Morales Navarrete who testified against Bosch in federal court," shredding the understanding of "one mission" reciprocity that had once been a staple.[314]

Bosch had wasted little time in becoming active again in anti-Castro organizing and its accompanying violence. He formed his Acción Cubana group (Cuban Action, translated) and fled the US for points overseas, violating his parole. At the time of Morales's car bomb in July of '74, Cuban Action's most recent success had been the mailing of a bomb to the Cuban embassy in Lima, Peru that blew off attaché Pilar Ramirez Vega's arm when she received the package.[315]

"She's a Communist," Bosch told reporter Hilda Inclán while he puffed on a cigar, "a member of Havana's Committee of Defense of the Revolution [which spies on Cuban citizens]...and we are at war."[316]

At the scene of the car bomb, Ricardo Morales spoke with reporters about the smoldering rental car before them.

"They're going to give me trouble when I take it back," he joked.[317] Then he became more solemn, burying his hands in his blue windbreaker, staring at the devastation in the road, and carefully crafting words that would certainly make the papers the following day.

"I'm not saying that it's Dr. Bosch."

★★★

Five-year-old Roberto was seeing his *Tia* Yolanda that day.[318] He was supposed spend the day with his father, but the visit was cut short, as their visits sometimes were. Time with his *Papá* was inconsistent in every way, with Ricardo's new position requiring nearly full-time presence in Caracas and wherever that took him beyond Venezuela's borders. *Robertico* was spending more time with his aunt and uncle than with his father.

Mimi and Ricardo had already split when he left for Venezuela, but it came to light that Morales had already been dating a woman named Pilar who lived across the street with her two daughters. This further cut into Roberto's time with his father, as his return visits from Caracas were now spent with Pilar and her girls.

On that July afternoon slated for time with Roberto, some unexpected business came up for Ricardo, and he deposited the boy at Yolanda's place yet again. Minutes later, as Ricardo drove off, his car exploded.

The passenger floorboard where Roberto would have sat was busted. Did the bomber simply wait for the kid to be dropped off before hitting a button, or had a timing device fallen in line with luck, sparing the little boy from disaster?

Danger, either way.

Roberto's mom was familiar with that kind of life, having been active in anti-Castro groups herself. Who would know, unless you'd lived another's life, that it wasn't normal for your mom to occasionally run into the room, throw a few of your outfits and toys in a suitcase, grab you by the hand, and rush out the door and into a motel for a week? Mimi was always ready to bolt when she sensed danger of some kind.

"She'd grab a bag," Roberto recalled, "grab a couple things, a couple of files, and it was seamless—seamless. We were never scrambling around. She was never nervous or worried. She would smoke her long More menthol cigarettes, get in the car, and drive down the street like it was nothing."[319]

Roberto's mom would head to work each day while they were hunkered down in a shitty motel on Flagler, and Yolanda or Pucho would come babysit. Sometimes, when they weren't available, it was some big man he didn't know.

Mimi had begun working for Rev. Manuel Espinosa around that time.[320] Espinosa was a controversial figure in Miami; he was a radical Pentecostal minister of the Christian Evangelical Reformed Church in Hialeah with ties to Cuba. He believed that the US should renew relations with Cuba and loosen the embargo—a stance seen as heresy by militant exiles who often clashed with his congregation. The threat of danger was real for Espinosa and anyone in his circle, including the rebellious Mimi and her young son. The men who sometimes babysat Roberto in the motel room were Espinosa's bodyguards, reassigned for a few hours.

One of those bodyguards named Johnny was very close with Mimi and eventually became a live-in boyfriend. He fell into a fatherly role despite Mimi's fierce independence. Roberto thought Johnny was cool; they got along.

Word got back to Ricardo, and he wasn't happy with the perceived paternal replacement. He'd left Roberto and Mimi behind, choosing to be free of entanglements as he moved to Caracas, and then took up with Pilar. But another man sliding into his role in Mimi's home was another matter altogether. Roberto heard this for himself when listening in on one of Mimi and Ricardo's arguments on the phone. He picked up an extension receiver and heard his father's voice.

"You tell him I'm looking for him," Ricardo said to Mimi, "and that if I see him with my son again, I'm going to kill him."[321] Mimi yelled back, asking rather correctly, just how the fuck Ricardo had the right. She didn't back down from Ricardo, or anyone, for that matter.

Johnny was aware of Ricardo's feelings, and occasionally the rides to school would become more adventurous than the average kid's.

"Your father is behind us," Johnny would say as he abruptly floored it and Roberto bounced around the backseat on wicked turns.

His half brothers Rick and Raul were older but still occasionally made time for him, teaching him judo at the YMCA. Other than those few times, Yolanda and Pucho were the only people in Roberto's extended family he'd see. Mimi was still considered the other woman and was estranged from the rest of the Morales family.

In addition to simply loving her nephew, Yolanda had an additional connection to Mimi and Roberto—her husband Antonio was an editor at *The Miami Herald* where Mimi also worked. The Monkey wouldn't be able to avoid newspaper coverage if he tried. Though, he never would.

Meanwhile, Magda had moved on, marrying a man named Jose Machin with whom she worked at the Shelbourne Hotel. The Morales children liked him, and they moved from Little Havana to a house in West Miami, a move upward by all accounts. The move offered something closer to a middle-class existence.

"The richer you got, the farther you moved from Little Havana," Rick, Jr. said. "It was the Cuban ghetto."

Ricardo's children from his first marriage had little interaction with Roberto. Beyond their impromptu judo instruction, Raul and Rick spent time with their friends playing basketball and hanging at the Y. Rick's obsession with sports also had him playing tennis on the only clay court in town, two blocks from their apartment.

The women in Ricardo's life all demonstrated a fierce independence and an uncommon strength. They had a ride-or-die loyalty to the mercenary's lifestyle. They were all strong women who needed no assistance. Once Ricardo left the picture and took up with a pregnant Mimi, Magda began working in the hotel business in Miami Beach. By the time Ricardo split from Miami and was in Venezuela full time, Mimi was working with Rev. Espinosa and climbing up the ladder at *The Miami Herald*.

Ricardo's newest woman, Pilar, embraced his transient lifestyle. Yolanda's youngest daughter, Annette, recalled Pilar being accepted rather quickly by her family. "She loved my grandma Ines and always treated her with a lot of tenderness," she said. "Even my mom liked her."[322]

On one occasion, Ricardo and Pilar showed up at Yolanda's after Magda finally went to the authorities about not receiving child support payments. She eventually dropped her pursuit of financial assistance, accepting his mother's plea to do so as her son was busy "fighting Cuba." As Rick, Jr. grew, he began to take issue with that, calling it bullshit as his father supported another woman's children. Pilar's daughters weren't even his own.

As Rick entered his preteens, some of the sting from his father's extended absences and lack of financial support would fade as he immersed himself more in sports. But he'd still have to reconcile inexplicable barbs, like Yolanda no longer extending invitations to Rick, Raul, or Sylvia to visit. Yolanda also abruptly cut Magda from all of the family photographs. She had no ill will toward Magda as far as anyone knew, and it was Ricardo who'd inserted Mimi into the picture. It was just Yolanda's way of distancing herself from the embarrassing situation she'd lambasted her brother for putting them all in.

It was *Abuela* Ines who worked to keep all of Ricardo's children in the Morales's lives. If his grandmother hadn't invited them to her house, Rick mightn't have seen Yolanda, Antonio, and their girls again. He was confused. His aunt had very obviously cut him and his siblings off, just as his own father had begun doing.

★★★

In DISIP, Morales honed his interrogation skills by requesting to sit in on polygraph sessions. He participated in the questioning, gauging his effectiveness against the needle of the machine on a couple of high profile cases. When American industrialist William F. Niehous, the general manager of Owens-Illinois Glass Corporation, was kidnapped in Venezuela, Morales participated in the polygraphing of company employees.[323] After the hijacking of an Air France plane by George Habash's terror organization The Popular Front for the Liberation of Palestine (PFLP), Israeli agents came to Venezuela for a hijacker's interrogation and polygraphing, which Morales helped facilitate.[324]

That wasn't Israel's only involvement with DISIP during Morales's tenure. He was soon part of a select group of agents entered into formal Mossad training.[325] Israel's powerful intelligence outfit sent a handful of agents to Caracas for training on its tactics and observations. They covered interrogation techniques, intelligence and counterintelligence, and the power of influence. Morales expanded on this during a 1982 deposition.

"There are five kinds of motivations," he explained. "Ideological motivation is the best one to work out." He said they were taught "how to detect the ideologically approachable individual."[326] This dovetailed into interrogation techniques.

Morales had been exposed to intelligence and counterintelligence during his CIA training for Operation 40.

"Intelligence and counterintelligence is a game," Morales explained. "Counterintelligence is the graft—where you find out what the intelligence services of the opposition are doing, either to penetrate your own service, to penetrate destructors of your government, your nation...the graft of counterintelligence is to detect them in their efforts, their agents."

Morales held the Israeli agency and their officers in high regard, later stating in deposition he respected them so much and would not discuss the details of what he'd learned. He completed the training at the top of his class, and his excellent performance in Mossad training is one of the things he was most proud of. His sister Yolanda recalled his carrying on about it, going so far as to report he'd been presented with a badge by Israeli Defense Minister Moshe Dayan as a gag. It simply said "#1."[327]

Israel's valuable training offered to Venezuela's intelligence unit was not just part of an exchange between friendly agencies. Morales's discussions with Yolanda during this period, over Cuban coffee and *natilla,* of course, revealed the opportunities it provided, such as learning some Hebrew and Arabic and doing undercover work for Mossad.

Following World War II, a decades-long prevailing antisemitism in pockets of Latin America sheltered Nazis that were fleeing Europe.[328] The channels of escape, called ratlines, had launch points in locations like Spain and Rome where clerics of the Catholic Church and other sympathizers assisted the escape of war criminals.[329] Argentina became a common destination due to President Juan Perón's admiration for fascist leaders Hitler and Mussolini, but other countries like Chile and Brazil played host too.

Mossad struggled to find these exiles and bring them back to Europe to face war crime charges. Of the Latin American countries that might've possessed both the might and stability to smoke out sequestered Nazis, Venezuela would've been a good choice at the time. Further, they had Ricardo Morales—top of the class under Mossad's training, a highly regarded asset for US federal agencies, and stationed at an airport with immediate access to flights all over the globe—who would certainly be a top choice to follow the trail of Nazis wherever it led. Morales's travel itinerary for DISIP also showed he was tracking targets outside the purview of communist threats to Venezuela. When asked in deposition for a complete list of countries visited while working for DISIP, Morales named Austria, Germany, Sweden, Ecuador, Guatemala, Columbia, Spain, England, Mexico, the United States, Costa Rica, and Panama.[330] According to a confidential government memorandum, Morales privately admitted to Asst. US Attorney Jerome Sanford that he assisted in the pursuit of war criminal Dr. Josef Mengele.[331]

While Nazis were high on the list of Mossad targets, Venezuelan-born Ilich Ramírez Sánchez was a priory catch as well.[332] Sánchez, more commonly known by the more arresting nickname "Carlos the Jackal," was an international terrorist who'd received training by the aforementioned PFLP in Jordan. He'd been garnering headlines for his assassination attempt on prominent Jewish businessman Joseph Sieff, bombing of a French café, and rocket attacks on El Al airlines in Paris.

Though Carlos and many prominent Nazis would evade capture for decades, Morales's efforts did not go unnoticed. He was presented with a medal of appreciation by Israeli Prime Minister Golda Meier.[333]

★★★

Back in Miami on December 3, 1975, Capt. Tom Brodie responded to the call of an undetonated bomb found at the Social Security building on on NW 14th Street. Ofc. Arnold Gibbs and Sgt. Rodney Sayre were dispatched to look for a possible explosive, finding a brown sack containing the device.[334] When Brodie arrived with the bomb squad, the bag exploded when he was just feet away. Miraculously, he suffered no physical injury.

There had been an earlier incident that night when two civilians picked up a brown paper bag in front of the State of Florida Unemployment Offices, thinking it might've been a discarded bottle of wine with something still in it.[335] Instead, they saw a bomb and called police who responded and disarmed it. Then, at 8:18 p.m., the madness began.

A pipe bomb exploded outside the FBI building on Biscayne Boulevard, shattering the windows.[336] Less than a half hour later, at 8:45, a pipe bomb blew up at the US Post Office at Flagler and NW 23rd.[337] At 9:03 p.m., the Post Office building at SW 8th Street and 68th Avenue suffered a shattered window and door when a pipe bomb detonated in a trash can outside the building. No one was injured in any of the incidents.[338]

As a pattern became evident, Miami police dispatched officers to as many federal buildings as they could hit, searching for more bombs. That's when Ofc. Gibbs and his sergeant came upon the brown bag at the Social Security building. The night ended without any further explosions, though a sixth bomb was found intact at Barnett Bank the next morning. Miami Bomb Unit Officer David Nye said the bombs indicated one set of actors was likely responsible.[339]

Miami investigators had been dealing with bombings long enough to know where to look. They soon realized Assistant Secretary of State William Rogers was kicking off a tour of South America with a luncheon and speech at the Dupont Plaza Hotel in Miami the following afternoon. The Cuban community vilified Rogers because he publicly wished for a better relationship between Castro and the US. Miami mayor Maurice Ferré had even warned Rogers of potential trouble if he showed up in the city.[340]

Sure enough, Cuban protesters lined the streets outside Rogers' hotel the following day. They carried signs reading "Rogers, the best friend of Castro and Communism" and "Down with the red traitor, Rogers."[341] Police had already been tipped off, and they beefed up security at the hotel, even assigning the politician an armed guard.

The terror spree didn't end there, and it wouldn't until widespread fear gripped the city. The following day, two bombings hit close to home for law enforcement officials as devices detonated inside both the Miami Police Station and the Metro Justice Building.[342] These events severed any once-sympathetic officers of Cuban descent from the anti-Castro cause. It was a bomb in their home base, where Fidel Castro didn't work.

"This is not a Cuban thing," said Major Gil Zamora. "To put a bomb inside a police station does absolutely nothing for the cause of Cuba."[343]

Police Chief Garland Watkins said, "The tragedy isn't that the Miami Police Department was bombed. It's that someone who disagrees philosophically with the government or police department is using this avenue to voice objection."[344]

Cuban radio station WRHC received an anonymous phone call from a man calling himself "El Condor" on the day of the law enforcement bombings. The caller claimed a letter was left for authorities in a phone booth on SW 8th St. at 24th Ave. in Little Havana.[345] The Spanish-accented caller directed law enforcement to open the Yellow Pages to page 1,043, where they found a small white envelope glued to the page. It contained a typed letter, written in Spanish, claiming responsibility for the bombs distributed on December 3 and 4.

> My name is El Condor. I am a member of JIN. The last activities we were forced to carry out because of the negative attitude of the traitorous system. We can increase our military strength and do great damage on a national level. This is only a demonstration.[346]

The letter went on to blame the FBI, therein referred to as "the Gestapo," for disrespecting the Cubans and for a murder and kidnapping. The letter called for the cessation of political jailing of Cubans, and it closed with a chilling threat to the citizens of Miami.

> If this demand is not satisfied within forty-eight hours, we will attack military objectives, and

a. There will be no warning.
b. The danger to innocent people will increase.
c. We will demand fifty million dollars to be given to minorities in this country.

-El Condor

FBI technicians were able to extract a fingerprint and palmprint from the letter.

Connecting the hellacious activities of those two days to other bombings in the past would be a challenge given the level of activity in the city. Prior to the eight devices planted on December 3, Miami had seen twenty-one other bombings in the calendar year. One of those had detonated in a locker on Concourse 5 at Miami International Airport on October 17.[347] No one was injured, but the blast sent fragments everywhere and was determined to be a "low-yield dynamite time bomb."

The significant thing about the airport bomb lay on the chrome handle of locker 5030's door, blown off by the blast. A fingerprint had been lifted and sent to the Dade County Public Safety Department, suggesting a possible connection between that incident and other bombings. Now, with another print found on the envelope at Specialized Services, a possible connection could be explored.

In Little Havana, the area most impacted, the community's sentiment regarding the exiles' sworn mission started to shift. While some residents remained steadfast in their "death to Fidel or bust" stance, others felt the cause eroding, its one-time nobility bastardized by undisciplined thuggery. A December 5 *Miami Times* piece posited the exile groups were recreating, ironically enough, "Havana, 1958."[348]

"They are harming our cause," Miami community school director Rolando Amador contributed.

Another prominent voice weighing in was that of Max Lesnick, who cited that the exiles "are behaving just like the Communists."[349] Residents hoped for the speedy capture of those responsible, fearing the struggle of their people would now become tarnished to the outside world, branded with the label of terrorism. "One mission," to the outsider, had been all but erased from the groups' activity.

And it may have been erased in the minds of the exiles themselves. Though the signature element of the groups' bombings seemed consistent—no casualties, no injuries—just how long could that go on as the targets became larger? The bombing of the police station and other buildings that serviced the community crossed the line for many.

A thin, gaunt, and pockmarked member of that community named Rolando Otero had been running a bolita operation out of his apartment.[350] He wasn't proud; running a gambling ring was an act of desperation. Otero was another exile who served the US in their fight against Cuba. He had been under CIA employ from 1960–1962 as a member of Brigade 2506, and he served the Bay of Pigs invasion as a demolition operative and intelligence assistant at just seventeen years of age.[351] He was one of the soldiers captured by Cuban forces and imprisoned for eighteen months on Cuba's Isle of the Pines.

Since being freed and returning to Miami, Otero applied for a taxi license and drove a cab while becoming active in the anti-Castro circles. Local and federal law enforcement eventually pegged him with responsibility for the nine bombings over two harrowing days, as well as the airport bomb back in October. They were preparing a federal indictment that would soon drop on Otero, charging him with thirty-nine felony counts.

But Otero, it turned out, had a flight to catch. On January 3, he was on his way out of the country and to the Caribbean, getting a step ahead of the charges that would eventually make him a fugitive. His plane ticket was purchased by Ricardo Morales.[352]

★★★

"Otero."

On December 26, 1975, Ricardo Morales was back in the US for the holidays, and he met with Detectives Raul Diaz, Eddie Mederos, Art Castro, and FBI agent Joe Dawson to give them the name of the man he knew to be The Condor.

"He drives a cab here in the city," Morales added.

Though plenty busy in Caracas, Ricardo had to keep his ties to US law enforcement strong by feeding them fresh kills. Who knew how broadly the connection he was managing between Venezuelan intelligence and US intelligence would extend? Besides, Otero would just have to understand the mercenary code of reciprocity. One can't help but think Morales derived a great deal of pleasure from a good game of chess.

Otero was aware the noose was tightening as he bounced around the streets of Little Havana. The cases were getting lots of coverage, and the "enough is enough" sentiment from the public was making him claustrophobic. His friend Morales had some advice: get out of town. Ricardo knew the feds had sufficient intel from his hand, and he realized he could stretch things out a bit by helping Otero stay a step ahead of them. If Morales controlled Otero's actions while also staying involved in the agencies' pursuit of him, then he could control the entire match. Morales would retain value with the feds by leading them down the paths he would create for Otero to walk. He purchased a plane ticket for The Condor and told him to get his shit together and get out. But not before the intelligence community's insufferable scamp had some fun.

Back a few days before Christmas, previous to giving Otero's name to authorities, Ricardo threw a Christmas party at his apartment.[353] Raul Diaz showed up and mingled with co-workers Art Castro and Eddie Mederos, as well as Agent Dawson and others from the Bureau. Morales had invited everyone in the law enforcement community with whom he'd been working.

And Rolando Otero.

To know Morales was to appreciate his sense of humor—that guest list was compiled for the amusement of one. The Monkey and his friends mingled and shared cocktails while Diaz and his guys wondered why Morales kept playing Simon and Garfunkel's "El Condor Pasa" (The Condor Passes) on the turntable all night.

Then on the 26th, Morales gave them Otero. The FBI lab confirmed the prints on the phone booth envelope belonged to Bay of

Pigs veteran Rolando Otero Hernandez. Diaz wondered just how many open bombings sitting on his books could be connected to him.

He immediately made the ten-minute trip to the Taxi Bureau.[354] Sure enough, they had a print on file for a Mr. Rolando Otero on his application, which Diaz retrieved and brought back to headquarters. They soon discovered that Otero's print matched one on the airport locker, too. Morales and the prints now connected Otero to both the October and December crimes.

Otero also looked an awful lot like the facial composite prepared by the police, which witnesses confirmed by positively identifying him. Otero's picture looked like another man authorities had met. In fact, they'd shared yuletide greetings with him only days before. The detectives and agents who'd attended Morales's party were in shock when they realized Ricardo had them partying with Otero days before he gave them their suspect.

Diaz had to laugh, and he laughed even harder when the straight-laced Dawson, ever the proper gentleman who never uttered a foul word, reacted to the revelation.

"That son of a bitch!" he barked as Diaz fell into hysterics. "He had us at the party with the fucking bomber!"

All roads now led to Otero. Every branch of justice was involved in the case, and preparations for a federal indictment finally began. Both Miami police and the FBI were satisfied, and Morales had extended the playing surface in a vast, intercontinental game he was about to play.

Morales warned his FBI handlers, "The Condor is about to fly."[355] They began to surveil Otero while they waited for the indictment to come down. But on January 3, despite the Bureau's watchful eye, Miami's most wanted bomber did, in fact, take Simon and Garfunkel's advice.

Otero landed in the Dominican Republic and in the care of retired Admiral Cesar de Windt at his estate on the outskirts of Santo Domingo.[356] The arrangement with de Windt was brokered by the Admiral's son-in-law, Frank Castro, who'd served with Otero in the Bay of Pigs.

At first it looked like Otero's escape might've been headed in a different direction. When he first got off the plane, he was detained by Dominican police at the request of the FBI. But after a short time, Frank Castro showed up to the jail, and the doors were opened. Otero was free.

"The Americans don't run everything," Castro told him.

If Otero wanted to lay low under cover of the thick foliage of the Caribbean island, he did a poor job. He thumbed his nose at US agencies by granting an interview to *The Miami Herald* while hosting a lavish luncheon with friends on de Windt's estate. The piece, called "Bomb Suspect Enjoys Dominican Hospitality," flaunted the pampering Otero received while also serving as a platform for his political messaging.[357] He proclaimed his innocence and framed himself as being a victim of US betrayal.

The article also made clear that the US government, if they chose to indict him, wouldn't have much help from Dominican authorities.

"[Otero] is a free man—here he can do whatever he wants," de Windt said, further stating the exile "will not be arrested here, will not be handed over to American authorities, and will not be deported."[358]

Otero's lavishing in the Dominican sun lasted until January 22 when the formal indictment was filed in Miami. Less than three hours later, Otero was on a flight to Caracas to meet Morales at the airport.[359] The DISIP commander greeted the exile-turned-pawn and led him through Customs checkpoints and into a DISIP car where he was told he'd be a guest of the Venezuelan government. Morales arranged for a hotel suite, complimentary meals, and even a driver for Otero during his stay, which Morales indicated wouldn't be permanent. US authorities had initiated extradition papers for the Dominican Republic and would likely do so with Venezuelan authorities upon learning of Otero's arrival. Morales and DISIP had a limited influence in harboring one of America's most wanted unless some sort of monkeyshine could be enacted.

The following day Morales showed up at Otero's hotel suite with his boss Orlando Garcia Vasquez in tow.[360] Morales and Otero then engaged in a scripted dialogue the two of them rehearsed the night before, wherein Otero expressed his desire to go to Chile, and Morales proposed DISIP could arrange that by hiring Otero for a covert mission. Morales offered Otero a $300 per month salary to volunteer for DINA, Chile's intelligence service similar to Venezuela's DISIP. Otero would only be responsible for reporting intelligence back to DISIP regarding planned activities that directly affected Venezuela. That limitation placated Otero, who'd expressed concern over being "a spy." Beyond that obligation, he would be free to work for DINA in a legitimate capacity and make a living there so long as he remained outside the tentacles of the US government.

Garcia Vasquez seemed pleased. He thanked Otero for his bravery and assigned three DISIP vehicles with a cadre of bodyguards to look after him until his exit. In just the two days Otero had been in Caracas, US Attorney Robert Rust had asked for copies of the extradition treaty between the US and Venezuela as authorities were tipped off as to the bomber's whereabouts.[361] Morales needed to keep a step ahead, so DISIP placed Otero on an Iberia Airlines flight to Santiago, Chile on January 24.[362] The Monkey then bought some additional time by telling the FBI that Otero was still at the Anauco Hilton in Caracas, where Morales kept residence himself. There was no reason for authorities to doubt Morales's intel, so the US remained one country behind Otero for the time being.

In early February, Otero did as instructed and walked to the Ministry of the Interior in Santiago met with the army captain. He recounted his history of anti-communist work in the US.[363]

"Your people have probably heard of me," Otero told him. After a thorough background check to verify his claims, Otero was then given his first assignment—a political assassination in Costa Rica, for which Otero was not prepared nor willing to carry out. According to Morales, the target was to be Pascal Allende, nephew of ousted Chilean president Salvador Allende.[364] Otero boarded a flight back to Caracas to report the proposed mission to DISIP and his reluctance to execute it.[365]

Morales, Otero, and Frank Castro met in Morales's apartment to discuss next steps. Ricardo was impressed with Otero's ability to penetrate DINA so quickly and receive such a priority assignment. After some discussion, it was agreed that carrying out the plan would benefit everyone present; Morales would have an embedded operative in DINA, having earned their trust, Castro's FLNC group would have prime positioning in Chile after brokering the deal, and Otero would have safe haven in DINA. Frank Castro suggested his group actually carry out the hit, as Otero was too hot a commodity at the time and might be spotted going to Costa Rica.[366]

It turned out DINA had a backup plan if the newest operative failed. Dr. Orlando Bosch, paroled from the US and making residence in Chile, was ordered to be the backup hitter in Costa Rica. However, the government there had gotten wind of the assassination plans, and Bosch was arrested at the airport and deported back to Chile. Frank Castro's FLNC had their mission foiled; Pascal Allende was not killed. But that put Otero in danger for blowing DINA's orders. On April 27, he was jailed in Chile. With great effort, the US forced his release and extradition back to the States to face his bombing charges. Morales's overreach was causing a headache for all involved, and no nation wanted any part of the Rolando Otero drama that The Monkey was orchestrating.

On May 19 at 9:50 p.m., The Condor was loaded into seat 31F in the back row of Flight 978 to Miami International Airport, with two FBI agents keeping the handcuffed passenger pinned in the window seat. A DEA agent assisted as well, sitting in the row ahead of the trio. Otero was wiry and fidgety after having conducted a hunger strike while being detained in a windowless cell with no latrine in Chile.

Before takeoff, Otero lost it, standing on his seat and screaming, then kicking FBI agent Robert Scherrer as the agent wrestled with him. Passengers began scrambling from the fracas as Otero was yelling, "There's a bomb on this plane! You're all going to die!"[367] Scherrer put his hand over Otero's mouth to muzzle him when the prisoner clamped down, locking his jaw and not letting go. The DEA agent in front of them jumped over his seat and onto Otero, who needed to be struck with a blackjack to release the bite. Blood spurted from Scherrer's hand as the chaotic scene caused the pilot to vacate the back eight rows so agents had room in case Otero fired up again.

At 6:40 a.m. the next morning, Otero, less one tooth, was led off the plane into the waiting arms of Miami detectives Vazquez and Rapado, as well as Agent Joe Ball and others from the FBI's Miami field office.

Raul Diaz, however, elected to stay away from the scene entirely. The FBI would've been front and center even if he had gone, and watching the feds prance before the cameras leading the prized catch would've been too much to stomach. Morales, who'd provided the glue in the case, was already Diaz's confidential informant. The FBI hadn't developed one lead that Diaz and Dade PSD didn't already have.[368]

The one thing the FBI did handle entirely was the surveillance of Otero once Morales had given the name. Ball and his fellow agents strode before the cameras at the airport, as Diaz was content to let him try and save face. *The FBI was responsible for the guy having left the country in the first place,* Diaz thought. *The Condor was under FBI surveillance back in January when he went to K-Mart and bought a large suitcase, underwear, socks, and toothpaste, and got on a fucking plane.*[369]

Go ahead, Joe. Walk him through the airport.

★★★

Law enforcement kept a close eye on their surroundings in case word of Otero's arrival had gotten out in the exile community. There was a good chance they'd make a scene if they knew, but the headline-grabbing extradition went smoothy once Otero was off the plane.

Otero's impending trial was moved to Jacksonville because officials feared the "pre-trial publicity" would've biased a jury pool from Miami. The case against him was strong. His fingerprints linked him to the October and December bombings, and Morales's testimony stating Rolando Otero had confessed to him before Diaz retrieved the taxi license application would serve as further evidence. The defense would contend that a CIA-trained operative like Morales had the ability to transfer fingerprints and therefore could've committed the bombings and framed Otero, though that was outlandish.[370] Morales would honor mercenary reciprocity one last time by ignoring the subpoena and staying in Venezuela, no-showing the trial. Without Morales's testimony, Otero was acquitted in Jacksonville.

In preparation for a possible, though unlikely, acquittal, the State put a contingency plan in place. If an acquittal did in fact come down in the federal case, Dets. Diaz and Mederos were to place Otero under arrest on the spot and transport him back to Dade County to face charges at the state level. Wihtout Morales's testimony, that's exactly what happened, and at 9:07 p.m. on August 26, the detectives walked Otero off Eastern Airlines Flight 199 at Miami International Airport. The next trial would again be moved out of Miami, this time to the Florida panhandle abutting Alabama where there might be a better chance for a conviction of a foreign bomber.[371]

Ricardo Morales's Venezuela was becoming a central point for Cuban exile activity in the summer of 1976. Dr. Orlando Bosch had recently been moved down to Venezuela in what was perhaps Morales's most strategic move of his tenure in DISIP.

In early June, Bosch and Frank Castro were in the Dominican Republic spearheading a meeting of several anti-Castro groups in an attempt at consolidation.[372] It was becoming tougher to garner funding for missions because of the increased level of violence many groups were employing. Additionally, the Cuban cause was fading from the headlines, and the passage of time had removed much of the urgency for Fidel Castro's removal. The Cold War was over, the Cuban exiles were making good livings in the US, and much of the public had moved on. Bosch had even resorted to floating his own "bonds" back in 1974 in an attempt to raise private funding for his newly formed Cuban Action group.[373] The Cuban flag was printed on one side of the bond, while the other featured the face of Jose Martí, with his quote: "He who has a homeland, let him honor it; he who doesn't have it, let him conquer it." The bonds sold for as little as ten dollars each and were not redeemable for cash.

Bombs were still exploding all over Latin America, though, and the consolidation of groups would create a centralized hub controlling actions against communism. The meeting in the Dominican capital of Santo Domingo was attended by Frank Castro of FLNC, Dr. Bosch representing Cuban Action, Roberto Carballo Diaz of Brigade 2506, Jose Dionisio Suarez from Cuban Nationalists Movement (CNM), Luis Posada formerly of DISIP, and Ramon Orozco Crespo representing the 17th of April Movement. That meeting was the birth of CORU, the Coordination of United Revolutionary Organizations.

FBI documentation shows CORU claiming responsibility for eighteen acts of terror in Latin America, the Caribbean, and Europe between June and November of that year, with Bosch orchestrating most of the attacks.[374]

Posada reported the content of the CORU summit back to Morales and DISIP, which included the designation of responsibility for actions along geographical zones.[375] The group had decided on targets including airline offices, consulates, and a Cubana Airlines plane. The coming months would plunge Morales into a centrifuge spinning nearly out of control.

Justice Raul Morales Despau. Photo courtesy of Morales Family Collection.

The groom on his wedding day. Photo courtesy of Morales Family Collection.

Magda and the calm before the storm. Photo courtesy of Morales Family Collection.

Ricardo with sister Yolanda and mother Ines. Photo courtesy of Morales Family Collection.

Ricardo serving the CIA's Operation 40. Photo courtesy of Morales Family Collection.

With Mimi at Benihana in Miami. Photo courtesy of Morales Family Collection.

Assembling a weapon for Uncle Sam. Photo courtesy of Morales Family Collection.

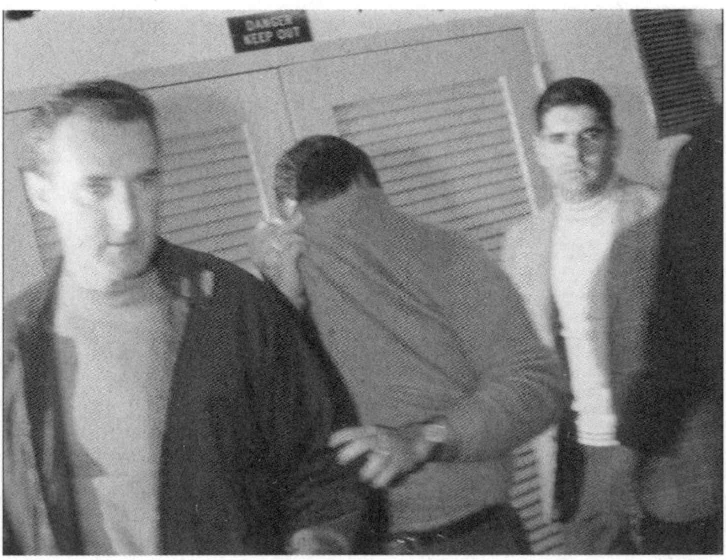

Ricardo sends a message with his right hand during his 1968 perp walk. Photo courtesy of Miami Dade College's Lynn and Louis Wolfson II Florida Moving Image Archives.

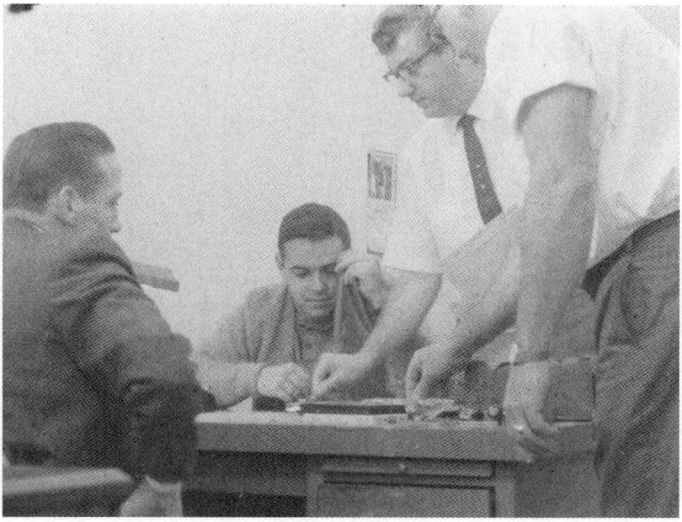

Sitting with his arresting officers.... Photo courtesy of Miami Dade College's Lynn and Louis Wolfson II Florida Moving Image Archives.

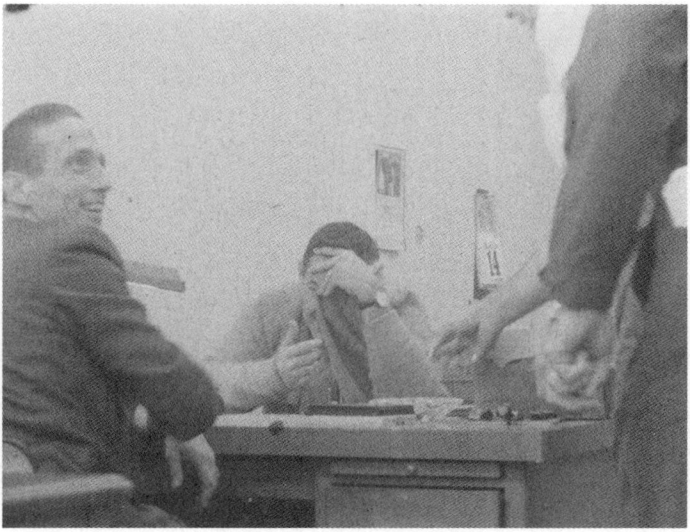

...and monkeying around them. Photo courtesy of Miami Dade College's Lynn and Louis Wolfson II Florida Moving Image Archives.

Raul, Magda, Sylvia, and Ricky Jr. Photo courtesy of Morales Family Collection.

Nazi hunting in Germany. Photo courtesy of Morales Family Collection.

A blast from below. Photo courtesy of Miami Dade College's Lynn and Louis Wolfson II Florida Moving Image Archives.

Morales heading into court in 1978, likely already knowing the outcome. Photo courtesy of Miami Dade College's Lynn and Louis Wolfson II Florida Moving Image Archives.

The outcome. Photo courtesy of Miami Dade College's Lynn and Louis Wolfson II Florida Moving Image Archives.

Hector Cornillot earning his revolutionary medal at Belle Glade prison. Photo courtesy of Hector Cornillot.

Rafael Villaverde, Monkey, Carlene Quesada, and Raul Villaverde and their brand of fun. Photo courtesy of Humberto Becerra.

Morales arrested. Again. Photo courtesy of Miami Dade College's Lynn and Louis Wolfson II Florida Moving Image Archives.

Lynette, Annette, and Uncle Richard. Photo courtesy of Morales Family Collection.

Chapter Eleven

JFK

Rick and his older brother Raul packed up the two rifles with scopes as they prepared to go shooting in the Everglades with their father. Ricardo's return trips from Venezuela were so sporadic they never knew when to expect him, so they cherished the time they had.

Rick had a memorable exchange with his father when returning to the car. As he opened the passenger door, Ricardo yelled from behind him.

"Hey! From now on you *always* have to look under the car first."

"For what?"

"Bombs."

They did, then got in and left.

As Rick looked down at the Barrett M82 in his lap, he remembered something they were covering in school. Rick's history teacher had said something about people thinking there were more shooters than just Lee Harvey Oswald. Rick told his dad what the teacher said.

Ricardo snorted. "He could never have made that shot. I saw him shoot at the camp."

And in just two sentences, Rick's world was changed. His father's prolonged absences had been shrouded in darkness. He knew he was a soldier of some kind, but Magda would never share where his father was and when they would see him again. Rick assumed his father didn't care and had found better things to do.

But no. It was more important stuff than that, as evidenced by the fact that he'd been at a training camp with Lee Harvey Oswald.[376] This was history—topics his teachers talked about in classes, written about in that big fat textbook in his locker. His dad was involved in some really important things if he was with the people mentioned in his books.

Rick wanted more. He pressed for more. But Ricardo was past the topic, ready for some target practice with his two oldest boys. He only offered that it was a CIA training camp, and they were being trained to fire guns, just like they were doing together there in the Everglades. And it sounded like the Oswald guy needed more training.

Rick lived for years never fully realizing the impact of what his father had told him. His childhood fascination about his father's admission was less about its historical implications than it was confirmation that his father was busy with important work for the CIA—the spy group he heard about on TV. Hot fucking shit.

As Rick grew, his questions about the whole CIA thing morphed more into questions about the whole JFK thing. Time with his father was less and less frequent, especially when he took some job for the Venezuelan government. But Rick didn't stop talking about JFK, and Ricardo kept moving past the subject.

"Ancient history," he'd say. "Like dinosaurs."

Later, Ricardo would be more open to the discussion, recounting the story of seeing Oswald, who stood out as one of only a handful of Americans at the CIA camp. As one of the more experienced operatives and better shots in the group of mostly Cubans, Morales assisted with some of the marksmanship training. He recalled Oswald as one of the trainees that needed guidance. Morales was later stunned upon seeing the newspaper image of Oswald as the man arrested for the assassination.

Some years later, Ricardo divulged that he was actually in Dallas when Kennedy was assassinated, though not in Dealey Plaza. He and a couple of Cuban exile CIA operatives were sent to a hotel, armed, with instructions to sit and wait for orders. They did, none came, and the day after the assassination, they were sent back to Miami. Morales told his boys he later figured they were a "cleanup crew" to be dispatched in the event of an error. Just who and what they'd be "cleaning" was anyone's guess.

That was the last discussion Morales would have about it. Later, Rick confirmed with his mother that Ricardo had, in fact, been out of town for two days in November 1963. She thought nothing of his handing her a go-bag before he left. He never spoke to her about Dallas or Kennedy. Magda was used to it; she knew only that there was a great deal of risk in the things he was doing and that her questions about it would not be answered.

★★★

There are over five million pages of declassified documents regarding the Kennedy assassination, and Cuban exiles appear often.[377] They were always involved in the narrative, if for no other reason than the administration's preoccupation with Castro and his threat to the US. However, the amount of documentation dedicated to exiles who served as CIA operatives is startling and significant. Ricardo Morales, Luis Posada, Orlando Bosch, and a slew of others, as well as non-Cubans like Frank Sturgis, who'd served Brigade 2506 and Operation 40, are prominent in the collection.

While no declassified document stands alone as a smoking gun, it is troubling that more than six decades after the incident more than fifteen thousand documents have yet to be unveiled. The backtracking of recent US presidents who'd promised to release them, pledging transparency in what their government had found, is more concerning still. President Trump promised to release all remaining files on the matter but recounted this claim in April 2018, citing national security concerns.[378]

President Biden was next, first advocating for the documents' release then reversing course, citing the COVID-19 pandemic and, alarmingly, a potential blowback on trust of government guidance. An October 21, 2021 White House briefing stated, "Temporary continued postponement is necessary to protect against identifiable harm to the military defense, intelligence operations, law enforcement, or the conduct of foreign relations that is of such gravity that it outweighs the public interest in immediate disclosure."[379] Both administrations' statements indicate the likely presence of information damning to US institutions. This has paved the road for still more theories in the hailstorm of countless books, articles, documentaries, and blogs on JFK's murder.

A woman named Marita Lorenz made an early conspiracy theory sized splash when she went public with a story placing culpability at the CIA's feet. She was Fidel Castro's mistress and assisted in a CIA operation to kill the dictator.[380] The extension of her CIA contact, she alleged, involved her accompanying CIA operatives to Dallas at the time of JFK's murder.

The first portion of Lorenz's claims, those involving Castro, were corroborated by CIA operative Frank Sturgis in his March 20, 1978 testimony before the House Select Committee on Assassinations. Sturgis had been working with the CIA to get to Castro. He testified to approaching Lorenz, whom he knew to be Fidel's mistress and secretary, about providing information for the US.

"I made an approach to Marita and the approach was successful," Sturgis testified. "I had to be very, very careful. She could have gotten me killed. And in making an approach to her, I did recruit her to go ahead and do some spying for me."[381] Sturgis was Castro's Director of Security while he was secretly moonlighting for the CIA, which made him a valuable asset due to his proximity to the despot.

Lorenz's story was brought into the mainstream courtesy of a 1993 *Vanity Fair* article in which she outlined her relationship with Castro, the CIA, and Frank Sturgis. In one story Sturgis confirmed in testimony, he handed her two botulinum toxin tablets with which she'd agreed to poison Castro. She botched the effort, having hidden the pills in her cold cream jar before boarding the flight to Havana, where they dissolved in the balm.

Lorenz's and Sturgis's stories diverge in the matter of JFK's assassination. In the *Vanity Fair* piece, Lorenz claimed to have trained at the Operation 40 camp under Sturgis in preparation for her assassination mission; at the camp she became immersed in the anti-Castro movement and its perpetrators. She also referenced the Mafia heavies she'd met in Miami through her association with the Agency, and alleged to have borne the child of Marcos Pérez Jiménez, the former dictator of Venezuela.

After his removal from power, Pérez Jiménez fled to the US and was jailed in Miami as Venezuela fought to extradite him on charges of embezzlement. Marita's connections to the anti-Castro movement continued once she moved back to Miami with him in 1962. She claimed to have run guns between Miami and New Orleans for them, and she attended a CIA camp in the Everglades that summer. While there, she met a new recruit named "Ozzie," who was Lee Harvey Oswald.[382] The next time she'd see him would be November 18, 1963, when she claimed she was summoned by Sturgis to meet him at "a small, shabby converted hotel" in Miami. Waiting there were Sturgis, "Ozzie," Pedro Díaz Lanz, formerly the head of Castro's Air Force, and "Gerry," Gerald Patrick Hemming of the CIA.

She said the group then moved to Dr. Orlando Bosch's house, where they met with the doctor and Guillermo and Ignacio Novo, the brothers who would eventually be convicted of the Orlando Letelier assassination years later. She watched the men load the car with guns, and they drove through the night to a motel in Dallas. E. Howard Hunt arrived at the motel along with Jack Ruby, with whom Marita got into a physical altercation after he questioned why "the fucking broad" was there. When she asked to leave, Sturgis drove her to the airport where she boarded a flight back to Miami on November 21.

Lorenz eventually went public with her claims, but they were refuted by all involved. Sturgis called her a liar and denied his involvement in the assassination in any capacity, testifying he'd never gone to Dallas or interacted with anyone about the assassination beforehand.[383]

Little of Lorenz's story has been corroborated on declassified paper, though one wouldn't expect the CIA to implicate itself in what has been accepted as a national tragedy. She's been filed away as a conspiracy theorist and, despite whether or not anything she presented bore fruit, her story sits beside a great number of unproven and unvetted tales suggesting more than a single unsponsored gunman with a lurid plan. One consistency that exists between Lorenz's tale and most other theories is the three concentric circles surrounding the assassination—the CIA, the mob, and the Cuban groups. And aside from the JFK assassination, there *is* a lot of documented verifiable overlap between these three organizations.

This book has spent considerable time detailing the relationship between the CIA and the Cuban exiles, but the mafia was also involved in the Agency's plan to get Castro. In US government documents declassified in 2017 as part of the National Archives' JFK assassination files, mafia kingpins Santo Trafficante and Johnny Roselli were considered by the CIA to eliminate the Cuban dictator.[384]

A couple of key elements of Marita Lorenz's story also line up with Ricardo Morales's confession to Rick. His version confirms that Oswald was trained at a Florida CIA camp used by the Operation 40 team, and it also verifies that CIA-trained Cuban exiles were part of the team dispatched to a motel in Dallas. Though Lorenz didn't report meeting anyone specifically named Morales, Ricardo and whoever he went with could have arrived after Marita went home on November 21. Also, Ricardo and his cleanup team could have been put at another hotel, so as to keep the groups separate and unaware of each others' presence. If it was someone in Sturgis's group that would need some cleanup, it was probably better they didn't know from which direction it was coming.

E. Howard Hunt, the CIA agent and Brigade 2506 organizer whose name was circulating in conspiracy circles, initially refuted all claims of his involvement, stating he was shopping with his wife in Miami at the time of the assassination. This was turned on its head in a 2007 *Rolling Stone* article that outlined how Hunt's son, St. John, allegedly obtained a deathbed confession from his father in 2003.[385]

Howard, eighty-five at the time and decimated by lupus, cancer, and an amputated gangrened leg, turned to his son and asked for a pen and pad of paper. The elder Hunt sipped his root beer, then, atop the clean sheet of paper, wrote the letters "LBJ" He then constructed an organizational chart of sorts, connecting the former Vice President's name with a line to "Cord Meyer," a CIA agent whose wife had an affair with Kennedy. Incidentally, Meyer's wife's murder in 1964 remains unsolved.[386] Mary Meyer was strolling the walking path alone beside Georgetown's C&O canal when she was executed by two bullets fired at close range.

Hunt wasn't finished. He connected Meyer's name to a "Bill Harvey," also of the CIA, and finally to "David Morales," as in David Morales Sanchez, the feared CIA agent who'd overseen, of all things, Operation 40 training. Once again, the CIA's band of assassins entrusted with the neutralization of Fidel Castro appears in JFK assassination text. With the formation of Brigade 2506 and Operation 40, the US government established the primary function of the CIA-trained Cuban exiles—performing the riskier tasks it could not, itself, be accused of.

In a 2023 interview regarding his uncle's assassination, politician Robert F. Kennedy, Jr. stated, "There is overwhelming evidence that the CIA was involved in his murder. I think it's beyond a reasonable doubt at this point."[387]

The Agency has continually denied any participation in the assassination of President Kennedy.

If the speculation in hushed tones is wrong and the CIA is verifiably innocent of any wrongdoing, one would think the release of the fifteen thousand remaining classified documents would help put such talk to bed. Yet the delay in releasing said documents due to matters of international security creates fertile soil for the blossoming chasm of trust in our government.

In October 2021, Rick Morales, Jr. went public with the story of his father's comments, his story covered by *The Miami Herald* and Miami's *Actualidad Radio* 1040 AM. *The Miami Herald* spoke with Democratic pollster Fernand Amandi who has extensively researched the JFK assassination, and says there is no doubt Morales's account has merit.[388] Rick, Jr.'s illumination of this possibility led to increased media coverage, including Rob Reiner and Soledad O'Brien's podcast *Who Killed JFK*? Ricardo's story was featured in an episode that covered possible involvement from the anti-Castro exiled soldiers.

In the variety of JFK conspiracies that exist in the world, Morales spotting Oswald at a CIA camp and later being sent to Dallas seems the least difficult to swallow. Maybe that's just a commentary on current public perception of our government agencies.

Chapter Twelve The Sky is Crying (1976)

Twenty-four members of the 1975 national Cuban fencing team, many of them still teenagers, boarded Flight 455 destined for Cuba. They'd just won every gold medal in the Central American and Caribbean Championships and were headed back to Havana from Guyana. They joined the forty-nine other passengers and crew, which included several Cuban government officials like Manuel Permuy Hernández, director of the National Institute of Sports, Jorge de la Nuez Suárez, Secretary for the Shrimp Fleet, Alfonso González, National Commissioner of Firearm Sports, and Domingo Chacón Coello, an agent from the Interior Ministry.[389]

Photographer Hernán Lozano also boarded, carrying just a toothpaste tube, and presented a Venezuelan passport bearing the name Jose Vazquez Garcia.[390] Lozano had done some freelance work for DISIP when his boss Luis Posada was a chief in the agency.[391] Lozano came to be a trusted source for Ricardo Morales and was even issued a DISIP ID card. Now he and his partner Freddy Lugo, who had also worked for DISIP, worked for Posada in his private investigative agency.[392]

Luis Posada had separated from DISIP in March 1974 and started Investigaciones Comerciales e Industriales (ICI), but he remained closely connected to his prized recruit Morales and DISIP as a whole.[393] According to CIA documents, he parted with DISIP because of allegations of drug trafficking. A 1973 Bureau of Narcotics and Dangerous Drugs investigation posited that Posada was facilitating the smuggling of cocaine from Colombia, through Venezuela, and ultimately to Miami.[394] The CIA, who'd maintained communication with Posada through his tenure in DISIP, expressed concern over the investigation and cut ties with him. DISIP followed suit in '74.

Lozano and Lugo got off Flight 455 during a layover in Barbados and didn't reboard, though they had left some personal items on the plane, namely Lozano's toothpaste tube in the restroom.

At 1:15 p.m., Flight 455 took off from Seawell Airport in Barbados without the two DISIP operatives, and it continued its journey to Havana with seventy-three people on board. Sixteen minutes later, a bomb exploded and plunged the aircraft out of the sky and into the sea, killing all on board. Turned out the C4 that was in Hernán Lozano's toothpaste tube hadn't detonated during the layover as planned. A CIA report cites a source inside the operation claiming "the operation had not gone as planned because it was intended that the bomb should explode before the aircraft took off from Barbados...apparently the timing mechanism on the bomb had not been properly set."[395] That would turn out not to be the case.

This horrific event came on the heels of a very public political assassination on US soil, right in Washington, DC. On September 21, Chilean diplomat Orlando Letelier and his American assistant and translator Ronni Moffitt were killed by a car bomb. The boldness of the execution in the nation's capital added to the incident's gravitas, and the violence from Latin America was brought closer to home. The assassination was eventually proven to be a state-sponsored directive in papers declassified by the Obama administration; it was ordered by Chilean dictator Augusto Pinochet through his head of intelligence Manuel Contreras.[396]

Letelier was once the defense and foreign minister under President Salvador Allende, and he was Chile's ambassador to the US until Pinochet's 1973 coup. After the new regime was established, the dictator targeted all Chilean exiles from the previous administration. Letelier had fled to the US and was working at the Institute of Policy Studies in DC when the car bomb went off.

As terrible as Letelier and Moffitt's murders were, American citizens could still find solace in the fact that they had no stake in the conflict with Chile. But Flight 455 was different. Terrorism in the air strikes a chord in everyone on the planet. With the Cubana Airlines incident, the exiles hadn't hurt Castro as much as they had everyone else in the world. It was bad.

DISIP's fingerprints were all over this one. Not only had the two bombers been working there, but it had leaked that former chief Posada helped plan the attack. Additionally, the logistics were facilitated by Commissar Ricardo Morales, who would later testify that the bombing supplies came from the Explosive and Disposal Division at DISIP headquarters.[397] Before the bombing, Morales's Division 54 agents had conducted a raid at the home of a suspected foreign intelligence agent, wherein a cache of explosives was seized and placed in evidence at DISIP.

"Later on," Morales said, "the explosives found their way into this Cuban Air Force plane."[398]

Through the years, Morales and others involved would repeatedly refer to Cubana Airlines Flight 455 as either an air force plane, military transport, or other designation linking it to Castro's army. Such labeling likely made it easier to distance themselves from the casualties. Though it is unknown whether or not the operatives were actually misinformed, there was no proof that the vessel was anything other than a passenger plane.

However, years later information emerged about a handful of passengers on the flight that deserves mention. In Luis Posada's 1994 memoir, *Los Caminos del Guerrero,* (translated *The Paths of the Warrior*), he reports the flight having been held an additional twenty-seven minutes at layover, which would account for the error in timing the detonation of the explosive.[399] More interesting, though, is Posada's explanation for the delay. The airline was ordered to wait for a handful of late arrivals on important business—a delegation of North Korean diplomats on their way to Cuba.

The strengthening of relations between North Korea and Cuba at this time indicated Cuba's alignment with the communist alliance. The Soviets first began training North Korean scientists and engineers on nuclear development back in 1956, and the two nations formalized this relationship by signing a nuclear cooperation agreement in

1959.[400] Moscow would continue to provide training and development of nuclear technology for the next thirty years.

The Yongbyon Nuclear Research Center was constructed in 1962 to house the IRT-2000 reactor. While nuclear energy itself isn't indicative of the development of weaponry, North Korean Foreign Minister Pak Song Chol wrote to their USSR Ambassador, "Who can impose such a [nonproliferation] treaty on countries that do not have nuclear weapons, but are perhaps successfully working in that direction[?]"[401]

In 1974, a couple of years before the Cubana Airlines bombing, North Korea's facility reached a power rating capacity of 4MW(th), doubling the initial rating of 2MW(th) back in 1965.[402] The team of North Koreans boarding Flight 455 for diplomacy talks with Cuba would have certainly sounded an alarm for operatives working to neutralize Castro's ability to acquire nukes. The plan for the airliner might still have been detonation on the ground, sending a potent message to Castro awaiting his North Korean visitors. But the twenty-seven minute delay they caused tragically invalidated the timing pencil allegedly set by Lozano.

The source of the device itself was complicated. No evidence could've been moved from the explosive-holding room at DISIP without security clearance, but Orlando Garcia Vasquez revealed a clue as to how that happened.[403] Sources stated that after the Air Cubana attack, Garcia Vasquez spoke with Carlos Fabri, bomb expert in the Explosive and Disposal Division. He informed Fabri that he would be expected to testify at any forthcoming trial regarding the bomb and its components.

"According to Garcia Vasquez," the report states, "Fabri became very nervous and Garcia Vasquez told source he believes that Fabri either made the bomb for this Cubana bombing, instructed persons on how to make it, or at least had prior knowledge of the bombing."[404] The same report indicated Fabri and Posada were arrested by Venezuelan authorities a few years prior for falsifying documents and, of all things, providing explosives to Dr. Orlando Bosch.

★★★

"A bus with seventy-three dogs went off a cliff and all got killed."[405]

Hernán Lozano waited on the phone for a reaction from Dr. Bosch. He didn't get one. Bosch said he didn't know what he was talking about and hung up.

It was one of several calls Lozano confessed to making from Barbados to Venezuela right after the explosions. After that, Lozano and Lugo flew to Trinidad, and they were arrested by the police within a day.

On October 16, Lugo was ready to talk. Corporal Oscar King, Superintendent Waterman, and Sgt. Anthony Jack sat with him and recorded his story regarding the bombing.[406] The following day, his partner Lozano called for the officers and, in turn, gave his side of things. He admitted to being attached to Bosch's CORU and said he'd recruited Freddy Lugo. Lugo, in his statement, said he saw Lozano with the C4 and the toothpaste tube at a restaurant earlier in the day, while Lozano's statement implicated Lugo and his cameras brought on board the flight. On the 26th, both men were on a plane to Venezuela to face their crimes.

Meanwhile in Venezuela, the Judicial Technical Police (PTJ) began to investigate the bombing, as it was becoming evident that the country seemed to have been a hub for the mission. Morales, Posada, and the two photographers were in the spotlight, and Bosch was indirectly drawing all eyes to Venezuela due to his presence there during the bombing. As those names began hitting the press, DISIP quickly took the case from the hands of PTJ in an effort to be the sole investigating agency.[407] And while all the attention was a problem for Morales, he'd actually engineered some of it. His uncanny knack for seeing the big picture and playing the long game indicated early on that he might need an escape hatch after the bombing.

Once initially receiving word of CORU's plan to bomb Flight 455, Morales reached out to Bosch and invited him to Venezuela.[408] DISIP gave him a safe haven in which to operate, provided the group didn't do anything on Venezuelan soil. DISIP's brass felt the best way to avoid conflict with CORU was to cut a deal with them.[409] The hospitable Morales even facilitated an apartment in the Anauco Hilton for Bosch, right beside his unit; much easier to keep an eye on someone when they're your neighbor.

Shortly after Bosch's arrival in September, DISIP's Morales, Garcia Vasquez, and former agent Posada attended a $1,000-a-plate fundraiser organized for Bosch and CORU, wherein he publicly proclaimed, "Now that our organization has come out of the Letelier job looking good, we are going to try something else."[410] It was yet another incident in which the publicity-thirsty Bosch had inserted his name. A comprehensive picture was being painted—Bosch was back in business in Venezuela, and it was no secret.

The CIA was playing right into the plan. The fundraiser dinner was reported in an October memo, as Morales knew it would be, and CORU's plans were documented by the CIA months before. Posada had attended CORU's group formation meeting in Santo Domingo in June. After that, he told Morales about their plans for Cubana Airlines, and that information was transmitted back to the CIA. A June 17 Agency memo titled "Possible Plans of Cuban Exile Extremists to Blow Up a Cubana Airline" cited Bosch's group's intentions.[411]

After the formation meeting, CORU had tried to hit Cubana Airlines twice and failed. Ironically, while those first attempts had fallen under Bosch's purview, Flight 455 hadn't. Morales admitted to being part of the planning alongside Posada and Frank Castro. After Lugo and Lozano did their thing and Bosch got wind of the news, his only comment to the group was, "You never blow up a plane while it is in the air."[412]

The press coverage was ramping up, and Venezuela stood alone in a narrow spotlight, which infuriated President Carlos Andrés Pérez. A week after the bombing, Morales and top-level DISIP officers were called to a meeting where it was demanded that a plan be hatched and put into effect immediately.[413] President Pérez insisted on a visible crackdown in which anyone and everyone suspected of involvement was arrested. Additionally, Morales was ordered to begin a propaganda campaign and divert attention away from Venezuela.

Before contacting the media, Morales played his ace hand. He called his on-again, off-again associate Orlando Bosch and informed him he'd be heading his way with another DISIP agent. Consider that a pre-arrest courtesy call. Bosch couldn't have been surprised considering the massive media attention the terrorists had garnered in Caracas. He was amiably arrested and was brought to headquarters by Morales.

Bosch's travel patterns arranged by DISIP implicated him in the bombing. The supporting intelligence collected on Bosch also made him a likely suspect, given his failed attempts to bomb a Cubana Airlines flight that summer. The doctor's quest for center stage had made him the face of such activity in the Latin American hemisphere. His arrest didn't shock anyone.

The other intriguing arrest was DISIP's detainment of their former senior officer Luis Posada. In addition to his attendance at the CORU meeting and his implication in Lugo and Lozano's confessions, his mouth was a ticking time bomb that might further implicate Venezuela.

"If Posada talks," Morales said, "the Venezuelan government will go down the tubes."[414] Without having been charged or convicted, Posada was plucked off the street and detained for years in an effort to keep him quiet.

"The Cubana bomb went off, the people were killed, and there were tracks leading right back to DISIP," FBI counterterrorism specialist Carter Cornick told *The New York Times*. "The information was so strong that they locked up Posada as a preventative measure—to prevent him from talking or being killed. There was no doubt in anyone's mind, including mine, that he was up to his eyeballs [in the Cubana Airlines bombing]."[415]

With Lugo, Lozano, Bosch, and Posada in custody, Morales focused on the next phase of the cover-up. On October 19, 1976, news reporter Jose "Pepe" Cabrera Riesgo at Miami-based Spanish radio station WQBA received a long-distance call from Venezuela.[416] The call from Ricardo Morales of DISIP was put through by Raul Diaz of the Organized Crime Bureau of the Dade County PSD on a three-way line from Diaz's office. Morales told Cabrera that he had a sensational story for air, and he requested Cabrera conduct an interview after specifically agreeing not to mention the Republic of Venezuela under any circumstances. Cabrera agreed, and he told Morales his superior Jorge Luis Hernandez would tape the interview to air on the radio program *Cubanissima.*[417]

After an introduction, Morales began his diatribe, starting by declaring the Rolando Otero trial "one of the biggest judicial monstrosities in the US, a matter of dreadful degradation against the true anti-communist fighters."[418] The triple agent then went on to accuse the agents of the FBI of beating the teeth out of Otero's mouth in an illegal flight out of Chile. Then after being found not guilty in Jacksonville, he was transferred "to the dungeons of Dade County jail, where he was brutally beaten by repressive employees of the American judicial system, to the point where two of his ribs were broken."[419]

He then exonerated Orlando Bosch of any involvement in the Letelier assassination, despite having personally arrested him. Morales instead blamed the "leftist" organization *The New York Times* for erroneously involving him in the investigation. The major Miami news outlets then fell into Morales's crosshairs.

"I am tired of putting up with the anti-Cuban campaign of *The Miami Herald,*" he told WQBA, "the anti-Cuban campaign of *The Miami News,* subsidized by the Federal Bureau of Investigation and the Central Intelligence Agency which these agencies, through their dirty work, their smelly work we might say, only want to slander once more the true anti-communist fighters."[420]

The next step of Morales's propaganda campaign seeking to sanitize Venezuela involved his new favorite tool, Dr. Bosch, and the highest-profile active terror investigation at the time, the Letelier murders. On October 18, Morales planted a story in the Venezuelan press which was carried globally the following day, stating DISIP had obtained information while Bosch was in their custody.[421] Morales reported that Bosch claimed the Novo brothers—Guillermo and Ignacio, leaders of the anti-Castro group Cuban Nationalist Movement out of Union City, New Jersey—were responsible for the bombing of Letelier's car.

The Novo brothers hadn't been on anyone's radar at that point and it seemed unexpected, given Cubans didn't seem to have skin in the game of Chilean politics and the violent transition from Allende to Pinochet. But Chile had been a friendly haven for Cuban exiles responsible for bombings, and a quid pro quo situation wouldn't have been impossible to fathom. If Morales and Rolando Otero's accounts were accurate, Chile's DINA had attempted to hire the Otero to hit Chilean president Salvador Allende's nephew Pascal when DISIP sent Otero to DINA to infiltrate the agency. The investigation into the Letelier murders seemed to suggest a political hit orchestrated by DINA. The link between the two countries had one commonality—Ricardo Morales. The chief of Chilean intelligence said, "The Monkey is a very dangerous man. He affects the entire relationship between Chile and Venezuela. We have to take special precautions because of that one man. He is a plague on us."[422]

Investigators in the Letelier case also questioned why Orlando Bosch would've had information about the Novo brothers' involvement. They started to speculate that perhaps the leak to the press about Bosch's accusations were orchestrated by The Monkey. No one would get close enough to Bosch to find out. DISIP made sure of that by denying US authorities' requests to interview him while in custody, and Morales felt he could handle any meddlesome reporters snooping around Caracas. For the moment, the media covering all things Venezuela now had a few arrests for the Cubana Airlines bomb and information that might crack the Letelier murders to run with. Maybe that, coupled with the WQBA interview, was sufficient enough diversion by Morales.

While the radio appearance could have been dismissed as the ramblings of yet another wayward terrorist, Morales's words were given weight. He was not facing charges for anything, and his well-known background as a dependable operative for the US made others take a second look at what he was alleging. His statement, once making its way back to Washington, prompted formal FBI denials of Morales's accusations in an October 1976 memo regarding the recorded phone call.

Ultimately, WQBA supervisor Jorge Luis Hernandez vetoed the airing of the tape, feeling the radio station would be open to excessive liability if they could not attribute the comments to "Ricardo Morales

Navarrete of DISIP, Caracas, Venezuela, or a similar title."[423] Morales had forbidden that as a contingency for doing the interview, so the station scrapped their plans to air it.

The day after the recording, the FBI met with Raul Diaz, who'd patched the call through and tape-recorded it on his end.[424] The detective made the cassette available for duplication by the Bureau and was then interviewed about its contents. He said he was personally put off by the statements and didn't fully understand why Ricardo was launching the campaign. He said Morales told him that over the past eight years he'd accumulated the names and salaries of all paid FBI informants and was planning to publish the list. He planned to return to Miami that week and "make *mierda*" (shit) of the FBI and CIA. Diaz felt he'd been coordinating with some other stateside media outlets, going into full muckrake mode.

The effects of what had happened in Venezuela with Flight 455 and in Washington with Orlando Letelier might have been lost on Morales as he played the final pieces, though that was unlikely for the savvy operative. The flurry of patching he was doing for Venezuela was probably needed as much for his own survival as for DISIP's benefit—stay afloat until the next round.

I don't play to win or lose; I play to stay in the game.

With the downing of Flight 455, most public support for missions against Cuba ended, as did the use of political leverage in the exiled mercenaries' cause. What the last of the freedom fighters thought would be an uppercut to Castro's chin ended up exposing their body. And even if you connect with a wild haymaker, it can still cost you the fight.

★★★

Rick's fixation on sports grew as he entered middle school. He threw himself headlong into baseball and football as part of an after-school athletics program. Though he had played since the first grade, he was now part of the travel team, and Rick was ready to bring his game to the next level.

Though the practices and games had filled a void in Rick, he still felt the lack of a close male figure in his life. Naturally, over time, Coach Javier was sliding into that spot. He'd been the man who encouraged him from age six. He picked up the players in his bus every day and brought them to practice where the first half hour was devoted to their homework. After that, they practiced for two hours, either baseball or football, depending on the season, then were driven back to their stops on the team bus.

Sometimes he'd call the parents and get permission to take the boys to ball games on their off time. Coach Javier was a blessing for the parents who worked long hours and needed someone to do something productive with their children.

Rick wasn't alone in his home situation. Several of the kids on his team were also living in broken homes and found refuge in Coach and his program. The team played a significant role in all their lives, and Coach was more than just the guy they played sports with. He bought them things, took them places.

Rick and two other kids on the team began spending time at Coach's house, checking out the electric race car track he'd built. He would call their parents and ask if he could get them pizza after practice, but they'd wind up at his home instead.

While Rick and his two friends hung out with Coach at his house, he began making advances, telling the three boys when people care about each other, there are things they should do to show it. Rick didn't know what to do or how to process that internally. It seemed neither of the other two boys did either, both also from fatherless homes. In short time, Coach began molesting them, and directing them to do the same to each other.

Beyond the confusion Rick felt, there was a sense of guilt brewing in him. Had he done something to invite this? Was this all his fault and, by proxy, had he caused his friends to endure it as well? It became clear this wouldn't be a onetime thing, and Rick would be fearful each time practice ended.

"It just becomes a nightmare," Rick said. "Every time you're going home after practice, you're praying that he makes a left instead of a right to take you home. And once in a while, when he doesn't take a left and takes a right, you know that you're in for hell."

The repeated violations further dragged Rick away from living any semblance of a normal kid's life. His familial situation was unstable as it was, and now his predisposition to blame others for his unhappiness was abruptly spun, and he pointed his accusatory finger at himself. Shame, guilt, and fear gripped the preteen. He didn't dare tell anyone about what was happening. Child molestation wasn't a topic openly covered with any sensitivity by media or in schools at the time, and even less so in the culture from which Rick's family descended. He was trapped. Rick had pent up so much he headed for overload.

"It's an awful thing," he said. "So, at that point, you just lose all trust in adults. I just shut down."

The abuse at the hands of Coach Javier—a pseudonym for these purposes—continued. Rick started doing drugs at age thirteen, starting with smoking pot. That escapism was just temporary, of course, and at three o'clock every afternoon he walked to the field, looking into the evil stare of what remained of his day.

He began acting out, less out of rebellion than a conscious attempt to get kicked out of the athletics program for his disruptive behavior. On one of Coach's field trips to the Seaquarium, Rick started a disturbance in the gift shop and was thrown out. They called his mother and when Magda arrived at the Seaquarium, Rick pleaded with her to take him home. He didn't want to go back on Coach's bus. But Magda refused, left, and made him sit alone on the bus, where he quivered alone at the thought of where it would deliver him in just a few hours.

★★★

Reporters Taylor Branch, John Rothchild, and Hilda Inclán boarded the same Pan Am flight on October 21, 1976.[425] The writers soon realized that the night flight to Caracas had a handful of parties similarly interested in the international web of intrigue that had unfolded in Venezuela in recent months. They were in the company of some heavy hitters: George Yoss and Hank Adorno, Asst. State Attorneys, and Sgt. Raul Diaz and Det. Raul Martinez of Miami PD. The fact that three reporters, two prosecutors, and two Miami detectives had landed on the same flight and were headed to the same destination served as confirmation that Caracas was a hotbed of intrigue.

Branch and Rothchild were going to try and interview Dr. Orlando Bosch while in custody at DISIP, and they ran into Inclán by chance. She was headed south for the same reason. She'd been the lead reporter covering Latin American terrorism for *The Miami News* and had snagged Bosch's last interview before his arrest, and she wanted an all-important follow up.

The clean-cut Cuban cops in fitted polos and prosecutors in suits were on the plane to meet with Ricardo Morales regarding Otero's forthcoming second trial at the state level. They wanted a hard commitment from Ricardo that he'd show up and testify this time.

Venezuela was where it was at.

During the flight, the seasoned and experienced Branch regaled Rothchild with stories about The Monkey—but only as many as he could fit in the three-hour flight. He'd interviewed Ricardo in Miami in 1974. Tales of his exploits made for spellbinding storytelling, but what lingered long after having dealt with Morales was his personal style. It was as if the death-defying operative was onstage at all times.

"He's one of the most cynical people I've ever met," Branch told Rothchild during the flight, "but I liked him anyway. He doesn't have any illusions about the business he's in, and he makes fun of all the people who do."[426]

Branch related a story that would be written about for years that Roberto Morales witnessed firsthand as a little boy. A reporter Branch knew had paid a visit to Mimi and Ricardo's place while Morales was in the shower. He was led to the living room by Mimi while *Robertico* played on the floor, and he placed his briefcase on the coffee table. Once out of the shower, Ricardo greeted him warmly and reached out, bypassing the outstretched hand of his guest, and instead took his briefcase from the table. He opened it and retrieved a tape recorder as the man stood speechless. Morales removed the batteries and stood them at one end of the table, then reached into his ankle holster and pulled out his Browning. He slid out the clip and stood it on the other side of the table, then placed the disarmed gun beside the disarmed tape recorder. He sat across from the man, not yet having uttered a word since coming out of the shower.

"Now," Morales finally said, reclining on the couch, "we can talk."

"I remember that vividly," Roberto Morales said, having watched the scene play out before his young eyes. "My mother and I, we were sitting like if nothing was going on. It's normal operating procedure."[427]

That was The Monkey.

Rothchild listened to his partner intently during the flight. Branch began the oral biography in Cuba, discussing Morales's CIA years, FBI years, his two assassination attempts, and finally landing on Bosch. Branch hoped to exploit his personal connection to DISIP and score some time with the imprisoned international bomber.

But after exiting the plane, Branch noticed a group of men standing at the airport entrance who were watching them intently. They broke their stares only to greet the Miami police officers and prosecutors who'd entered the gate behind the reporters. As Branch, Rothchild, and Inclán got in line at Customs, the men approached.

"Give me your papers and follow me," a man in a turtleneck sweater and leather jacket said, hospitality absent from his voice. The reporters did so, with the group of stone-faced men flanking them on each side. They were led to a separate room and served a summons printed on DISIP letterhead to appear at an address the following day. The reporters were released and grabbed a taxi, which was tailed by a car for the entire ride to the hotel, ensuring they went nowhere but their designated lodging.

The following morning at 5:30 a.m., Morales appeared in their hotel room leading a team of DISIP agents. They wrangled the reporters while Ricardo seized their passports and airline tickets and darted around the room barking staccato commands.

"Pack!"

"Close those bags."

"Let's go!"

The glaring disparity in reception the reporters and law enforcement had received from Venezuelan intelligence wasn't surprising given the climate in Caracas. The cops and prosecutors were there to curry favor with the comandante of DISIP's Division 54, while the reporters were there to meddle, probe, and get Bosch and Posada to say something revelatory. That shit was simply not going to happen. Morales's tornado through the hotel that morning had set a tone that kept the writers obedient and silent. Their focus was narrowed to getting through the next thirty seconds with their freedom, maybe their lives.

They were led outside into a car and drove in silence to the airport. Once arriving, Morales marched them up some stairs to the DISIP offices, where the three reporters sat down on a worn couch. Morales bounced between rooms, making calls, speaking with other agents, and ignoring questions from the reporters. Finally, he stood before them, acknowledging their presence with a smile.

"Is anybody hungry?"

In a bewildering reversal of tone, the enigma led the group to an employee dining room, where they were served a full breakfast.

Morales's charm was now on, full blast. The trio was in his custody, having been kept caged and away from others, and they would soon be on a flight out of the country—Ricardo could now kick back and relax. This was the real him. Maybe.

They chatted casually over breakfast, as Branch and Rothchild later recounted colorfully in their *Esquire Magazine* piece titled "The Incident." Morales was full of quotables.

On the current World Series: "It is just like the world everywhere: the Reds are winning and the Yanks are losing!"

On Inclán, and all women, working as investigative journalists: "Women should be at home having babies and making their men happy. Nothing else."

On Inclán's objection to that, telling him he's a hundred miles from reality: "You are a hundred *miles* from reality, and I am a hundred *years* from reality. You understand the difference?"

On his having been described as "nice" by Taylor Branch: "I am not nice. You know what I used to do in Cuba when I was a kid? I sent anonymous death wreaths to my friends. All the time. Is that nice?"

On their desire to interview Dr. Orlando Bosch: "Never heard of him."[428]

They were eventually sent to their gate with a DISIP escort, but to Venezuelan airliner Viasa's gate, as Morales seemingly disappeared into the walls. Though, the dutiful reporters would not be so easily dismissed without a fight. They staged a sit-in of sorts by occupying the runway stairs to the aircraft and refusing to move. The plane's captain got involved, confronting the Venezuelan soldiers below who had drawn swords in preparation to poke and prod the reporters up the steps and onto the plane. The captain was unhappy with the scene and called for an immediate resolution.

Rothchild goes, Inclán and Branch stay. For the time being.

Resistance was futile, and soon the two non-compliant reporters were on a flight back to Miami with their Venezuelan visas permanently revoked by DISIP. That was a clear indication of how Venezuelan authorities planned to handle inquiries into shadowy activity in Caracas. External agencies couldn't expect much for their efforts; the journalists lost their story, and despite the smiles and palm-pressing with Miami prosecutors and detectives, Morales no-showed the second Otero trial. Everyone got fucked in Caracas.

★★★

As foreign entities suffered through the Morales migraine, Venezuela began to cover its tracks. On October 27, the Venezuelan government issued a news release stating "there is no Ricardo Morales Navarrete in DISIP," and people answering calls to his office at the airport and his apartment said they knew of no such person.[429] Morales called Pilar in Miami and said not to contact him because "he didn't exist any longer." He told her he'd reach out for her when appropriate.

DISIP played cleanup as well. The agency's Director General Raul Giminez claimed to have officially relieved Morales as chief of Division

54, and the records announcing Morales's removal were backdated to October 1, a week prior to Flight 455's bombing.[430] Further, he ordered the confiscation of a circulated memo listing Morales's assignments with DISIP, though he was unsuccessful in locating all copies.[431]

While Morales couldn't have been surprised, he was angry and took the snub as a blow to his ego. He later testified to getting in a physical altercation with Orlando Garcia Vasquez when learning he'd been replaced.[432]

While public sentiment had already soured for the exiles' cause, the staunchest holdouts in the anti-Castro community finally lost all hope that the US had an earnest interest in their cause. Upon returning to Miami, Branch was stunned by the shift of the Bay of Pigs and Operation 40 veterans, as he articulated in "The Incident."

> The most loyal veterans of the CIA—people who had spent years denouncing and exposing terrorists as a detriment to the anti-Castro cause—now supported the terrorists and expected nothing but opposition from the Agency. 'If you don't help the good people fight Castro,' said one old CIA Cuban, 'then we have to help the bad ones do it. There's nothing left but terrorism.'[433]

The purpose of Morales's October 19 recorded phone call to WQBA was twofold. His public denunciation of the FBI and CIA was calculated and served him beyond just the deflection he'd promised DISIP. After being ordered to launch the propaganda campaign, he could've gone about it a thousand different ways. But Morales's public rebuke of the CIA and FBI was his attempt to engineer a safe landing back in the US. Morales knew his time in Venezuela was running out. He needed to get back to Miami, but a friendly homecoming was unlikely as things stood. Many exile groups had been decimated by not only the convictions to which he'd contributed, but also the arrests of Posada and Bosch in Caracas. The US federal agencies wouldn't want their ongoing association with him to be mentioned anywhere near

Flight 455. His shaming of *tres letras* in the media would placate the bombing groups and possibly lessen the call for action against him. Simply put, the feds were the lesser of the threats to his existence. Creating a safe landing in the US by satiating supporters of Otero and Bosch was a desperate final move on the chessboard that Venezuela had become.

Raul Diaz saw the path Morales was on and began stepping away. Ricardo had provided plenty of arrests for law enforcement, but his machinations in Venezuela had resulted in a mess. Cubana Airlines Flight 455 certified that future mentions of anti-Castro efforts would yield nothing but contempt from Americans. What had started as political bombings on targeted locations with no civilian casualties had now become outright terrorism. Despite any intel about the flight having been a disguised military shuttle, the presence of the North Korean ambassadors, or the timed bombs errantly detonating during the take-off rather than on an empty plane at a layover, seventy-three innocent people were now dead. In the eyes of the global community, freeing Cuba now engendered fear and anger, not support. Venezuela was left holding the bag for this calamity, alienating one of the US's cooperating nations in the tumultuous Latin American region.

Government agencies purportedly had little tolerance for the execution of people for political gain.

PART THREE

RICKY

Chapter Thirteen New Miami (1978)

Only those who knew Miami before the city's meteoric boom of the '70s would've been shocked its development. New Miami had big-city buildings, big-city businesses, and big-city residents that weren't modest about flashing their status. Rolls-Royces and three-hundred-foot luxury hotels fit in South Florida's pulsing neon picture perfectly; one would never have believed the explosion of affluence was nearly an overnight occurrence. Miami's rise had lifted the industries that floated in its waters: real estate, tourism, and banking.

Real estate and tourism benefitted handsomely from the boom, each showing earnings of $12 billion and $9 billion, respectively, by the '80s.[434] But the banking industry had never seen anything like the windfall of profits caused by the paper currency flying into its coffers in the late '70s. Banks were required to report large sums of cash deposits, but many simply didn't. The Senate Banking Committee held hearings about it, but it was difficult for bankers to know for certain that deposited money came from clients' illegal activities.[435] And, well, who had the time to probe that extensively when everyone was busy taking those deposits in the front door, hauling them in bags, boxes, and even twenty-gallon trash cans?

Miami banks "are the financial centers for the drug traffickers," said Allan Pringle, special agent in charge of the Miami DEA. "The Wall Street of the dopers."[436]

In 1980, at a time when very few states had any surplus whatsoever, Miami's Federal Reserve had a cash surplus of $5 billion.[437] That figure was more than the country's twelve Federal Reserve Banks combined.

The Federal Reserve Board was willing to give the benefit of the doubt. "We make every effort to cooperate with drug enforcement authorities," Fed member John Ryan said. He added the Fed was of the opinion that "the overwhelming number of bankers" do not knowingly launder money.[438]

Beyond the participation of the friendly international banks, Miami was perfectly positioned to become the capital of the drug word. Geographically, with more than three thousand miles of South Florida coastline and 550 square miles of Dade County waterways, law enforcement had no way to efficiently patrol all of it. They were outnumbered and ill-prepared to fight the trafficking surge. Additionally, many of the smugglers, having been former CIA operatives, were savvy enough to avoid detection.

"They found [drug smuggling] absolutely child's play when they started out here," a former commando leader told the *St. Petersburg Times*. He said US law enforcement "didn't have that type of defense." The head start, plus the smugglers' skills, made them nearly unstoppable.[439]

The smuggling activity grew at a daunting speed. In 1970, Customs seized 108 pounds of cocaine.[440] By 1975, that figure was up to 729 pounds. At Miami Airport, cocaine seizures increased from 37 pounds to 271 in the same period. Considering the difficulty law enforcement had in intercepting loads, it's no surprise that exponentially more made it into the country undetected. According to the DEA, by 1979 the South Florida illegal drug trade was the state's biggest industry, worth $10 billion a year.[441]

Miami's massive Cuban population had more relaxed attitudes toward cocaine. Cubans' opinions on the drug had some carryover from the old country and its link to class. Back in Cuba under Batista's rule, cocaine was the candy for the wealthy, while marijuana was for the lower class. Heroin, far more dangerous than the magic powder, was to be avoided altogether.

"Some Cubans think that the cocaine is like the violation of the tax," commented one Cuban journalist. "But the heroin is a vice."[442]

Before the '80s, cocaine was seen as the more innocuous and recreational of illegal drugs by US agencies, its reputation not yet established as an addictive substance.

"Cocaine," wrote Dr. Peter Bourne, drug advisor to Jimmy Carter and Special Assistant for Health Issues, "is probably the most benign of illicit drugs currently in widespread use." He acknowledged a case could be made for its legalization and described the drug as "short-acting...not physically addicting, and acutely pleasurable."[443]

Attitudes were changing beyond just the classification of narcotics. The topic of Castro and the mission to unseat him had fallen far from the lips of most in Miami. The Flight 455 bombing had not only closed a door for most Cubans, but also for Morales himself. All his skills would need to be rerouted, used for other ventures or for survival alone.

Since returning to Miami from his post in Venezuela, Ricardo Morales discovered the newest venture in the city was populated by a fair amount of his comrades from past missions. As early as 1972, a *New York Times* piece identified the industry's surge of those once having served the CIA's efforts against Castro. The article states, "Among those who have moved into the trade, well-placed informants say, are certain members of the ill-fated Assault Brigade 2506, which landed at the Bay of Pigs on April 17, 1961."[444]

Those Cuban mercenaries, though a significantly small percentage of the dutiful Cubans serving 2506, were neither the first nor the only group to move significant narcotic contraband into the US. Corsican heroin and cocaine traffickers, having settled in South America after World War II, began exploiting their relationship with ex-US military fighter pilots who'd been smuggling traditional consumer goods.[445] After dropping in South America, they filled their planes with the drugs and brought them north.

France's Marseille coast had long been an exit point for Corsican smugglers moving South Asian product. Although Europe remained the primary source of heroin and opium throughout the '60s, South America's global positioning was central to all points across the Atlantic and Pacific. It was an ideal hub, and that became more obvious as the smuggling industry matured.

By the '70s, Brazilians, Argentinians, Colombians, Chileans, Uruguayans, and Panamanians would have some hand in the game.

But Miami was a Cuban stronghold, and so too was its business. CIA mercenaries, albeit a minority, who'd sacrificed their lives for a pittance and believed in the promise of a free Cuba sought to struggle no more. Their haphazardly financed bombing missions in Little Havana bore few results and no money. Many were living on the fringe, their mission forgotten by the US, and themselves discarded along with it.

Now there emerged an industry in need of young blood with a unique bravado and fearlessness. Those skilled with weapons and in counterintelligence would excel in that business, and they were hiring.

There was a man known throughout South Florida, as much reviled as he was revered in 1977, who checked all the requisite boxes for someone primed for New Miami's startup industry. His resume was on display for all, printed on newspaper stock in Miami, Venezuela, and elsewhere, with headlines to prove he was not simply a candidate for hire but a highly qualified recruit for anything clandestine.

Ricardo Morales boosted the credibility of anyone for whom he worked, which was crucial in an industry where reputation was everything. And he was on his way home.

★★★

Morales climbed the side entrance steps into the Mutiny Club, located ten million miles from Cuba, Venezuela, and reality. The two floors of decadent extravagance simmering to the beat of '70s disco was a monument to the success of South Florida and its denizens dappled in gold and fueled by coke.

The club, located inside the Mutiny Hotel at Sailboat Bay in upscale Coconut Grove, was central to the South Florida cocaine scene. It was Cinderella's castle to the newly appointed Miami royalty, dashing about in threads spun by magic dust, their tattered rags and floor scrubbing not too distant a memory. Competing warriors in Miami's new industry glad-handed warmly and sent bottles of Dom Pérignon to each others' tables. On the busiest weekend nights, the place would go through ten cases at $125 a bottle.[446] Waitresses, the ever-elegant "Mutiny Girls," were stars in their own right, featured in the venue's brochures with bios under their photos like a Broadway *Playbill*. It was a big, flashy, expensive show that ran every night.

The architects of New Miami worked and partied at the Mutiny. They made phone calls from the tables surrounding the dance floor upstairs and tipped staff in fifties, hundreds, and little baggies. No one gave away the good stuff; coke tips were usually from the loads that came in less pure, cut a little too much with baby laxative, Mannitol, or similar filler.

Interspersed in the crowded room were cops in plainclothes. The not-so-undercover officials were wholly recognizable and on first name basis with many of the regulars. Feds would slip in also, keeping an eye on the players in the room and trying to determine who was making the most moves based on their activities in the club. The *tres letras* were easy to spot as well, strangers though they might've been—they never looked quite comfortable in their own skin.

Ricardo Morales first entered the club as a guest of Carlos "Carlene" Quesada, who he'd known casually since 1972 when Carlene ran a used car dealership in the city. Membership to the Mutiny was just fifty bucks a year, ensured by the presentation of a gold card bearing the club's iconic caricature of a pirate's head. The more important members didn't even need the card; they just came up the back entrance and cut through the kitchen, where they could tell Manny the head chef what they wanted before even finding their table.

Those tables, with numbered cards atop each, were reserved for the CEOs. Table 14, for example, was for Carlene and his crew, which included his beefy muscle nicknamed Humberto "Super Papi" Becerra, Fausto Villar, Franklin Sosa, and Carlene's business partner Rudy "Redbeard" Rodriguez. Rudy came with his own cadre of personalities on the payroll, including his Puerto Rican hitman "Mon" Perez-Llamas, who was still wanted for murder charges back in his native island, and traveling pianist Sunshine Sammy. The latter was often zonked on quaaludes but musically brilliant, on Rudy's staff for the express purpose of providing beautiful music in any room Rudy occupied—he had pianos in all his properties. The hostess might sit someone else at

Table 14 for dinner before ten o'clock, but after-hours belonged to the CEOs, and diners were told as much. No one objected.

The seating area that overhung the valet downstairs was the prime spot in the club. Known as the "the terrace," the space could seat a medium-sized group and offered the benefit of seeing everyone who arrived. Maybe you wanted to see them, maybe you didn't, and you could plan accordingly. It was a favorite spot for a young up-and-comer named Willy Falcon, who would later grab headlines with his partner Sal Magluta as *los muchachos*, "the boys," in the Cocaine Cowboys days.

There was a consortium of dark history in the club every night; any of the patrons' individual stories was an espionage novel unto itself. The tall guy with the comb-over making his way around the room was Bernardo de Torres, who'd served Brigade 2506 in the Bay of Pigs. He was held captive by the Cubans and released only after the personal intervention of President Kennedy. The CIA operative was investigated by both the House Select Committee on Assassinations and the Warren Commission regarding JFK's assassination.[447]

Walking past Bernie at the club and exchanging pleasantries might be Mario Tabraue. The menacing figure with a piercing stare was referred to in some circles as the "Chairman of the Board" of a marijuana trafficking ring that smuggled five hundred thousand pounds of product.[448] He'd reportedly maintained the most extensive list of Miami law enforcement officers receiving regular payouts. At that time, long before his being featured in the Netflix documentary *Tiger King*, Tabraue's love of exotic animals led him to open a store and ranch wherein he dealt in big cats, cobras, and parrots. Some he acquired legally, others perhaps by alternative means. Many feel he later became the model for Al Pacino's character Tony Montana in *Scarface*. The character certainly channeled Tabraue's intensity.

The young guy being paraded around by owner Burton Goldberg was a writer named Oliver Stone who'd recently written the screenplay for the film *Midnight Express*.[449] He visited the club to research his new script about Miami's Cuban exiles in the drug trade.

Morales didn't have any steady work lined up in the US when he returned. Payments from the federal agencies were finished after the

Venezuela debacle, and he needed money. Upon returning to Miami, he followed a trail that led right to the doors of the Mutiny Club. Morales's senses were highly attuned to action, and he knew he'd find some there.

For such a showing of personalities prone to violence, there was rarely an issue inside the walls of Mutiny. For one, the place was revered. It was an escape for so many, and no one wanted to put a magical place like that in jeopardy. Besides, eccentric owner and micromanager Goldberg would handily rescind anyone's membership who acted untoward or simply failed to dress the part in the upscale club. Image was important—the Mutiny was not to be a den of iniquity.

"First of all," began the club's former GM Chuck Volpe, "as managers, we wore three-piece suits—expensive suits. We wore ties at all times. We looked like gentlemen. We didn't have a shirt open and all that shit going on."[450]

Ricardo's reputation preceded him at the Mutiny Club. He may not have owned any thousand-dollar suits, but The Monkey walked in that door wearing twenty years of mythology, and he was a guest of Carlene Quesada of Table 14. And that all meant something in New Miami.

According to testimony, before Morales ever hooked up with Carlene and stepped into the Mutiny, he had partnered with a friend, Franklin Sosa, and agreed to help him move a shipment of marijuana.[451] Sosa brought Morales to Carlene Quesada's house, who Morales remembered from the car dealership. Sosa had agreed to unload a sizable shipment, several thousand pounds, but he had no outlet for it. By that time, Quesada was a major mover, and Sosa enlisted his help.

They entered Carlene's house on SW 16th St, nicknamed Villa Lola by his crew, and on November 15, 1977, Detective Raul Martinez snapped the first photo of Ricardo at the residence.

Staking out Carlene Quesada's residence was a regular detail for the department, given the amount of activity that generated from there. Two of Carlene's men, Fausto Villar and José "Pepe 70" Gonzales, had been providing information to law enforcement. This cleared the way for surveillance and, eventually, a wiretap of Quesada's phone.

"The cops were always outside," said black belt bodyguard Super Papi Becerra, who lived there with his boss. "Every morning I'd go to teach judo and see them out there, and I'd flip them off."[452]

Carlene introduced Super Papi to Morales.

"I want you to meet this guy because he's a good friend of your dad's," Carlene told Becerra, whose father was a police chief in Cuba. The Morales family's connection to the courts kept them in the same circles in Havana before things got out of hand.

"We hit it off because he was just like me, man," Becerra said.

During that first visit, Sosa told Carlene of the impending pot shipment.

"I've got some friends in Lauderdale who are potential buyers," Quesada told them.[453] Sosa and Morales went off to line up the deal, and on December 17, 1977, they delivered three thousand pounds of marijuana to "a couple of Anglos" in Fort Lauderdale. Carlene, Sosa, and Morales split a $75,000 payment for the delivery, which was summarily blown by Christmas.[454] This was Morales's entrée as a special guest of Table 14.

"It was spent freely at the Mutiny," Morales recalled. "We bought cocaine. We bought champagne. We bought wine." They gave everyone at the club Christmas presents.

And like that, he was in. The Monkey was officially part of the scene.

Given the number of guests who'd also served Brigade 2506 and Operation 40, Morales couldn't have felt too much like a stranger to that scene. Ricardo was struck not only by how many exiles were now active in that world, but how well they seemed to be doing. Some who he wouldn't have bet on to cross the finish line were tearing up the track, sipping champagne and sitting with pretty, young, sparkly ladies.

Though not everyone there had fled Castro and carried a rifle for the CIA; there were other interesting stories in the room with origins in less traditional places, like that of the spritely and spunky Mollie—a Mutiny girl from a conservative family in the midwest learning the ropes very much on the fly, but doing rather well at it. Or Owen Band, the Ivy League Jewish drug dealing kid from New York who'd taken a route on the other side of the highway from his prosecutor brother Michael who'd put away some of Owen's friends.

"It was a big happy family," Mutiny girl Mollie Scruggs recalled. " You'd stop at a table, have a drink and a hit."[455]

Countless celebrities in Miami for work or play found the Mutiny Club. Those with a proclivity for the kind of fun offered up by the late '70s did so, anyway. "Superfreak" Rick James's fast-lane lifestyle ensured he was a repeat visitor, and musician David Crosby was a frequent guest.[456] Even stars with less of a reputation for debauchery got sucked into the Mutiny, such as Sally Field and Paul Newman who were in town filming *Absence of Malice*.

Beyond the celebrity clientele, there was one curious thing many of the regulars at the Mutiny had in common—nearly all of them had been providing bits of information to law enforcement. Everyone there was moving *something* for cash, mostly marijuana and coke, and feeding local law enforcement a bite now and then could work in their favor one day. It was a small insurance policy, and all the players seemed to make use of it—even the guys at the top of the food chain, like Rudy and Carlene.

★★★

The Quesada and Rodriguez families were both from the Surgidero de Batabano region of Cuba, a straight shot south of Havana. Rudy and Carlene knew each other from childhood; both families were descendants of fishermen, as nearly all of the men in the small province were. In 1961, in the wake of Castro's revolution, the families loaded as many members and friends from the village as would fit on Rudy's father's eighty-three foot sloop.[457] They brought enough fuel to make it to the United States.

Twenty-year-old Carlene and twenty-two year-old Rudy settled in Miami. They started working in the auto business, with Carlene eventually co-owning a used car dealership with a partner. Rudy soon started a boat manufacturing business that Carlene joined him in. They made three molds—twenty-four, twenty-six, and twenty-eight-footers—that were great racing boats. But when the 1973 oil crisis struck in the US, sales went belly up.

Carlene wasn't a stranger to law enforcement. His rap sheet dated back to 1969 for a "violation of narcotics laws" wherein he was given three years probation.[458] In 1971 he was arrested in possession of a firearm as a convicted felon, though that was abandoned by the State Attorney. He was picked up twice in 1972, one for a breaking and entering charge and the other for an assault charge. Neither of those stuck either. He kept plugging away at the boat business with Rudy until their last shot at legitimate money died at the hands of the oil crisis.

Fortunately a stroke of luck came for the two entrepreneurs sitting on a bunch of unsold boats. Carlene knew some men in Florida who needed help getting their illegal product from their manufacturers in South America into the United States without detection. Not everyone could pull that off. Navigating the Caribbean was a harrowing prospect, and anyone who didn't know what they were doing might get snagged crossing Cuba, which would've been a death sentence. Carlene and Rudy decided to help the enterprising group import their loads of smokable plants.

Their pickups were in Colombia, where the pair soon learned the least of the threats to their runs was the local Colombian law enforcement. The launch point for their loads was in the country's shore town of Santa Marta in the Guajira Peninsula, where the entire town seemed to be in on the business.

Rudy Rodriguez, Jr., who joined his father and Carlene in the business at age fourteen, said local Colombian police were part of the business.

"Everyone was on the take down there," he observed. "The sheriff, fucking everybody. It was a business. They'd bust you, then help you load your boat afterwards, and send you off."[459]

The duo successfully moved product into the US for the Colombians, though after a while they realized they were leaving money on the table. Once they'd mastered the route from Santa Marta and saved up some cash from their runs, they began transporting loads that they purchased themselves from the Colombian manufacturer. Every dollar they could make by selling the pot themselves would be profit.

The two entrepreneurs began making serious money and invested in next steps. They bought more boats since they were losing some on the routes, though not unintentionally.

"You run three boats," Rudy, Jr. explained. "You give one to the cops, and two go in. That's it. You made your money." The cost of doing business.

In addition to their boat routes, Rudy and Carlene soon added a Rockwell International twin-engine turboprop plane to their operation and began flying in loads as well. The increased traffic necessitated new, efficient ways of communication. The team began using mobile phones before the widespread adoption of the technology, employing them to stay ahead of law enforcement. Using a car phone, Rudy and Carlene's crew now had the ability to securely communicate the minute details about their flights into and out of Colombia.

The pair quickly expanded their product lines, realizing that the money made from importing tons of bales of pot could be made with just some bricks of cocaine. They would deal in both, but the preference soon became coke. The issue was the quality of their marijuana remained fairly consistent, but the cocaine supply was all over the place. A lot of the Colombian coke they were bringing in was too acidic and had a yellow tint to it. Its processing in the jungles of Colombia was haphazard, containing additives like diesel fuel that was more easily accessible to the cooks, but made for inferior product. It was good for smoking, but no one wanted to snort it.

In this, Rudy saw opportunity.[460] He seized on this challenge and built a processing operation that would churn out product of unrivaled quality. He took the inferior Colombian coke and reprocessed it, making a product nearly 99 percent pure. Rudy then became the wholesale supplier for the locals.

Carlene was the man on the street, the social member of the team who everyone knew as a reliable distributor. Rudy slunk back to his lab, and Carlene worked the showroom. They'd found a rhythm that complemented their individual personality types. Rudy was more comfortable in the shadows, an eccentric whose dyed crimson facial hair earned him the "Redbeard" nickname. He was the workhorse of the duo, grinding it out for three or four days at a time then partying for an equal stretch, visiting the Mutiny and smoking his *basuco*—freebased cocaine rolled into cigarettes that gave off a distinct and unpleasant smell.

"He smoked that shit right in the club," Mollie said. "It's terrible. He mixed that shit with ammonia and all these other chemicals. It's terrible."[461]

While Rudy was more reclusive than Carlene, he wasn't averse to flaunting his CEO status. He kept his fifty-eight foot yacht named *Graciela* docked directly across from the club in Sailboat Bay. Partying with him was tricky—if he was whacked, he became unpredictable, antisocial, and nasty. No one wanted to be near him at those times.

Carlene was more laissez-faire than Rudy, eternally visible at the Mutiny, dressing the part and signaling success. When Ricardo returned to Miami and reconnected with him, Carlene was different, wearing silk shirts and lizard-skin shoes. This slight, mustachioed slickster wasn't the little car salesman that Morales remembered. He'd been at the dance clubs with Carlene in '73—he hadn't been wearing this shit.

In '77, when Morales first stepped into the Mutiny, he wasn't sporting anything of that quality either. But things would change after that one night at the corporate headquarters of New Miami, Inc. Carlene Quesada led his friend into the boardroom and introduced him to his partner Rudy Rodriguez, who was already well aware of the operative's history. Hell, everyone in there was, and Carlene's crew was honored to have him at Table 14.

★★★

Carlene and Ricardo pulled onto the nine acres of land at 114th Street and SW 87th Avenue that served as not only Rudy Rodriguez's living compound but also his laboratory. One of the three buildings on the property was designated as the cooking lab, and Rudy, Jr. was tasked with maintaining it and overseeing the reprocessing of the impure

Colombian coke. The key to its success was access to the proper chemicals.

Rudy, Jr. was gifted with his dad's ingenuity and got a student chemist's license from University of Miami, or something that looked like one anyway. Flashing that at a chemical supply house in Miami allowed him to purchase an abundance of acetone, muriatic acid, and ammonia to stock his dad's lab. The process was tedious and dangerous, given the fumes and flammability of the mixture.

First, Rudy, Jr. would mix the powder coke in water and ammonia, making a fine paste.[462] Once it dried, he would chop it up as finely as possible until it floated and add it to an ether and acetone mix. Rudy would then add hydrochloric acid as a chemical accelerant and sit back and watch, in his words, "the wonder happen." Crystals would begin to cling together and form a cone.

The resulting product was an almost totally pure cocaine that allowed their purchasers to cut it with filler, double their load, and still have a product more than 80 percent pure. That meant they could cut it yet again and still deliver superior quality to buyers. More than that, the cleanliness of the reprocessed drug made for easy use. It didn't burn when snorted, and users didn't need to use much at all—one dab would keep the partier going all night long.

After passing the gorilla gate by the entrance, Carlene and Ricardo pulled toward Rudy's house. Carlene preferred moving the white powder instead of pot; it was easier, very much in demand, and more profitable. He and Morales were there to pick up some pure coke and bring it back to Carlene's to cut and store.

Waiting for the guys back at Villa Lola was Super Papi, who guarded not only his boss's body but also his inventory.[463] They'd cut a kilo, double the load, then repack it. Carlene had created a hollowed wood block press that would densely pack the cut load into a brick, just like the fresh, uncut loads coming into the country. With the purity of Rudy's product, even the most expert nostrils would accept the load as uncut or barely cut. Kilos of pure cocaine were going for $60,000 each back then, so stretching your load meant exponential gains and a windfall of cash.

After their initial pot deal with Carlene, Morales and Franklin Sosa continued to move more grass, and Carlene started to bring them into small coke deals.

"I was getting into the drug business, the drug mentality," Morales said of those months.[464]

But Morales couldn't be fully entrenched just yet because he was still volleying between Miami and Caracas, wrapping up his time in DISIP. It would keep him away from Carlene until he was ready for a permanent return to the States.

During that time, Morales dodged a bullet by not being near Villa Lola on March 25, 1978 when police raided the home on March 25, 1978. Pepe 70 Gonzales had become disgruntled with Carlene after having to forfeit his home to the drug kingpin after an unpaid drug debt. His subsequent arrest for the undercover sale to Detective Raul Martinez of two illegal silencers forced Pepe's hand, and he reportedly offered up his boss.

Carlene's residence wasn't the only location raided that day; Rudy's house was busted as well. The seizure netted fifty-six pounds of cocaine and $913,000 in cash.[465] Shortly after the raids and with Carlene out on bail, Morales and Sosa returned to the Quesada home to discuss next steps. While visiting, Sosa made a quick phone call and arranged an impromptu marijuana deal to get the crew on track and earn back some money.

"Out of the blue sky," Morales stated, "Franklin Sosa got up some sort of connection with this guy Roberto who claimed he was going to give us twenty thousand pounds [of marijuana]." It was a deal that Quesada authorized on the spot, feeling somehow safer with a pot deal at the time. "Quesada said he agreed that he would go along with us in that shipment because cocaine was getting very rough for him."[466]

★★★

Rick, Jr. left the basketball court and walked toward the equipment closet where Coach Javier had summoned him. Now in eighth grade, Rick was getting bigger and had begun physically resisting Coach's advances. If he pushed back, somewhat forcefully, perhaps the abuse would end. He was hoping this would just be a talk in the equipment closet; they were on a field trip, and who knew what staff might enter.

Rick pushed the door open and stepped inside, but he didn't see Coach, just an empty room. With a thump and a blast to the back of his head, Rick's legs were taken out from under him. He fell to all fours and was struck again and again. Rick rolled over to see Coach wielding a phone book; he'd been waiting behind the door when Rick entered and had a clean shot at the back of his head.

Rick fought back, throwing everything he could at Coach to stifle the assault. Rick landed a couple of shots and scrambled out the door and through the gym, disheveled and panting.

Several days after that at the field, Rick was running laps and trying to avoid Coach Javier as best he could. The laps were a punishment for not bringing his football pants to practice—another deliberately defiant action. If you weren't suited properly, you ran punishment laps and couldn't work out with the team. Rick was the starting quarterback, so his defiance would put the team—and Coach—at a disadvantage all day.

He was acting out of instinct, unsure about his next moves, but he'd seen that fiery rage in his coach's eyes. He was breaking away from Coach's grip. All this was a gathering tornado in the boy's mind as he ran his laps when he noticed something in the distance. There was his father, back in Miami somehow, wearing aviator sunglasses and leaning on a maroon Cadillac, watching him run. Ricardo hadn't visited in quite a while; Rick was as shocked as he was happy to lay eyes on him.

Ricardo waved his son over. Rick jogged to the lot and hugged the ghost, confirming he was real. They made small talk, covering the stuff that was the least important after years of not talking with each other at all.

Rick was called back to the field.

"You have practice tomorrow?" Ricardo asked.

"Yeah."

"I'll come pick you up after. Wait for me here, and we'll go hang out."

Rick jogged back to his team with a hopeful feeling that would not leave him all night. Maybe his father was back, having completed the top secret stuff that kept him away from his family all these years. He'd come there specifically to see Rick. Maybe he had a dad again. Maybe this was his chance.

After mulling all of that over, something else began jabbing at Rick. His father could be the tool to free him from Coach Javier. He'd tried to do it himself, and though the sexual abuse ended, it now seemed that physical beatings might replace that. Rick couldn't allow himself to be tortured, and here stood a rare opportunity to get out of it.

But how to tell his alpha soldier dad? What words would he use to describe the sexual nature of the abuse, or would he report just having been roughed up? He'd have to lay it all out there; he didn't want to be mistaken for just having a tough coach. There was a chance his dad would kill the guy right on the spot, but Rick couldn't lose this opportunity to unbind himself from three years of terror. He decided—the following day when Ricardo picked him up from practice, he would tell his father everything that had happened. All of it.

Rick spent the next day's practice distracted by a tense anticipation, an eye on the parking lot the entire time. Eventually Coach loaded everyone on the bus, and Rick told him of his alternate plans. He went to the parking lot, looking for that maroon Cadillac he'd seen the day before. It was good the coach had pulled out before Rick's dad arrived; it would prevent a scene from occurring in front of the team.

Then, after pulling himself out of those distractions, he realized a half hour had passed without Ricardo's anticipated arrival. He decided not to wait for him any longer, that afternoon or ever. Rick wouldn't tell his father about the man who'd spent infinitely more time with him in the past two years than he ever had. And he'd never tell him how they both destroyed him. He grabbed his duffel bag and walked home alone, leaving behind sports and a certain hopefulness that had shown a flicker the day before.

★★★

"I tell you all the time, you cannot leave anything *anywhere*."[467]

Lynette expected that from her mother. Yolanda was every bit the Cuban mom, offering no empathy when there was a lesson to be recited. And recited. And recited again.

"And you ignore me, so now someone has stolen it."

Her jacket. Lynette only owned two suits while in graduate school at Princeton, and she desperately needed all components of both. She'd just begun teaching as an adjunct professor at Hunter College while also giving professional talks on art history. Her housing was subsidized through Princeton, and Yolanda and Antonio could only help her out with fifty dollars a month. She was poor as anything. Losing the jacket to one of those suits was very significant. Half of her wardrobe was gone.

Lynette had been studying at her favorite spot in Marquand Art Library at Princeton—the basement—where she could pore over hundreds of pages of precious art history, virtually undisturbed by all humans. All, that is, except the person who'd swiped her jacket off the back of her chair while she was at the bookshelves.

Lynette tried every lost and found location at the university to no avail. Now she'd have the unpleasant task of telling Yolanda that she needed a new jacket she couldn't afford to replace. And she knew her mother never passed on an opportunity to wax about what was to be learned from such irresponsibility.

In the typical course of his checking in with his sister, Ricardo got the whole story from Yolanda.

"You should call the damn school and—," Ricardo began.

Yolanda raised her hand. "I got it."

She hadn't invited her brother to run her household just because he'd been in the newspaper for the better part of the '70s.

"Antonio and I will handle it. And we're not calling anyone. She's a grown woman. It'll teach her never to leave her stuff laying around."

Morales's increased profile in the city posed some challenges. The danger quotient went up on the street, naturally, but something less expected, and less considered, was the ancillary pressure on his family. His older sister, never having less than full control of any given situation, would forever see Ricardo as her little brother. When he came into her home, irrespective of having returned from Operation 40 missions into Cuba, a war in the Congo, or a bombing in Miami, he was just a bit player in her show.

So she was particularly annoyed a couple of days later when Lynette called and reported campus police had returned her jacket, which was followed by a phone call from her Uncle Richard.

"I heard you got your jacket back," he said.

Lynette thanked him instinctively.

Whether he'd had any influence couldn't be proven, but Yolanda and her girls had lived through the evolution of Ricardo's myth and all the events that erected it. He survived a car bomb and a gunshot to the head, not to mention his escape from Castro's secret police in Cuba. These events were etched in Miami history. If they got a call that Ricardo was seen walking on the surface of Biscayne Bay, no one in Yolanda's household would dismiss it out of hand. Begrudgingly, perhaps, for Yolanda. When Ricardo next stopped by for a taste of *natilla*, he was met with an icy Yolanda.

"I should make you drive to New York and throw that jacket in the garbage in front of Lynette," she said, working the stove and not turning to him. "She doesn't deserve it. She lost it."

"It was stolen."

"Who cares. She needs to learn from it."

Ricardo sighed. "My niece doesn't have to suffer because some asshole stole from her. The world will make her suffer plenty on its own."

Yolanda turned, feigning shock. "Oh, you're gonna let that happen?"

Morales considered the proposed scenario and his place in it. "Probably not." He surveyed the kitchen expectantly. "Where's the *natilla*?"

"Maybe Magda's house. With your children."

It was becoming a sore spot. Ricardo spent significantly more time with his nieces and Pilar's daughters than he did with his own children he shared with Magda and Mimi. Rick, Raul, Sylvia, and Roberto barely saw him anymore.

Despite Yolanda's dig about Ricardo's negligence, she took full advantage of the uneven attention given to her daughters. While Lynette was busy up in the northeast, Annette, ten years younger, was in high school and beginning to date. In Ricardo, Yolanda had her own personal intelligence agency, complete with background checks. She'd feed him the boy's family name, and in a couple of days he'd return an "all clear" or "forget it."

Uncle Richard's attention made Annette feel special. He'd given her a Cartier Tiger Eye watch, and when visiting he'd occasionally slip her a one hundred dollar bill over Antonio's protestations. Though just a teen, Annette was mature enough to understand the inequity—her uncle was being entirely negligent to his own children.

"I totally felt special," Annette said. "But I don't like to say that because that man was absent from his children's lives."[468]

Occasionally when something was going down with her uncle, he would blow into their house barking and cursing about it. Yolanda would say she'd heard about whatever was going on from Antonio or had read it in the newspaper, and Morales would then warn her to lay low.

"Don't let the girl go out," he'd say as he darted out the door. That meant Annette was now under one of the many lockdowns her mother enforced at Ricardo's orders. Annette would call her girlfriends and say she couldn't go out because her uncle was in trouble again.

Antonio never shied away from covering his brother-in-law's antics in *The Miami Herald*. To think he might omit stories or sugar-coat details is not to know Antonio Bosch (no relation to Dr. Orlando Bosch; Bosch a common Catalan surname). He had a framed poster titled "The Ethics of Journalism" hung in his office, and he would point to it as a reminder during contentious discussions in the newsroom. It worked on reporters as well as family. The job kept him out of the home more than everyone would have liked, but journalistic integrity came above all else for the editor.

After Yolanda's jab about his children and the realization that no *natilla* was coming, Ricardo pulled himself up and started for the door.

"I treat your girls like gold," he said.

"Yes, you do. And you are their *tío*—beloved *tío*, maybe favorite *tío*—but still their *tío*."

Morales paused at the door. "I'm leaving because I'm sad about the *natilla*."

Battles of will between the Morales siblings were two Sherman tanks playing a game of chicken. Though it could be debated whether he was safer on the streets than being the subject of Yolanda's ire, he sauntered from the house equally nonchalant about both.

★★★

Detective Raul Martinez had come to the Special Investigations Section that year from the Narcotics Division. The SIS investigated high-level crime as opposed to the street level drugs of the Narcotics Division. Martinez made the leap in less than a year.

Martinez, like his colleague Raul Diaz, had come to the US via the Pedro Pan policy at age twelve without his parents. He was earmarked to be sent to a Catholic boarding school in Iowa, but an aunt and uncle living in Miami intervened, offering to board him in their apartment with their young daughter. It was a tough living arrangement while he awaited his mother's exit from Cuba.

"I didn't see my mother for sixteen years," Martinez said. "She was not able to get out. She was taking care of my grandfather, who was too old. He didn't want to leave—he was hardheaded. When he finally passed away, my mother and my grandmother were able to go to Spain and come here."[469] He was working a surveillance detail when he got word his mother had just stepped off a plane in Miami. He pulled himself off the job and went to meet her at the airport.

Pepe 70 and Fausto Villa were one of several informants in and out of Villa Lola, but their specific information about Rudy and Carlene's operation proved valuable enough to land full-time surveillance approval and a wiretap on Quesada's phone. That wiretap would remain in place after Carlene's and Rudy's arrests and releases, and it caught the phone call from Franklin Sosa on April 6 arranging the large pot shipment.

Sosa arranged for a friend to leave a furniture truck at his father's house on NW 125th Street, which would be used the following day to haul five thousand pounds of marijuana. Sosa had been promised the shipment on the tapped phone line. After the load was packed into the truck, Morales was to drive the lead car for the drop off.

Carlene's group wasn't the only crew who knew the details of the plan. Detective Martinez and his officers in the SIS division had already been sitting on the empty truck for twenty-four hours. Nothing was happening, and Martinez hadn't slept in a day. No one working a case wants to miss the big moment, but one can only deny biology for so long.

"I was being relieved from my surveillance post," Martinez recalls. "And the second I got on the expressway to head home to get a couple hours of sleep, the other guys got on the radio. 'The truck is moving, the truck is moving!' I had to turn around and go back."[470]

Ricardo Morales, driving a '78 Oldsmobile, had arrived at the location with three men—Cary Wayne Clark, Edward Lewis Dunbar, both of Miami, and Richard Joseph Prino of Massachusetts—who then moved the truck to a home on SW 123rd Avenue.[471] They loaded the box truck with bales of marijuana from that location. Though Morales had been monitoring the police radio traffic on the scanner in his car, the SIS detectives and police arrived unexpectedly.

Arresting officers charged at Morales with their guns drawn and shotgun pumped. He felt they were a touch overzealous, and he was uncertain what the unnecessarily jacked cops might do with their big fish on the line. He heard a frenzy of activity coming over the radios. Morales joked in deposition about the walkie talkie chatter.

"The things they were saying over the radio about me being armed, dangerous, Dracula, and things like that."

The initial search of Morales's car yielded not only a concealed .45 caliber automatic weapon but also something that would baffle police on the scene and the law enforcement community at large.

In addition to finding his police scanner, investigators opened Morales's glove box and found a list of confidential radio frequencies for the DEA, Coast Guard, FBI, Secret Service, Florida Highway Patrol, and police departments in Miami and Miami Shores.[472] The FCC said it didn't even have some of them. His possession of the frequencies of land and water agencies was another indicator of his value to the underworld.

"Intelligence," Rudy, Jr. said of what Ricardo added to his father's operation. "He had inside knowledge, and knew a lot of people." Everyone in the community knew Morales had his hooks in both sides of the law. "It's helpful. You want to be moving product from one place to another, you want to be able to know where the hell you can work at it."[473]

Super Papi also knew Morales's reputation was helpful in making others think twice. "People wouldn't fuck with us because he was with us," he recalled.[474]

Various agencies of law enforcement also saw imminent value in Morales while he was locked up for the pot bust. His attorneys petitioned Judge Wilkie Ferguson, Jr. for protection from all local and federal law enforcement agencies "including but not limited to the FBI, CIA, Internal Revenue Service, Drug Enforcement Administration, US Customs, Immigration service, and the Treasury Department."[475] They won that order from the judge on April 25, and Morales remained in custody in lieu of his posting a hefty $350,000 bond, which was outsized compared to the others arrested due to his possessing Venezuelan credentials. At the arraignment hearing when bail was set, Morales told family and friends, "Don't try and raise my bail. I'm safer in jail for now."

That astronomical figure was set after Assistant State Attorney William Richey relayed a third-party message he'd received to the judge that stated, "If Morales were able to make bond, he would leave and it would be impossible to get him back."[476]

The official that sent the message?

Raul Diaz. He'd had enough.

Morales wasn't anyone's traditional confidential informant. His information came with a price for agents of the law trying to maintain clear dividing lines between right and wrong. Diaz knew his informant was still a well of information and was needed to benefit active cases. But it was clear Ricardo was moving toward something very different from the anti-Castro group activities of the early part of the decade.

But with every arrest came an opportunity for more information. Diaz knew The Monkey was capable of magic at any given turn, and it was worthwhile to deal with the pain in the ass.

★★★

Rick watched his handcuffed father be led into a police car. He'd been flipping channels past the news and stopped at the sight. It was a story about a big pot bust for which his dad and three gringos were arrested. What the hell was his father doing hauling truckloads of marijuana in the boondocks with them? He was a soldier, probably still stationed in Venezuela. This was ridiculous, an obvious mistake. All fourteen-year-old Rick could do was laugh.

The news about Morales's new line of work made its way through the family to mixed reactions. His older brother Pucho would split from him due to the drug involvement, disapproving of this brand of criminal lifestyle. Setting bombs to fight Castro may have been one thing, but pumping drugs into the streets was another.

Yolanda was initially annoyed by the news but had to answer a call to duty. She'd spoken to her brother from jail and was given an assignment to visit him every day. Though American jails were very different from those in Cuba, Morales wasn't taking any chances. She was to visit him every day, look at him, make sure he was coherent and not visibly injured.

That didn't mean Yolanda was as accepting of the situation when in private. She cursed the newspapers for running the story, always with pictures of him, nearly every day. When *The Miami Herald* was mentioned, Antonio would just shake his head. Yolanda belittled everyone involved, always branding them "American communists." Annette vividly recalled that title flying around the home.

"This is a label she bestowed on anyone who was remotely sketch. Which meant they were just on the wrong side of the issue from her, but probably six degrees from Fidel."[477]

Annette herself was scared by the news. Uncle Richard was an impenetrable force in her life. He was brave and placed a forcefield around her through her teenage years. What would happen to him now?

At the time, Rick was working his first job as a bellboy at the Seville Hotel on Miami Beach. Magda had been working nearby at the Shelbourne and would get a room for the kids during the summer. This allowed the family to sleep at the hotel rather than make the hour drive back home. Rick had been spending the summers there with his mom and siblings since age thirteen—too young to work, but not too young to tag along with sixteen-year-old Raul when his older brother went partying. Young Rick was tall, and his drinking and smoking acumen helped him blend right in with the high schoolers.

At fourteen, Rick began working at the Seville during the summer. His partying continued, and carrying travelers' bags was the perfect job to meet visiting girls. His summers living on the beach were unforgettable; so much so that he preferred them to school and began cutting all the time. Magda worked nights and slept days. Rick would leave in the morning and party all day, making sure to snag those truancy letters from the mailbox while mom snored in the background.

Sometimes arriving guests at the Seville would lower their voices and lean in to the young man wheeling their bags to their room.

"Hey, do you know where I can get some…stuff?"

Rick always had quaaludes or pot on him, so he'd offer some for sale to the guest. After all, that was hospitality, right? Make the guests happy at all costs.

"Welcome to Miami."

It began happening frequently enough that when Rick got paid and bought his supply, he bought more at lower prices. And right there, starting in the hotel business at a young age, taught him all he needed to know about finance. Buy wholesale, sell retail, advertise to the thousands of guests checking into the resort all summer, buy an even larger supply at an even lower wholesale, sell more product at retail, repeat. Young Rick was growing and learning on his own.

His father, facing charges of conspiracy, possession of marijuana in excess of a hundred pounds, carrying a concealed weapon, and possession of a firearm in the commission of a felony, finally had bail posted for him, and he walked from jail after over a hundred days.

Chapter Fourteen The Cost of Goods Sold (1978)

Ricardo Morales was sprung from jail just two days before the start of his trial, which began on July 19, 1978. Morales's attorneys planned to ignore the haul of marijuana altogether.[478] What can you say about being caught sitting on five thousand pounds of weed? They instead went after the source of the entire case—the wiretap on Carlene's phone line.

The discovery evidence identified Fausto Villar and Pepe 70 of Carlene's group as the insiders who gave the information that got the police department clearance for the tap.[479] Pepe 70 was facing the gun charge for selling to Detective Martinez, and word was that Villar had a personal grudge against Morales after Carlene moved him up in his organization so quickly, usurping Villar. They had reason to open their mouths.

But now they also had reason to second guess that plan. Pepe had already been sentenced and was doing time in federal prison in Indiana, while Villar was wandering Miami a free man. It's still up to speculation if they rethought the plan organically or if they were forced along by someone with knowledge of that discovery evidence. Regardless, the pair backtracked their stories. Once they heard they were named in the documentation delivered to the parties and to Morales specifically, the two would-be witnesses pivoted and said they hadn't actually spoken with authorities.

Judge Wilkie Ferguson ruled. "The law requires informants to be reliable. In this case…the reliability is seriously open to question."[480] He barred the prosecution from using the wiretap evidence containing Franklin Sosa's phone call—the entire basis for the case. Prosecutor

Sam Smargon presented what little he had left, which was basically Morales standing by a truckload of pot and driving a car in front of it.

The prosecution pressed on anyway, with Detective Martinez wheeling a load of the seized contraband into the courtroom, past the jury.[481] The investigator sensed the case was in trouble when the fragrant evidence passed a juror who whispered to his neighbor, "That's good stuff."

Judge Ferguson publicly agreed the state's case was "pretty flimsy" when the defense asked for a directed acquittal in the absence of the wiretap evidence.[482] Despite his observation, Ferguson denied the defense's motion and sent the case to the six-member jury, who returned an acquittal for Morales in two hours and fifteen minutes.

Ricardo left the courtroom looking smugly amused, healthily tanned and trim in his tan leisure suit with open collar. He was greeted by Pilar and a group of well-wishers as cameras caught the exile's exit from the courthouse.

Morales went right back to work, having spent months in jail awaiting trial and losing out on money-making deals with the crew. Quesada and the others arrested for the July bust had been out on bail and working. The plan now?

"We started dealing right away," Morales said. "On the 29th I won my case, and on the 30th we were in business."[483]

Returning to Carlene's wasn't simply a work detail. There was a sense of brotherhood and family with all members intertwined, like any other start-up business. Rudy, Jr. had been working with the group from his early teens, and Carlene had family involved was well. Rudy, Jr was godfather to Carlene's daughter, and Rudy, Sr's triggerman Mon was Jr's godfather.

"That's how involved we are in each other's families," Rudy, Jr says.[484]

Many of the people traversing Carlene's doorstep shared connections beyond the business they were there to discuss. The Villaverde brothers, the childhood friends of Morales's from Havana and cousins of the priest that had given him last rites in the Havana hospital, began popping in and out of Villa Lola. The oldest of the brothers, Rafael, had spent a lifetime in Morales's periphery, from their childhood jaunts to the Woolworth in Havana to their service together in Operation 40. They once again converged for social and business purposes at Carlene's.

Rudy, Jr. would soon become more permanently connected to Morales when he married his high school sweetheart—Pilar's daughter. He referred to Morales as his stepfather-in-law, recalling visits to his and Pilar's high-rise apartment on the bay.

"We used to steal pot from him," he recalled. "He'd always have pot and we'd grab his smoke. He didn't give a shit."[485]

Rudy, Jr. was also witness to Morales's obsession with intelligence and counterintelligence.

"Remember, he was a spy—an *eccentric* spy." Rudy, Jr. and Morales's stepdaughter would often happen upon him looking out over the bay. "He'd sit out on his balcony with his binoculars. Who knows what the fuck he's looking for, you know? We would always laugh together. I guess he was waiting for something to come after him or some shit."

Morales soon left that place and Pilar. He became a more permanent houseguest at Carlene's SW 16th Street home after Carlene extended an invitation to move in with him and Super Papi.

The thick bodyguard felt an immediate bond with Morales beyond his father's friendship with him in Cuba. Ricardo was something of a big brother to him. Becerra was impressed when Ricardo would beat them all to the day, waking before anyone and heading to the kitchen.

"We'd get up, and we'd see Ricky already made us breakfast, man," Becerra recalled fondly. "He would make us breakfast. Yeah, man, there's a lot of things that people don't know."[486]

More than that, Ricardo would privately express concern about the big guy's weight, telling him it was all about his diet.

"I was in martial arts, and I'd worry about gaining weight, and he goes, 'Look man, you gotta do what I do—I eat a little bit, a bunch of times a day, but just a little bit.' And he would show me. He was just a great guy."

One member of their makeshift family proved not to be. Right after everyone's acquittal on the pot charges, Franklin Sosa, fresh from picking up the hot telephone in Carlene's house and starting the whole fiasco, took off. Moving out would have been one thing, but he didn't leave empty-handed.

"He ran away with almost everything we got," Morales remembered, including, "the door, the lamps…he took everything. Even the toilet paper."[487]

More critical than those damages, however, was that Sosa had taken all their money from the stash. At that crucial time, having just come off the court charges, it was a blow. There was only one way to recuperate, and that was get back to work more profitably. Their choice of product line was key.

"Cocaine," Morales recalled. "Cocaine taught me everything about the trade." He pledged to work in the diamonds of their trade—smaller in size and much more lucrative. "Never in my life again am I going to touch a bale of grass. It was getting on my nerves to see a house loaded with bales."[488]

Carlene's crew stayed away from Rudy for the time being, instead getting their product from a Colombian nicknamed "Larry" who was dating Carlene's sister.[489] According to testimony, she started putting together some deals for the crew, and in time they were getting between twenty and twenty-five kilos a month. They cut it at Carlene's house, his sister's place, and also a condo they rented in Kendall on 147th Ave. That initial twenty-five kilos was stretched to fifty, which could sell for over $20,000 per kilo at the time.

They had a series of smaller distributors with names like "Shampoo" and "Flaco" in place to push product in South Florida. As was standard in that business, one's long-term success depended entirely on how reliable their associates were on all ends of the distribution chain. That was arguably as great a risk as that posed by law enforcement, evidenced by Franklin Sosa absconding with their money and anything else he could carry.

Rudy and Carlene's family ties in their operation may have insulated them from some trust issues that permeated larger organizations, but even that wasn't one hundred percent. Morales testified that a member of Carlene's wife's family took five kilos from Larry, their main supplier, and disappeared. Additionally, their distributor Flaco was clogging the flow of money back to Larry.

"He was holding about a couple hundred thousand," Morales testified, "and we [had] some discussion with Larry."[490] After that discussion in mid-December 1978, Larry paused dealings with anyone in Carlene's organization.

Morales and Quesada held out for a month or so, but in late January 1979 they realized they couldn't just stop earning. They had no trouble finding another supplier—it was 1979 Miami after all. According to Morales, Carlene tapped a Colombian import team, Isabel and Ruso, who were also reportedly supplying coke out of the country.[491]

Morales testified that in late January, they received their first load from the new Colombians, twenty kilos, which Carlene's crew cut into forty.[492] Moving the load wouldn't be a problem, as Flaco guaranteed the sale of up to a hundred kilos via his West Coast connection, "Fat Man Wheels." But after that, Isabel and Ruso proved unreliable and dried up as a source, and going back to Rudy Redbeard wasn't an option for Quesada's crew. Morales testified that Rudy had started "a war" with Carlene, and it seemed all supply lines had dried up at the same time.

How serious could a "war" be between people that considered each other family? Rudy and Carlene's families knew each other from back home when Rudy's father's boat brought the entire village to the US. Families fight. Rudy and his childhood *hermano* were no exception.

"And like family," Rudy, Jr. explained, "they fuck each other over, and they talk shit about each other. Blah, blah, blah. That's just the way it is, you know?"[493]

★★★

Assistant US Attorney Jerome Sanford had come up empty in the Rolando Otero federal trial, one of the most high-profile cases in South Florida. Sanford and his office were in preparation for the upcoming case against Rudy and Carlene, stemming from the March raids on their homes that netted over $900,000 in cash and a bunch of coke.

Quesada had barely slipped the trap when acquittals were awarded in the truck pot bust, and he might do the same thing again.

Ricardo Morales should've been the last face Jerry Sanford ever wanted to see again. The exile was responsible for sinking Sanford's Otero federal trial by not showing up to testify, which then he did again in the state case. Sanford knew Morales had just been acquitted in the pot case and he was clearly in bed with his defendants in the upcoming cocaine trafficking case despite not facing charges himself.

However, in a most unlikely turn, the opposite happened—Sanford took a liking to Morales. The prosecutor began dropping in to visit him while Ricardo was held on bail for the pot bust.

"Ricardo," he'd say to the prisoner, "do you need anything?"

Morales always politely declined the offer, though he never forgot it. After his release, he kept in touch with Sanford and didn't talk business at first.

"We would bullshit about the KGB and the CIA," Sanford recalled, "about who did this and who did that."[494]

Sometime around January 1979, their meetings had turned toward business. There was no formal agreement between them; it was more like Morales was unpacking the minutiae of his day, complaining at the dinner table about his tough day at work. But in those complaints and seemingly innocuous stories was a wealth of inside information into the Miami drug scene. Sanford had been pursuing a federal grand jury investigation into Jose Alvero-Cruz, purportedly the biggest major pot smuggler at the time, and Morales seemed to know everything about everyone.[495]

Eventually, Sanford brought DEA agent Avelino "Bill" Fernandez to his meetings with Ricardo.[496] Bill would learn quickly what it was like to deal with Morales when the operative arrived to one of their clandestine meetings wearing a straw hat. But the lawmen knew it was worth it. They hit pay dirt at a January meeting in a local bar when Morales said he wanted to become a confidential informant for them. He opened the floodgates at that meeting, talking about everything from a new, young cocaine dealer on the scene named Willy Falcon to Alvero-Cruz, the target of their most recent investigation. They shared a laugh when he said Alvero-Cruz was upset about the indictment Sanford had handed down on him, but not because of the charges—rather because the two low-level dealers he was indicted with would make him lose stature.

Agent Fernandez nudged Morales for more than just information, saying he needed go all the way, get on the team, and nail Alvero-Cruz with them. That would mean testifying as a government witness. Morales was noncommittal at first; it was an aggressive ask.

He then expressed the singular enticement he could never refuse.

"If I'm going to do anything, I have to be the only one, the only witness."[497]

Hot shit. *He wants to be the star,* Sanford thought, *like he was in the Orlando Bosch case in 1968.*

Plus, the rascally prick owed him for no-showing the Otero trial.

Sanford and Fernandez next met with Morales in February in the lounge at the Ramada Inn on NW 72nd Ave. He'd been thinking about their offer and how he'd go about getting Alvero-Cruz, a savvy operator in his own right.

"I can't do it with drugs," he told them. "He won't sell directly to me."[498]

While that took some air out of DEA agent Fernandez, Morales's proposed solution definitely perked him up.

"Alvero talked to me about me about putting contracts out on four people." The targets, Morales told them, were a couple of associates, one confidential informant, and Bill Fernandez himself.

Morales offered to approach Alvero-Cruz about that and wear a wire to get the planned murders on tape. But again, Ricardo reiterated, it could only be him working as the star witness.

During the meeting, Sanford noticed two investigators from the State Attorney's office, Bill Reilly and Marty Dardis, pass their table. They'd certainly seen Sanford, Fernandez and their guest, who'd been kept off the radar to date. The investigators made two quick phone calls from the lounge pay phone.

"I'm blown," Morales said cryptically, then changed his tone. "This is even better. Don't get up. Act naturally, let them look. Now this is really a challenge. If word leaks out, we'll know where it came from." He seemed excited at the prospect of word hitting the street that he was involved in active investigations again. "This is like the old days!"

Sanford tried to reason with him about being made a source, but Morales carried on, full of bluster and passion.

"If this was a CIA operation they'd call it off," he said. "We can still try and make it go. Remember, it's my life and I can take care of myself."[499]

They did as he instructed and waited out the State Attorney's investigators at the bar. Later, when the two were alone, Morales leaned in and gently placed his hand on Jerry's forearm.

"You know too much," he began. "You know everything I have told you. I'm not going to let you get away from me; I'm going to be right with you. I'm going to know who you talk to, I'm going to know when you talk to them, and I'm going to know what you said."[500] This was Morales emptying the batteries from the reporter's hidden recorder all over again.

Now we can talk.

Sanford left the bar realizing how important danger was to Morales's existence. *He thrives on it,* he thought. And so too should anyone riding with The Monkey.

★★★

The Quesada crew's dry spell lasted until August 1979 when Carlene's sister and her boyfriend Larry returned to the picture.[501] That meant the Colombian supply was back in effect, wholesaling their coke for between $45,000 and $50,000 a kilo. Colombians were driving up the price of coke in Miami as they took over more of the market, eventually cutting the Cubans out of their supply chain altogether. Carlene eventually broke from Larry and the Colombians altogether; they were too expensive.

Enter the Bolivians.[502] Carlene and Morales took the proceeds from the last forty kilo deal with the Fat Man and used it to open new supply lines. They sent two of their men down to Bolivia to arrange for a load.

That fall of '79, Sgt. Diaz got word that Rudy Redbeard was hoarding a sizable amount of quaaludes on his yacht. He got a search warrant and boarded the docked vessel with his team. They seized the targeted pills and a stack of VHS video tapes, one of which would change the trajectory of the pending case against Rudy and Carlene. Diaz put it in the VCR and knew he'd just been given a magic wand.

"One of the video tapes was of Rudy fucking Carlene's wife," Diaz recalled. The investigator put the damning video tape into evidence.[503]

The pair had been spending less time together, each working with their own crews. They were having their own separate issues as well. Carlene Quesada's crew had rip-off and payment issues, while Rudy's *basuco* use was becoming more frequent and leading to more paranoia and unpredictable behavior. To the observer, it didn't seem like the partnership would last for long.

Super Papi got firsthand confirmation of this when he was approached by Rudy to switch teams. He'd asked Becerra to come work for him more than once.

"No, man," Becerra said, rejecting his advance. "Rudy, Carlene is my friend, man. He treats me well."[504]

Becerra had also seen Rudy's increasing instability and had concerns. He'd heard the kingpin was high all the time now and was giving his hitman team more assignments. "He'd smoke that shit, and then he sent those idiots to start shooting people."[505]

Carlene's business issues were wearing on him. He began drinking hard liquor at the Mutiny, which he hadn't done before, getting shit-faced and mumbling about having to "kill someone." Mutiny girl Mollie didn't know the particulars, but she knew the one-time partners were falling apart.

"I knew Rudy and Carlene as friends," she said in Roben Farzad's book *Hotel Scarface*. "Then all of a sudden you had to pick sides."[506]

On the night of October 17, 1979, Carlene was driving home with his new fiancée—he'd split from his wife on Rudy's tape—when his new Datsun 280ZX was sprayed with twenty-eight rounds of submachine gunfire from the darkness.[507] Quesada instinctively put the car in reverse and navigated the entire ride back to his house looking in the rearview mirror.

He took five rounds to the body, but the shots were superficial with most grazing Quesada and a couple getting wedged just under the skin. His fiancée hadn't suffered anything but a horrific fright. Super Papi went to Carlene's house and brought him into the bathtub, where he leaned his guy over the edge and picked the .45 caliber slugs out of his back. Carlene was fine, but a message had certainly been sent.

Word was a trickling out that Mon, Rudy's hitman, was responsible for aerating Carlene's ride.[508] One would think that if Rudy had sent an experienced hitman like Mon to actually kill Carlene, the job would've been done. Rudy Redbeard later confirmed as much.

"Please," he's quoted as saying in *Hotel Scarface*. "If I wanted Carlene dead, he would not have survived."[509]

Quesada was vulnerable, at his lowest point personally and professionally. The time was ripe for police to show Carlene the Rudy sex tape.

"Yeah," Rudy, Jr. acknowledged of his dad's actions. "That's where he fucked up."[510]

★★★

Morales owned a copy of Sun Tzu's *The Art of War*, and in the Cuban operative's ability to use existing conditions in the universe to his advantage, he'd mastered a concept espoused by the ancient warrior and self-help guru.

Sanford passed Morales in the hallway of the courthouse.[511] There wasn't time for a chat, as Sanford was on his way to an appeal hearing. A quick greeting would have to suffice, but that was fine with Morales—he only needed one sentence.

"What would you do if Quesada flipped?"[512]

The chess master stopped Sanford in his tracks. Was that even possible? There had been no talk of that. Carlene and Rudy were both in the bag; the investigation and resultant raid netted both of them. They were partners from back in the old country. Could this really happen?

On October 23, 1979, Morales led Carlene Quesada, his attorney Jack Denaro, and five Miami PD officers for security into Sanford's office.[513] Carlene's mind was made up. He said he'd testify against everyone as early as the next day at the wiretap hearing Sanford was scheduled to attend. Quesada was officially switching teams. It was announced in court to the defense attorneys that Carlos "Carlene" Quesada would now be a witness for the government, testifying against Rudy Rodriguez and everyone else.

"This is the first witness we have ever had who can help us penetrate the upper echelon of the narcotics trade in South Florida," Sanford said in court.[514] He told Judge Sidney Aronovitz they would be dismissing all charges in exchange for Carlene's testimony.

Attorneys for the defendants were furious at the last minute bombshell. One of the defendant's lawyers said, "They have struck a deal with the man their original witness identified as one of South Florida's biggest drug dealers. They are throwing out the baby and keeping the bathwater in this case."[515]

Morales had arranged things perfectly for both Carlene and Sanford but not so much for Rudy, who Morales figured was nearest to going off into the deep end. His increasing use of *basuco* and impulsivity was making him self-destruct. Like Sun Tzu reading the terrain and weather, Morales guided the players along the path that was developing naturally before them.

He knew Carlene was at his wit's end and had no other choice. Upon seeing the Rudy sex tape, he had flown into his house in a rage, going right for his ex-wife and swinging wildly at her.[516] Fortunately Super Papi was there and dove between them, restraining Quesada before it got worse.

"He was about to pull his gun," Becerra recalled. "I'm telling you right now, if I wouldn't have been there, she would have been dead."[517]

For the time being, the government was prepared to present the argument that Rudy was the big fish in the partnership, complete with hitmen at the ready, front companies to wash the drug proceeds, and a lab on nine acres of gated, secured land. That story would work; everyone thought it was enough to put Rudy away. Perhaps there would come a day when they'd both be locked up for their crimes, but for now Carlene was absolved of his transgressions.

And that absolution meant business as usual for Carlene's crew. The Bolivian investment had paid off, and forty-four kilos of cocaine came in, locking in a new supplier.[518] The first Bolivian load landed on a small air strip in Vero Beach, Florida, flown in by a gringo Eastern Airlines pilot they found named Skip. It was then flown to San Francisco where the Fat Man's organization was poised to move it for the hefty sum of $67,000 a kilo.

The Bolivian connection was working, and once Carlene and company saw the prospects, they invested even more capital into the operation. They paid $25,000 to have a second air strip paved in Santa Cruz, Bolivia.[519] They next arranged for a massive eight-hundred-pound load valued at $1.2 million to come in, but it was picked off by the DEA. At the same time, another one of Carlene's guys took $180,000 from the group and disappeared, never to be seen again.[520] The two blows were a major setback because that money had been earmarked to purchase two planes. They'd planned to get their own full-time pilot as to not rely on others, removing another liability. But now they had a paved airstrip and nothing to land on it.

Around this time, Morales and Carlene moved in together in a town house on 72nd Ave after Super Papi left the group. He didn't like where Carlene's business seemed to be headed, and he had taken an offer from an up-and-comer in the game named Jose "Coca Cola" Yero.[521] Carlene's main man walked away from a situation he knew to be deteriorating.

"It was that Carlene got to a point he wouldn't listen to nobody, man."[522] True as that might have been, with the repeated rip-offs and DEA bust that left nothing in the kitty, Super Papi more than likely wanted the opportunity for upward mobility in Coca Cola's rapidly expanding organization instead of the mess that Carlene was in. Plus, dealing while being a federal witness probably limited Carlene's days.

Then in a shocking development, before the start of the government's case against Rudy, Sanford turned in his resignation letter to US Attorney Jack Eskenazi.[523] Dade PSD detectives had told him information from a credible source. The source claimed a collective of Miami drug dealers was planning to send a message by executing someone symbolic of the government's efforts against them, and Sanford was the name they'd chosen.

After receiving that initial word from the PSD, Sanford ran into PSD Major Steve Bertucelli. He confirmed what Sanford had learned: "Have you heard the talk about hits on prosecutors, especially you?"[524]

Sanford wondered if his days were numbered, or worse, if his family was in jeopardy. Once he resigned, the case against Rudy was placed under Assistant US Attorney Sam Smargon's direction. On May 9, 1980, Carlene Quesada's testimony did the trick, and Rudolfo "Rudy" Rodriguez Gallo was convicted and sentenced to fifteen years.

Carlene's crew held off on any activity until that summer—a reasonable enough respite for the federal witness who'd had thirty years' worth of charges dropped in exchange for testimony. He and Ricardo still lived together at the condo, but did no business, choosing instead to lounge around and wait for the storm to pass. "It was getting into drinking matches, doing cocaine, talking about the same baloney," was how Morales described it. He continued to see Jerry Sanford, though, and with Sanford having stepped down from the US Attorney's Office, their relationship became more personal.

"I don't fully understand the relationship," Sanford wrote in his personal journal, "but he wants it to last."[525]

Morales still railed about the trials and tribulations in his business. He complained about a Bolivian colonel at the Santa Cruz airport who took payoffs for cocaine shipments, and he told Sanford of two German mercenaries he thought to be responsible for the assassination of Nicaraguan President Anastasio Somoza.

"I never really knew why he kept giving me information like this, unless it was just because he wanted to tell someone he trusted," Sanford wrote.

One night while talking at Captain's Tavern Restaurant, Morales looked over at the former prosecutor and revisited his favorite film, *Casablanca*.

"This could be the start of a beautiful friendship."[526]

Chapter Fifteen Telling Time (1980)

One of the benefits of becoming a government witness is locking up your competition and returning to business with a smaller field. After some mishaps and the moratorium on dealing, the Quesada crew was still in need of money. One of Carlene's associates was sent back down to Bolivia to try and line up another load, and Morales was dispatched to San Francisco to deal with a new issue.

Flaco's connection, the Fat Man, was not paying for the load fronted by Carlene's crew. Ricardo testified to having flown there with a partner in early August 1980 to collect "half a grapefruit," which amounted to $500,000.[527] Loads in the millions were referred to as grapefruits. Morales was flown to San Francisco in a private Learjet, and Flaco put up the two pilots in the Marina District while they handled business. Morales or Flaco would reach out to the pilots in a few days when they were ready to fly home.

One of Fat Man's distributors was scheduled to fly up from Los Angeles that afternoon to deliver $250,000 of their debt to Quesada. The guy came as planned, but only had $17,000. Morales took it and met another one of Fat Man Wheels's distributors slated to pay, who only had a little over $100,000 available. Morales would have to return to Carlene with considerably less than the anticipated half million.

When Morales was ready to fly back, Flaco was nowhere to be found. He called his house in the hills of Sausalito and got no response. The pilots didn't respond either, and when Morales called the airport they couldn't find the Learjet. Frustrated by Carlene's disorganized operation that was coming apart at the seams, he called Quesada and told him he wasn't going to remain a sitting duck in the Hilton. He was getting back on his own. He took a cab to the airport and got on a Pan Am flight back to Miami.

When he returned, the $117,000 earmarked for Quesada's desperate crew was instead given to a group of Colombians to whom Flaco owed $490,000.[528] Once again, they were broke.

Morales and Quesada moved out of their townhouse when Carlene got married again. The newlyweds got a condo in Key Biscayne, and Ricardo began staying on South Bayshore Drive with a new girlfriend named Silvia.

Though Morales was a cold-blooded operative with only a sardonic sense of humor to indicate he was human, a distracted paranoia began to creep in. One afternoon at Crandon Park, Morales pulsed with fear when he saw a young dark-skinned man with a machete coming toward him.[529] His fight-or-flight instinct waned when he realized the guy was a park worker trimming the bushes. But he acknowledged that something deep inside him was signaling he shouldn't trust anyone.

Morales always drank—Johnny Walker Black, rocks—but his cocaine use since working with Carlene and partying at the Mutiny might've been crossing his wires. He began using more Valium to try and find equilibrium. His initial reason for taking the sedative was the series of recurring nightmares that kept him from sleeping soundly. It was a remnant of war; he dreamt of the Congo girl he'd left in the hands of the Congolese soldiers, and he thought about her long after waking. Had they kept her safe? Had her apparent savior left her to an uncertain fate?

Jerry Sanford, by then in private practice, also started seeing changes in Ricardo. He was drinking more heavily during their meetings, and he more than once broached the subject of his own pending assassination. The attorney suggested he just leave Miami, but Morales said he wouldn't.

"I'm going to be hit," Ricardo said, "but my body won't be dumped in the Everglades. It'll be left on Flagler Street for all to see."[530] He thought there was big money on that contract for his head.

On April 16, Sanford spoke with investigator Gaeton Fonzi, called by *The New York Times* "one of the most relentless investigators on the House Select Committee on Assassinations" about the Kennedy assassination.[531] Fonzi said he thought Morales had something to do with it. Sanford was to meet with Morales that night and wanted to ask him about it, but based on his recent moods, decided not to bring that up.

Ricardo became emotional when Sanford mentioned a return to Cuba, his eyes misting up. He said he had a love for Cuba but had been away so long he no longer felt Cuban. Sanford asked why and explored that sentiment, but Ricardo became confused, puzzled as to why Sanford was asking about it. He seemed all over the place.

One afternoon, Morales walked into Sanford's office with Carlene in tow. As a result of his testimony resulting in Rudy's conviction, it was on the record that Carlene had made $3 million in the drug business. And, while his testimony was in exchange for the dismissal of his pending drug charges, no one said anything about his taxes. The IRS sent a bill for taxes on the unreported $3 million.[532] Morales asked the former prosecutor if he would handle the civil tax case against Sanford's former star witness. That competed the Quesada trifecta for the attorney—the drug dealer in his office had at different times been his target, witness, and now client.

For Morales, there was no denying that business with Carlene was deteriorating. Their most recent intended load from Bolivia had an issue—the money was delivered, but nothing came back. There was also a load of cocaine base that arrived and had to be returned for being too oily. A new distributor named Kathy lost one load in a rip-off and had three of her other deals busted by the DEA.[533] Everything Carlene was touching was turning to shit.

Morales began fighting with Carlene. He felt their terrible string of luck occurred because Quesada was becoming careless and desperate, working indiscriminately with new people that were problematic. There were fights breaking out among these new people in public, and guns were often drawn. Then there was the cash flow from Bolivia; the region no longer seemed to be a viable source, unless everyone else in those deals knew something Ricardo didn't.

"I didn't know what was going on, exactly, down in Key Biscayne," he testified in regard to Carlene's new residence.[534] Maybe money was indeed coming back but not making its way to Ricardo. Was he just paranoid? Didn't matter. The Carlene thing wasn't working out any longer.

Morales also took note of the new crowd showing up around Carlene.[535] He knew a couple of them: Frank and Ronald Condom-Gil, brothers who'd served at the Bay of Pigs for the CIA, and the Villaverde brothers, Brigade 2506 veterans.[536] Frank Castro, the Bay of Pigs veteran and FLNC anti-Castro group leader, who was present at Orlando Bosch's Santo Domingo restructuring meeting, was also with the group now.[537] They all spoke with Carlene of planned ventures in coded terms, repeatedly referencing "stocks," which Ricardo felt to be out of place. He had been around the block a few times and had a suspicion as to what that veiled talk meant.

"The only time there is secrecy is when heroin comes up," Morales later said of the stock talk. "That's the only time you might hear anybody saying 'I sell pot, ludes, coke.' You will never hear anybody saying he sells heroin. I have never heard anybody say that."[538]

Any suggestion of stocks had to be bullshit. Morales had not exactly seen Carlene cutting lines of coke on that day's *Wall Street Journal.* Morales thought the Condom-Gil brothers might've been mixed up in the Cuban side of the "French Connection" case he'd informed about in the early '70s, and he testified as much.[539] They'd been arrested in a major international cocaine smuggling ring back in '73, but they'd never been arrested or convicted of heroin dealing.[540] When he first saw them at Carlene's, he approached Quesada and asked what they were doing there.

"I know Ronnie from Cuba," Morales testified. "We used to work at the same place at the airport, and Frank I met over here, but everybody knows they are heroin, you know. It's not a secret. And I said besides that they are dealing in all kind of racketeering things, you know. They are con people and what are they doing here?"[541]

Their presence at Carlene's place and at the Mutiny plus all the talk of getting into new "stocks" was the giveaway for Morales.

He repeatedly told others how morally opposed he was to heroin and anyone involved in it. To that point, it hadn't been an issue. The pot and coke business was plentiful in Miami, and while others were obviously handling heroin, Rudy and Carlene's crew weren't.

Two days prior to Halloween in 1980, there was a meeting at Carlene's about raising enough assets to buy these stocks. Morales looked on, silent in his displeasure and gravely disappointed by Carlene's desperation. Was his business in such shambles that he'd agreed to this?

Carlene was serious about raising assets. Morales testified that Quesada gave the Condom-Gils his two Rolex watches and just about every dime he had for this investment.[542] Another associate gave them his boat. Carlene was buying in, big time.

Morales got him alone at the Mutiny during their annual Halloween party, at which the CEOs of New Miami partied all night and into the next day. Morales, Carlene, and the new crew had been drinking for fourteen hours when Morales finally cornered him.

"Listen, Carlos, don't come up to me with this story that there are stocks because you don't know anything about stocks."[543]

On the off chance the new business actually involved stock, Morales knew it wouldn't be legitimate if Carlene was involved.

"I don't know anything about stocks," Morales advised his friend, "and if the stocks are stolen, you know, that's it. That's the SEC, there is no way. Playing with funny money, the Secret Service gets after you right away. You don't play with those things."

"We will have to discuss it more intently because of the profit," Quesada replied. Morales would testify that Carlene explained the margin was so big, that "with only five, we can do what we are doing with twenty." Morales took that to mean there was a 4x profit multiplier in the new business. Did stocks really come with such a guarantee?

That Halloween ended in a shitshow when Morales found himself in a big fight with a group of Venezuelan men, who he later suspected were hitmen sent from Caracas.[544] It started in the club but spilled out into the lobby where the bouncer had to pull his gun to try and get control.[545] Super Papi, who'd been there with his new Coca Cola crew, followed the fracas, also pulling his gun. He mightn't have been with Carlene's guys anymore, but some random dudes were fucking with The Monkey, so he stepped in.

But Morales had a better way to disperse the crowd—he held up a hand grenade and pulled the pin.[546]

"Trick or treat," he said. The unarmed Venezuelans scattered, and Morales slid the dummy grenade—an empty case he'd bought from a guy in Nicaragua—back into his belt line.

The entire city seemed to be heating up. Colombians had recently ratcheted up the violence as they began to control more of the cocaine market with ruthless abandon. That behavior was creeping into the business across all ethnic pockets, as the way of the gun was becoming the way to do business and stay alive.

Tensions eventually extended to Table 14 itself. One night Sanford sat on pins and needles as Morales and Rafael Villaverde got into what started a simple discussion about historical events, namely the assassination of Orlando Letelier in Washington.[547] As the two threw competing conspiracies at each other, Morales added pats of butter to his points, tossing them across the table with each retort. They bounced off Villaverde as he and Carlene tried to ignore the disrespectful act.

Morales was spending less and less time with Carlene, but that didn't seem to faze Quesada. In November, Morales happened upon Carlene holding a 2 p.m. meeting at the Mutiny, which was wildly outside the daily timeline of anyone of importance at the club. Quesada and his new friends were now apparently "day people," and Morales was still firmly on the opposite side of that clock.[548] Moreover, Carlene lied to Morales about his whereabouts. Morales had caught him—a violation that kills partnerships.

"He started lying to me which was an agreement that we always got—not to lie to each other because once you lie to me, that's it. That's it."[549]

He walked in and saw Carlene and the Table 14 crew, Mach-2. He sat and as the rest of them talked, he realized he was far out of the loop.

"I was off, [dis]placed completely," Morales said of the meeting. "I was getting news of what they were doing after they [had] done it."

Daytime meetings would be impossible for Morales. His nightmares continued, as did his efforts to use narcotics to keep them at bay. In the middle of the night on December 7, 1980, Jerry Sanford's home phone rang. It was Morales in a full panic.

"Jerry, what's your address? They're trying to kill me...with M16s, everything. I've got to see you right away!"

Sanford figured it was probably the drugs, but he gave him the address anyway. Sanford told his wife Jeanine what had just happened, and she took out a .357 Magnum and sat at the kitchen table with the gun on her lap. They waited. Fifteen minutes later, he called back.

"Jerry, how do I get to your house? I'm coming right now."

He never showed up.

He called Sanford's law office the following day in a normal state. He never mentioned the phone calls, but he did have a request. He asked Sanford to call the Assistant US Attorney on his behalf and ask about arranging his entry into the Witness Protection Program.[550]

★★★

Roberto, now entering his teenage years, hadn't seen his father for a long time. He'd grown content with occasional check-ins—little indications that his dad was still out there and cared about him. Like the times he'd chase Johnny's car as Roberto was being driven to school. Or the time he called the house, screaming.

Roberto had been playing sandlot football with some friends when a photographer showed up and snapped some action shots of the kids.[551] He got their names and told them to check the newspaper the next day. Roberto was excited to see the paper had run it—a big photo of him and his friends with their names printed below. How awesome.

Within an hour of seeing it, Roberto heard Mimi yelling into the phone at someone. He asked what was wrong, and she waved him off.

"Go to your room."

His father was on the other end of the line. "How could you let that happen? You work at the *Herald*!"

After the call, Mimi came into Roberto's room, soft but firm.

"You can never let that happen again."

"What?"

"Come out in a newspaper. Your father is worried about your safety."

This didn't bother Roberto. It meant his father was looking out for him, wherever the heck he was.

Over at Magda's house, Rick, Jr. had just started high school at South Miami High after having gone to all-white Catholic school for eight years. He'd decided to give sports a shot again, trying out for the school's basketball team. They ran drills for the coaches, but Rick, Jr. was the only White kid in the gym, and none of the Black kids passed him the ball. Rick was cut the next day. He then transferred to Coral Park High School, but something was triggered in him, and he decided not to try out.

"I was not gonna put myself under the grip of another coach," Rick recalled. "Sports weren't worth it to me anymore. So I decided to follow my father's path. I don't need to go to school. I live in Miami—I'll just deal drugs."

Rick dropped out of school for good. Magda grudgingly made the trip down to the high school and signed the required paperwork. He'd stopped attending and would've failed everything anyway. What choice did she really have? He could go back someday and get his GED. At least had a job at the hotel, although Magda suspected he was doing more than that. Rick was using drugs steadily, and it was pretty obvious when he was out of it. When she spoke with his dad on the phone about their son dropping out of school, Ricardo mentioned he'd heard about Rick dealing. He was pissed off about it.

Rick's family had been struggling for so long without support, so his father's disappointment did nothing to dissuade him from making a little money however he could. As a matter of fact, if he was so concerned, maybe now was a good time to pay up. Rick's friends were all planning a trip to New York City, and neither Rick nor Magda had the cash on hand for something like that. It was time to collect some of that child support Rick's dad had neglected for over a decade.

Rick didn't know where his father was staying since returning to Miami, so he began cruising by the only place he thought he'd visit regularly—Carlene's house. If the news was correct, his father was dealing with him, and Villa Lola's address had been listed in all the newspapers as the operation headquarters. While cruising the neighborhood with friends, Rick would have them pass Carlene's to see if that maroon Cadillac was parked behind the gates. When it was, Rick would get out and ring the bell, but he never received a reply. He'd leave notes, asking his dad to reach out. Those overtures also went unanswered.

One day Rick and his friend Angel were cruising scenic Bayshore Drive into Coconut Grove when they passed Ricardo's car. It was parked outside a condo complex building, where each unit had a marked parking spot below. Angel pulled over, and Rick went to the corresponding apartment door, ready to ask for money. Well, money, but probably so much more.

"It's like subconsciously you're hoping for help," Rick said, "but in reality you'll settle for basic assistance—money, something. Those are the two ends of that spectrum I was hoping to gain. Maybe just get my frustrations out, maybe let him know what a bad father he was."

Unless he was invited inside, that was a lot to ask for whatever short interaction they'd have. But Rick had suppressed a lot, and it wouldn't take much to make it bubble over. There was a good chance this wouldn't go very well.

Morales opened the door.

"What are you doing here?" he asked.

The coldness of the greeting put Rick on the defensive. He explained he had to seek him out because he and his family needed help. It degenerated from there, with more than a decade of unanswered questions firing from the young man's mouth.

Finally, "Why don't you take care of your family, you son of a bitch?"

They went at each other, but Angel held Rick back as the woman tried to pull Ricardo into the house.

"Look at you, *qualupero*," Ricardo yelled at his son, invoking the slang for a pillhead.

"Me?! Look at *you*, you fucking hypocrite! Big-time drug dealer calling me names."

"Fuck you!"

"All your drug money and your family has *nothing*!"

They barked at each other like rabid dogs until the woman got Ricardo inside and slammed the door.

"Come on, man," Angel said, pulling Rick away. "The cops are gonna come." They had a car full of pills downstairs. They left, not speaking to each other.

Rick knew there was something terminal in that last exchange. When his father hadn't met him after practice, it was Rick that had made the decision to cut off hope for a future with his dad. But this day, seeing his father's face when he opened the door and the exchange that followed, he knew definitively that his father wanted out of his life. He wasn't going to sit there and whine about it to Angel. They'd just go off and get high, like they'd done every afternoon before that.

★★★

On the afternoon of December 16, Ricardo Morales entered room 310 at the Holiday Inn in Coral Gables.[552] Assistant State Attorney Rina Cohan, Raul Martinez, and Detective Diosdado "DC" Diaz (different Diaz than Raul Diaz) were waiting for him there. The Monkey was prepared to sign a waiver of immunity and give deposition outlining his dealings with Carlene Quesada's crew over the past three years. Ms. Cohan would ask the questions, legal reporter Margie Sanders would record the answers, and the two cops would ensure everyone's safety and also glean details for their upcoming investigation.

Cohan began. "Let me start out by saying that I am only interested in your activities with Quesada, Villaverde, and that organization. I am not interested nor will I inquire as to any criminal activity you may have had outside the fact."[553]

That was right in line with Morales's plan. His activities in New Miami since returning in 1977 would now be scrubbed completely in exchange for delivering the heads of some associates. Whereas others might dread a process like that, Morales was most comfortable in that environment. His most harrowing days had come when he was detached from all agencies entirely and from Carlene's group. Where there was no action, Morales would create some.

During the deposition, Morales reminded Cohan about the witness protection deal. Three days ago, he gave a sworn statement at the State Attorney's office predicated on his placement in the US Marshalls' program. That statement became probable cause for another court-ordered wiretap on Carlene Quesada's phone and the planting of a bug in his residence, where the majority of their dealings were discussed. After Morales was sworn in and all the preliminary discussion had finished, The Monkey spent several hours outlining Carlene's operation, displaying his remarkable memory. He was able to list exact dates, names, kilo weights, and dollar amounts for every conversation and transaction for which he had been present.

Morales reiterated on record his reasons for approaching the government with this information, or at least the reason he'd decided to advertise as such.

"The pressure of the drug business is getting to me," he began, "and there has been a change in the drug dealing of the organization that I used to belong to—from cocaine and pot to heroin, which goes against my own belief and religion."[554] He said he flatly refused going along with their new enterprise.

Stocks, my ass.

After Morales's sworn information was on record, the Miami Police Department took over. Their target location was Carlene's Villa Lola, as Morales testified it had been business as usual over there while Quesada's new wife was at their condo.

Wiretapping the phone line wouldn't be challenging because the process occurs entirely outside the residence. The bug would be another matter. They'd need to get into the house and actually plant it. DC Diaz, Martinez, and the team went into action. Carlene's residence was already under fairly constant surveillance, so keeping an eye on his whereabouts was easy. He employed a housekeeper who was to remain inside whenever Quesada was out.

Except he didn't. Police sitting on the house observed that when Carlene left for an extended time, the housekeeper would leave and hit local bars. This would be their opportunity to get inside. But how?

The answer came when a member of the investigation team observed the housekeeper on one of his jaunts, carrying a knife that seemed longer than legal.[555] The team immediately devised a plan to both get access to the residence and buy some time inside.

They found a wall clock identical to the one hanging in Quesada's living room, bought it, wired it, and waited. The bug stood at the ready.

Operation Tick Talks was born.

One day the housekeeper left while Quesada was out, giving the team the go-ahead. Police stopped him a few blocks away and arrested him for carrying the illegal knife as planned. He was processed and his possessions were taken into custody—all except his key ring.[556] They made copies of the house keys, then returned the originals to the caretaker's personal belongings. The entry team took the new keys, entered Villa Lola through the front door, swapped the clocks, and were out in a flash. They had to be quick about it. Despite Carlene being under surveillance to ensure he didn't come home, there was a chance someone else in the crew might stop by the house and run into the investigators. But everything went perfectly.

The bug was operational instantly, and police recorded discussion between Quesada and all his visitors, nearly all of it in Spanish. Literal translation of the conversations would leave any Anglo reading the transcript scratching their head. But any Cuban in a courtroom would know that *perico* didn't mean the literally translated "parakeet," rather, it was the Cuban term for cocaine.[557] This word was derived from the cokehead's tendency to chatter excessively when high, like a parakeet that won't shut up.

With the investigation in full swing and seemingly bearing fruit, Martinez and the team delivered the State's star witness to the US Marshalls for entry into their Witness Protection Program.[558] Morales's official acceptance into the program was actually facilitated by the IRS for a case against Jose Alvero-Cruz, on which he was assisting Agent Raul DeArmas.[559] As was often the case with Morales, multiple agencies were always in play, and the Witness Protection Program would serve all of them by protecting The Monkey.

On February 5, Morales turned over his MAC-10 machine gun to Martinez in preparation for his entrance into the program. He was put up in a hotel at Miami Airport where Agent DeArmas and the Marshalls took custody of him and whisked him away in a plane to parts unknown.

As police began filling hundreds of cassette tapes from the bug, their wildcard informant interjected himself into the investigation, maybe inadvertently, maybe not. During a recording, investigators heard a very familiar voice on tape threatening Carlene on his answering machine.

"I'm gonna get you," Morales's slurred voice said. "I told you I was gonna get you, and I'm gonna."[560] The cops laughed, wondering if he was so drunk he forgot he was calling a tapped line that his testimony had precipitated. Rather, anyone who knew Morales would realize the restless operative knew exactly what he was doing. The tapped line was part of the investigation for which he was given immunity. He could give his former friend a piece of his mind without facing the consequences.

He was going out of his mind in Witness Protection. He wasn't the type to hide undercover, and the Marshalls placed him in Houston's Chinatown section, which felt like a cruel joke.[561] Of all the languages he spoke, Chinese wasn't one of them. Was this the US government's final "fuck you" for publicly flaming them after Flight 455?

Though his placement seems like the punchline to a joke about the operative's tenure with *tres letras,* closer examination shows some logic. The main goal of the Marshalls' WITSEC was to keep a high-profile government witness safe and undetected. Morales might've stuck out like a sore thumb if placed in a white community when his Spanish accent crept out, and putting him in a Latino area would've ensured his unveiling, as his picture had been in all the Spanish newspapers over the years.

Chinese communities in the US were fiercely insular. There was an embedded fear and skepticism regarding US police agencies, and the majority of the inhabitants didn't speak English. They kept to themselves and kept their mouths shut, rarely even calling police to report problems. Morales, or Guillermo Anibal Martinez, as he'd been renamed after being moved out of Miami, might've looked weird wandering around Chinatown, but its residents weren't reading Spanish newspapers and minded their business anyway.[562]

He didn't care. He complained to anyone who would listen and Guillermo Anibal Martinez was soon out of Texas and living on 216th Street in Bayside, Queens, NY, where he choked down all pride and applied for work as a gas station attendant.[563]

Back at Villa Lola, the bug was working well and investigators were optimistic until they looked at the calendar and saw catastrophe ahead. They'd been meticulous about everything—getting the keys made, finding the exact replica clock, and installing it quickly and clandestinely. How could they have forgotten about April 26?

Daylight savings time.

While Americans were preparing to set their clocks ahead one hour, the cops were shitting themselves. The mechanism in the back of Carlene's clock would surely be seen when it was taken off the wall and adjusted. They had to find a way to keep Carlene and anyone in the house away from that clock.

Their saving grace was that Carlene occasionally provided intel to police about competitors' loads. Law enforcement sometimes breezed through the Quesada home, and the Operation Tick Talks team took advantage of that. A member of the team to whom Carlene had previously given information rang the bell at Villa Lola and was let inside.[564] He met with Carlene in the living room under some bullshit pretense of clarifying a previous tip about another dealer, and he was relieved that Quesada had been so forgetful.

The investigator looked up during their chat. "Carlene, you never set your clock ahead," he said. "Let me help you." The cop did it, and that was that.

With the hundreds of hours of chatter caught on the tapes, one thing never appeared—the mention of heroin. Coded talk about pot and cocaine loads were deciphered, but there had been no talk about branching out, trying new suppliers, or even delving into a new product.

That's because, it turned out, all talk of "stocks" was, in reality, talk of stocks.[565]

The Condom-Gil brothers were privy to an exciting business opportunity and had come to Quesada to shore up sizable investment capital. They'd somehow come across an inventor who was looking for venture capitalists to invest in a product he was patenting. The Condom-Gils and Quesada saw a future in the revolutionary invention—a circuit breaker for one's home that would illuminate when the breaker was tripped.[566]

Carlene Inc. was prepared to do something legitimate with his new executives, and splitting the shares too many ways would diminish returns. That explained Morales' unexpected entry into their daytime meeting at the Mutiny. None of the usual heads would be there at two in the afternoon. They could talk business without the anyone looking to leech onto any kind of deal.

This most unlikely misunderstanding had launched one of the biggest drug investigations in South Florida.

★★★

By 1981, crime was so out of control it had formed Miami's new identity. Even the palm trees, beaches, and the Dolphins couldn't compete. A convergence of events had changed the city from a vacation destination to a war zone to be avoided. A popular travel ad in the '70s showed a bikini-clad woman soaking up the sun below the phrase "Experience Miami Like a Native." A parody T-shirt sold in the early '80s kept the phrase the same, but replaced the girl with a gun.

Carole Masington, a resident of a South Miami suburb and wife of an attorney, told *Time Magazine* reporter James Kelly in 1981, "We had two manhunts in my neighborhood in one week. One friend was mugged, another was assaulted and raped. My favorite storekeeper was beaten and hospitalized, and my mother was robbed twice. And I am just one person."[567]

The magazine's now infamous profile of Miami, titled "Trouble in Paradise," spotlighted the city's violence and its widespread effects on quality of life and tourism. Even celebrities living in the most exclusive areas weren't exempt from the epidemic. The Bee Gees' three Gibb brothers lived in Miami Beach and contributed to the story, recounting how their dad, Hugh, had been mugged, and Barry Gibb's wife Lydia had her purse snatched.[568] Gun sales in the city rose 46 percent in 1981 with a record 66,198 weapons purchased.[569]

Vacationers stopped visiting. Tourism was a $9 billion a year industry for the region, and hotel occupancy rates saw a 25 percent drop in one year.[570] The local real estate market had gone cold as well. As if it wasn't enough that all this was happening organically, *Time Magazine* had just published the worst travel brochure in history.

The change in South Florida's climate was not gradual. The crisis was triggered by a few factors that had a rapid effect.

A surge of new Cubans entered the US after May 1, 1980 when Fidel Castro opened the Port of Mariel. He allowed anyone to leave the country if they could acquire transportation.[571]

"Those who have no revolutionary genes," Castro said in his May 1 speech, "those who have no revolutionary blood...we do not want them, we do not need them."[572]

Many Cubans who were already established in South Florida still had family left behind. When US President Jimmy Carter said America would grant asylum to up to 3,500 people under the Refugee Act of 1980, Cubans living here grabbed the opportunity.[573] A rare window of time had opened to get their parents, grandparents, siblings, and cousins out of Cuba and, in President Carter's words, into America's "open arms."[574]

Miami's exiles sprung into action, commandeering fishing liners, shrimp boats, and a host of ramshackle floating vessels and sailed south. 1,700 boats arrived at Mariel and were loaded with anyone wanting to flee the island. Cuban exiles picked up their relatives and loved ones but were also forced to load those who wanted to leave but had no one to take them. The US stood prepared to accept and process their promised 3,500 refugees but was instead inundated with more than 125 thousand people. Carter and the Cubans ended the Mariel deal in October 1980, and a great majority of those refugees remained in South Florida, with an estimated ninety-two thousand residing in Dade County alone.[575]

The overcrowding and strain on resources was immediately evident. A quarter of Miami's Mariel refugees were still without jobs a year after arriving, driving Dade County's unemployment from 5.7 percent to an estimated 13 percent.[576] Classrooms in the county exploded in size as an estimated sixteen thousand children were added to public school rosters. The exponential burden on the county was later exacerbated by the Reagan administration reducing refugee aid to Florida for fiscal year 1981–82.[577]

The Mariel immigration had another hidden feature that was damaging the city. Mixed in with the boat lifts of family and friends was a number of outcasts that Castro hadn't advertised nor had the Carter administration anticipated. Castro saw this as a rare opportunity to cleanse the land of citizens he deemed *escoria*, or "trash." Twenty thousand of the Mariel refugees loaded onto boats were convicted criminals, committed mental patients, and those otherwise jailed for being socially undesirable to the Castro regime, which included many people accosted for simply living an LGBTQ lifestyle and anyone living on the autism spectrum, undiagnosed.[578]

The dump of Cuba's jails and institutions into Dade County caused a rise in crime. Though the majority of Mariel's refugees were working people and a positive addition to the community, the criminal segment became very busy, very quickly.

"In terms of percentages, they are few," Metro homicide Lieutenant Raul Gonzalez told *The Miami Herald*, "but you put one thousand hardcore criminals in a city, and they tear you apart."[579] In two years since the Mariel operation, 69 percent of incarcerated Dade County Latinos were Mariel refugees, and just 19 percent were pre-Mariel Cubans.[580] The murder rate alone surged 60 percent in those two years. These refugees were branded "*Marielitos*"—a new pejorative created by Cubans who'd arrived in the US before them.

In the drug trade specifically, there had been a rapid increase in violence irrespective to Mariel. Miami had ruled as the sole leader in drug traffic for a decade, but never before had there been such a violent spike. The *type* of chaotic violence was degenerating into something more uncivilized. Florida's coastal paradise was becoming a third world nation, with dealers openly mowing down their competition with automatic gunfire. Bloody bodies were dropped in broad daylight on street corners, and dismembered body parts were left on roadsides in cardboard boxes. Representatives from Colombian cartels were arriving illegally, now plying their trade in US cities. As their participation in the cocaine trade shifted from mere exportation to distribution, territorial killings also began on US soil.

"At one point the Colombians were bringing it in and the Cubans were distributing it," explained Martinez. "And then at some point the Colombians said, 'Hey, we can make more money if we handle the whole ball of wax.' Because the money is in how you sell it. And that's where the cocaine wars started and all the killings for the fighting of the turf."[581]

In addition to targeting Cuban syndicates like Rudy and Carlene's, Raul Martinez and Raul Diaz were on the front lines battling the Colombians and their new brand of violence. Though there were few Colombian illegals in the South Florida drug trade, never more than a few hundred at the time, the degree to which they outgunned police put law enforcement at an insurmountable disadvantage. It was bad when the drug industry first overtook South Florida. Now, with the Colombians taking over, they held a potentially fatal edge over the cops. After Diaz and his officers had a shootout with Colombian hitman Pablo Melo, on whom police were executing a warrant for a double homicide, Diaz used some crime lab data from that incident to petition his supervisor, Major Robert Windsor, to make changes.

"The other eleven detectives [on the scene] were carrying .38s," Diaz began, "because the department did not allow them to carry semi-automatics. So we had eighty rounds among all twelve of us. When we got Pablo that night, he had a MAC-10 with sixty rounds, a MAC-11 with sixty rounds, and a model 59 Smith and Wesson with twenty-eight rounds. So here we got a guy who's got 148 rounds."[582] One man against twelve police officers, and he still had them outgunned nearly 2–1. Upon hearing that, Windsor approved fully automatics for Diaz's department.

With 569 homicides in 1980, up from 369 in 1979, and with 1981 on track to surpass 600, that would amount to nearly twelve per week for Dade County Medical Examiner Dr. Joseph Davis to house.[583] Making matters worse, since many of the murdered were illegal Colombians with no paperwork, they were admitted to the morgue as John Does and held while authorities worked to identify them.[584] Bodies piled up beyond what the facility could handle, so Davis had no choice but to get resourceful. He rented a refrigerated box truck from Burger King at $800 per month in which he could store the overflow from the morgue.

By the time prosecutor Rina Cohan was ready to bring the case against Carlene Quesada and more than thirty other defendants, she had some wind at her back. The ladies and gentlemen of the jury knew the city's drug violence. Would they really be able to make the distinction between Colombian cartel violence and the Cubans' civilized business? They were being called to judge the proprietors of a large drug dealing ring, and drugs were the reason bodies were piling up in their streets and making them keep their children inside.

Chapter Sixteen Trial and Error (1982)

Morales lasted only seven months in the Witness Protection Program. He would testify to having been moved around from Houston to New York, which he deemed a "security risk."[585] Handing a gas station manager a job application posed an indigestible reality that he wouldn't accept. Risk may have been his justification for wanting out, but pride had certainly been the main factor for someone like Morales.

He began reaching out to all available resources to spring him from the program, but that required him to forfeit his monthly living expenses from the government. He'd still have to testify for the IRS and Ms. Cohan for their respective cases, so someone should be pitching in to keep him going, right? That was the logic Morales used. If he wasn't heard, he could just bail on WITSEC and take off somewhere. Their trials would be screwed, Rolando Otero style.

Morales stated he spoke with Cohan, Martinez, and Major Paul Oboz, head of PSD's Special Investigations Department, regarding his exit from the Marshalls' program.[586] Doing so would require someone covering his living expenses for the next four months, which he estimated would cost $6,000. In September 1981, he was given that amount without objection and was summarily bailed on the protection guaranteed by the US government.[587]

In early April 1982, the defense team got their chance to depose Morales. For nine days, defense attorney Douglas Williams would try extract information but mostly spar with the sardonic operative. More than once it seemed the two would come to blows, and the other parties in the room had to cool things down.

Williams tirelessly led Morales through all phases of his professional life, zeroing in on details of his exploits from Cuba, Miami, and Venezuela. It was clear the defense wanted as much of Morales's life on record so they could punch holes in his credibility once taking the stand. Rina Cohan was present to object when she had to, and more than once the proceedings were stopped when Morales would refuse to divulge information he deemed to be irrelevant or protected. Much of what was discussed on record involved the *tres letras* in the US and overseas agencies like DISIP and Mossad.

In their quest to build an unreliable witness, Williams had a lot to work with. Morales was forthcoming about events like the murder of Eladio Ruiz, bombing of Cuban interests in the city, and his participation in the drug industry. The attorney also established that Morales received payments from various agencies in exchange for information while he continued to operate in illegal activities himself. It wasn't hard to deduce he was working toward the argument that Morales cut deals out of desperation to absolve himself of his criminal ways.

> Q: And, you know that there are several different circumstances and situations that could arise in the legal system in this country, in which the value of information received by a person depends directly upon that person's credibility or believability, correct?
>
> A: That's correct.
>
> Q: And, you know that another thing that determines reliability or credibility, is the past conduct of the person who is supplying information as well, correct?
>
> A: Not necessarily. That's not a correct statement.

Williams broke it down.

> Q: If Jack the Ripper, for example, walked into a police station in London, and said, 'I'm Jack the Ripper, and I slashed those ninety-seven ladies to bits, and now I

> want to give you information about somebody who stole a cow from my farm two days ago,' right? Based on his background? [588]

That was the shelf upon which the defense would try and sit Morales.

In March of 1982, an eight-week series of pretrial hearings began, and the one thousand hours of recorded conversation were placed at the forefront. A series of inquiries took place based on what was captured on those recordings as Judge Gerald Kogan weighed the admissibility of the tapes. The South Florida press coverage grew, and the Tick Talks hearings were covered daily. They were devoured by the public, hungry for the outrageous and provocative stories that came out of the courtroom.

Fiery headlines baited readers to dig into the smoldering details:

- "Drug Dealer Tried to Bribe Him, Officer Says" covered Detective Diosdado Diaz being called to the stand regarding the Tick Talks tapes. In his testimony, he divulged Carlene Quesada had tried to bribe him with a $12,000 gold Rolex watch and a Walther P-38 automatic weapon, among other things.[589]
- "Cop Relieved of Duty Over Drug-Dealer Link" was about the wiretap operator in Operation Tick Talks, Officer Raul Puig, who was relieved of duty due to his allegedly fraternizing with a man indicted on federal drug charges in 1978.[590]
- "Operation Tick Talks Gave Inside Glimpse of Drug Smuggling World" in the *St. Petersburg Times* recounted the "specific details of the bizarre and sometimes slapstick saga that is known as Operation Tick Talks."[591]

In the course of the extensive pretrial hearings, language would become an issue. The court went to great expense to have the Spanish recordings translated, paying $169 per cassette.[592] Given the number of tapes, the court would give great attention to the transcriptions. It was the foundation for the government's entire case.

But the amount of idiomatic nuance in the transcriptions was difficult to communicate to English-speaking jurors, as illustrated in the previously cited "parakeet-cocaine" example. Judge Kogan ruled simply:

"It is not for the translators to interpret what they hear or to say what they think was said, but to translate it exactly as it was said. If somebody else wants to interpret what was said, it is for other parties to do and for the court to listen."[593]

But grabbing most of the headlines during the eight-week press frenzy was The Monkey. His extensive depositions were on display as the court weighed motions and heard witness testimony from the outrageous events he recounted. Tales of his overseas missions, work for US governmental agencies, and crimes for which he served no time made for great fodder and further elevated the myth of South Florida's most famous spy.

Morales's depositions wrought havoc on the pretrial proceedings as well, as the defense began to pursue Morales's claims against two more Miami law enforcement officers. Morales gave testimony to Guillermo Zamora and Charlie Black participating in his bombing operation with Lefty Rosenthal. Morales had mentioned it to Doug Williams in his depositions, so it was now fair game in the Tick Talks case. Defense attorneys brought it up at pretrial, seeking to upend the state's case by tying Morales to a corrupt Miami police department, and Kogan wanted to know what had become of it.

"I want to know if they did investigate or if they didn't investigate," Kogan ordered. "I want to know everybody he's talking about."[594]

Miami Assistant Police Chief Robert Warshaw issued a segment contradicting Cohan's confirmation that there had been an investigation into Zamora, and Detective DC Diaz stated the department determined Morales had mentioned Lieutenant Black in error.[595]

Another revelation from the pretrial proceedings involved the Florida Department of Law Enforcement (FDLE) and their passing on the Quesada investigation. The state police had a shot at Tick Talks before the Miami cops undertook the case, but Rolando Bolanos,

FDLE special agent in charge of South Florida, testified they passed for one reason.

"These agents felt Mr. Morales would not meet the standards of a credible, reliable informant." Bolanos's team decided not to begin the exhaustive operation if the end result would be compromised by having to use Morales. "The members of the squad brought it to my attention about his background. He is a controversial individual to work with."[596]

Morales and the tapes were the one-two punch that the government threw at the accused. If the tapes were admitted into evidence and the defense would try and prevent that, Morales would take the stand and interpret for the jury anything that might've been misconstrued. Once he confirmed that any recorded discussion of loads of *perico* being delivered was actually not the delivery of a shit ton of little pet birds, the jury would obviously have some foundation to believe it. Morales would validate the tapes based on everything he'd told Rina Cohan at her deposition and the nine deposition sessions he'd been subjected to by the defense.

The defense spent a significant amount of pretrial courtroom time trying to discredit Morales. They'd amassed a lot of ammunition to paint him as unreliable and try to exclude him from the proceedings. If the tapes were played for the jury and Ricardo took the stand, the defense would have a monumental task ahead, but if they could get the tapes and/or Morales tossed, they'd have a far better shot.

The media lapped it up; each day bore new fruit and they never had to work hard at conjuring something titillating coming out of Dade Circuit Court during those two months. There was shit going down every day, and Morales hadn't even shown up yet. Judge Kogan was even forced to issue an arrest warrant for one of the defendants who'd seemingly disappeared.[597]

★★★

Back in August 1981, the gregarious and robust Rafael Villaverde was forced to resign from his longtime post running the Little Havana

Activities Center.[598] The facility, a community fixture that looked after elderly Cubans, held a final gathering for the Cuban exile regarded as a hero by the men and women at the center. He'd just been arrested that Tuesday in a big cocaine smuggling case the newspapers were talking about. Despite the outpouring of support, Villaverde requested the executive board suspend him from his post as director until the case was resolved. He believed an unpaid suspension would be necessary for the center to retain its reputation and continue to receive federal funding. Amid embraces from many of the teary-eyed old ladies of the community center, many who called Rafael "son," the board obliged. The old men shook his hand, and their wives danced with him as a Cuban band played from a stage. They knew in their hearts that a man so honorable and kind would be cleared of false charges.

"I am innocent," he told the assembly of around four hundred. "The courts will declare it that way."[599]

Villaverde, who served dutifully in Brigade 2506 and Operation 40, was charged in Operation Tick Talks alongside his two veteran brothers, though charges against Jorge Villaverde, the youngest brother, would eventually be dropped. The family's ties to the Morales family extended back to Havana, but their most recent reconvening, unfortunately for the Villaverdes, was their work with Carlene.

On March 31, 1982, as the extensive pretrial motions were underway, Rafael and six friends thought it a fine time to venture out into international waters for what they'd describe as a fishing trip.[600] Three of these friends were his co-defendants on bail, including recurring operative Frank Castro. The seven men boarded a thirty-six foot cabin cruiser, towing a smaller twenty-eight foot boat, and set out before tragedy allegedly struck.

The harrowing details were recounted for *The Miami Herald* by Raul Villaverde, who wasn't on the excursion with his brother but said he'd spoken with all the survivors.[601] He said when the group was just off the coast of the Bahamas, the larger boat, the *Michele,* caught fire from below somehow. Six of the passengers safely jumped from the *Michele* and swam to the twenty-eight footer that was conveniently being towed.

Rafael, the other passengers said, was not as lucky. He ran up from the lower compartment, his body on fire, and dove overboard to extinguish himself, but he never surfaced. The twenty-eight footer, whose engine wouldn't start, drifted until getting a tow from a schooner into Great Harbor Cay. The stranded boaters were questioned by Bahamian authorities, and they were then turned over to the US Coast Guard who stated they were uncooperative. Good thing for authorities the brother who *wasn't* there had all the details for them.

The Coast Guard then initiated a two-day search of the waters near Berry Island and found nothing—no boat, no Rafael, not even a shred of debris from the burned vessel.[602]

A week later, Judge Kogan sat in the courtroom and listened to the story. He then issued a warrant for Villaverde's arrest. He gave the bondsman ninety days to determine whether he was alive or not, at which point he'd seize the bond; Villaverde wouldn't be at trial.

The entire incident was met with skepticism by mostly everyone but the defendants. Martinez didn't know what to think initially, but he was swayed when his team surveilled the Villaverde house the day after Rafael's disappearance. The family was hosting a large party on the property.

"It looked to us like a real weird way to commemorate somebody's death," he said.[603]

Some felt Villaverde was morally incapable of pulling such a ruse on anyone and stuck with the story they were given. Zoraida Rodriguez, the seventy-four year old maintenance woman at the Little Havana Activities Center, felt this way.

"I think it was something wicked they did against him," she said, attributing it to jealousy over the "openness" of Villaverde's personality.[604]

Rafael's fiancée, Lily, didn't believe much of what she was hearing either.

"There are lots of rumors that he is in Cuba, Martinique, here and there," she said. "But he would never do that, he would never have abandoned his family and his little girl."[605]

Ed Carhart, Rafael's attorney, said of the incident, "I really don't buy the story that this is some kind of faked disappearance."[606]

Back in the Miami courtroom, the main event was up next. Morales was scheduled to stand before a defense table of familiar faces. Minus one.

★★★

Morales's decision to shirk the Marshalls' program while he was in the newspapers was a liability. In the new Miami, things were handled differently on the street, with retribution murders common and no target off-limits. All of his actions were being laid bare for the public, placed below headlines in large print like "Monkey Morales Admits Murder and 15 Bombings" in *The Miami News*.[607] Was he even aware that he was entering the most dangerous time in his already dangerous life?

But this was Morales's grandest stage to date. He was intoxicated by the attention of the press, as many articles mentioned his work for the FBI, CIA, DEA, and others. It was a public certification of sorts, and he further grew into the persona the media had either reported or created.

Sitting before him at the defense table would be a few dozen people from his life, with many of them garnering their share of notoriety in their own right. Names like Frank Castro, the Villaverdes, and Frank Condom-Gil were known to those on the shadier side of Miami's streets. But Morales was certain to make himself the star of the show, and it was all but guaranteed the disruptive raconteur would take the stand and wrap the defendants in the yarns he spun. What more might be revealed about the operative when questioned? Jesus, what was left?

Those questions were scheduled to be answered on Wednesday, May 19, when Ricardo Morales would take the stand. The defense had planted every seed possible in their nine days of depositions, each a landmine they hoped to detonate the case with. The prosecution had their arsenal at the ready as well. Morales's answers would validate a thousand hours of recordings. Everyone in the room that morning passed through additional security measures, further amplifying the gravitas of the day. The drama of the pending entrance was elevated when defense attorney Douglas Williams addressed the bench.

"Your honor," began Williams, "I think Mr. Morales himself should be searched." Judge Kogan smirked and denied the request.[608]

Then there was nothing. The room had quickly settled, and everyone on both sides of the room and in the gallery took a breath. The press perked up, preparing for days and days of testimony that they could repurpose a hundred ways in headlines. And then the doors opened.

Morales entered the courtroom, casually dressed and maybe smaller than the spectators thought a man of such lore would be. He'd aged a little past the recirculated photos in the newspapers; he was grayer and carried a puffier waistline. Police officers led him into the courtroom, past the spectators, and toward the bench.

Morales stopped unexpectedly at the defense table. He faced the men he was there to expose, scanning all the eyes locked on his. More than a handful of those faces were fellow Brigade 2506 and Operation 40 veterans, guys who decided to risk everything for their shared, idyllic vision of their homeland; a home they would never return to. They'd worked in service of self, sure, but also of country—both theirs and ours. Their exile to a new place and its resultant missions, battles lost, damage done to others and themselves, and death of a dream had broken all of them in that room. Ricardo may have been standing on a different side of the table, but did anyone really think he was different?

Then Ricardo Morales Navarrete, soldier #2449, straightened himself, outstretched his arm, bent it at the elbow, and saluted the men before him.[609] The air left the room. His gesture of respect was returned by the CIA operatives at the defense table, who then leaned over the wooden barrier and hugged Morales. They shared a laugh and a quiet exchange in Spanish with him. Ricardo then shook hands with the other defendants, lawyers, and made his way to the stand.

It was now the prosecution's show as their star witness sat expectantly. Rina Cohan didn't have much of a poker face that day; the disgust she must've felt was visible to the press in the courtroom. Everyone waited as the prosecution conferred. What had the orchestrated homecoming at the defense table done for their argument? Did it reinforce that Morales indeed had a relationship with these men as he testified in deposition? That would work toward the prosecution's efforts to certify his credibility.

The larger question was about Ricardo himself. Cohan had seen him be difficult as he challenged Williams throughout the days of depositions. Proving himself the smartest man in the room seemed a preoccupation for him. Though she felt him to be totally credible, Cohan knew he was undoubtedly a wildcard. What would he say once questioning began? She certainly wouldn't have thought to remind an experienced informant that he was working for the prosecution, and therefore fraternizing with the defense table would work against them. But he did it. Was he reversing course, having seen the fellow soldiers? What the hell might he say now?

It was too much to risk. Rina Cohan told the court the prosecution had no questions.

The defense, having no direct examination on which to base cross questions, were precluded from asking any.

They turned to Judge Kogan.

"So, why do we need Mr. Morales?" he asked.[610]

The room sat in silence. The judge continued.

"Well, the state has no questions. The court has no questions. The defense has no questions. Therefore, Mr. Morales is excused."

Ricardo rose and thanked the judge before passing the awestruck assembly, offering the crowded room nothing but a big shrug. And with that, he was gone, concluding eight weeks of testimony in Dade County Circuit Court's longest-running pretrial hearing.

A quote from a *Harper's* magazine profile of Morales from earlier that year was ringing in everyone's ears.

"One of Morales's abiding talents is to arrange things so that nobody ever feels completely defeated on his account."[611]

★★★

Though the final arguments were heard in June, Judge Kogan's ruling on the admissibility of the Tick Talks tapes didn't come until September

1982. Unimpressed by what the prosecution had presented, especially their failure to vet Morales's testimony that led to the initial approval or have him corroborate any of the recorded material in court, Kogan prepared a twenty-nine page ruling that tossed the recordings.

"One thing we have learned," he wrote, "is that we judges ourselves perhaps have made it a bit too easy to obtain wiretap interception orders."[612]

Kogan went on to criticize the police's execution of the recordings, and he faulted the State for failing to adhere to some technical procedures.[613] The State hadn't provided any background information on Morales to the judge who signed the wiretap order, as his deposition was the entire basis for the application. Further, the prosecution hadn't notified that judge of prior requests for wiretaps of those people recorded on Tick Talks, which was a violation of a basic legal requirement. Additionally, State Attorney Reno's office hadn't properly bonded the Miami officers as state attorney investigators before they manned their wiretap intercepts.

The cops weren't off the hook either, as Kogan claimed they used an unauthorized third recorder and then erased those tapes. Kogan thought the investigation rushed past basic procedure to get the intercept order signed. Further, the judge deemed Morales "a man known to sell his services to the highest bidder."

With the tapes eliminated from the State's case and The Monkey put on mute, there wasn't much left on which they could proceed. State Attorney Reno prepared the written reply to the judge's ruling, and it was a bombshell.

She dropped the case, setting all thirty defendants free.[614]

Reno wrote, "We believe there is an adequate basis upon which to appeal each and every one of the adverse findings by the court. But… we believe the court's order would be affirmed (by a higher court)."[615] It was front-page news; the investigation initiated more than a year and a half ago fizzled before everyone's eyes.

While it may have been back to business for everyone else, Morales's image had swelled exponentially. There were cover stories about him in two magazines that year—"The Informant" in *Harper's* and "License to Kill" in *Newsday*. He was the most salacious part of the Tick Talks coverage for the newspapers. While that degree of mainstream exposure might work to one's advantage in a different line of work, it euthanized Morales's value to law enforcement and made him a walking virus to anyone in the narcotics industry. He bailed on witness protection and found himself very much alone in the world. He clung to those closest to him, few as they may have been.

He ended up occasionally crashing with Mollie, his favorite Mutiny girl. Ricardo always had a fatherly thing with her, more so than the rest of the old Cuban guys at the club that gave her healthy tips and baggies of blow. More than the other Mutiny girls who might've stirred up something more, er, primal, in the men, Mollie could hang with the guys.

"Oh my god, we used to laugh," she says with a smile. "They were always looking over their backs, so they never got a chance to just be fun and light-hearted. And I am *just* fun and light hearted. I love to make people laugh. I like doing goofy things and you know, I think they just liked having me around. I was kind of like entertainment."

But Morales sometimes went uncharacteristically dark while at Mollie's. He'd occasionally wake up crying, and she'd hold him as he spoke of the late night visions of the Congo. In his sleep he'd walk among the dismembered villagers, slaughtered at the hands of the cannibalistic *jeunesse* tribe.

The Congo girl he saved would always appear. She never approached him; she only watched, with the largest, darkest, blankest eyes. Then she'd walk off into darkness, into the uncertainty in which Ricardo had deposited her.

The nightmares came more frequently now, with lifelike vivacity, as if the ghosts had waited for him to be less distracted by the fortress of chaos he'd always used as a shield. He was alone, and now that he was unprotected.

Sanford kept contact with Morales and summoned him to his office on December 14.[616] After the usual chitchat, Sanford asked for Morales's assistance with a new project—a search for Dr. Josef Mengele, the Nazi war criminal in hiding. Sanford had been part of a near miss back in 1979, but Mengele was tipped off and escaped. Based on Ricardo's experience working with Mossad in Venezuela, Sanford looked to the operative.

"Jerry, that's dangerous," Morales replied in his office. "Do you know what you're getting into?" But he ultimately agreed to help. Was there a mission Morales wouldn't go on?

At that meeting, Sanford noticed the changes in Morales. Sanford described him as "grayer, heavier, and looking tired."[617] But after he accepted Sanford's mission, Morales seemed to metamorphose at a cellular level, actually standing taller, broader, and walking with a more confident gait as he left Sanford's office. He promised to call the attorney in a week after he put some leads together. He was still needed.

He also spoke with Sanford about a book he was writing about his experiences, titled *Death Beam*.[618] Morales had asked him about it previously, casually wondering if something like that would sell. But this time Morales said he was working with a writer in New York to bring his story to life. He never told Sanford her name nor did he share any pages, but he claimed to be actively working on it. There was no way he'd allow himself to be shelved. And that worried Sanford a bit.

★★★

For some, a god complex can foster a perceived invincibility, a state of grace created by the ability to engineer a reality to their design. Once fully invested on that quixotic path, the individual cannot go home because that home is no longer there. They carry it with them. And in that committed journey, it's easy to forget about the ledge.

On December 5, 1982, Miami independent TV station WDZL Channel 39 aired a bombshell interview. The Spanish language program *En Una Hora* (*In One Hour*) aired host Francisco Chao Hermida sitting with Ricardo Morales for a no-holds-barred interview in an episode titled "A Story of Intrigue."[619] In it, Morales publicly detailed his version of the Cubana Airlines plot in what can only be described as an offensive.

Morales began by first accepting responsibility for the terrorist act.

"You helped put the bomb on the Cuban plane," Chao said.

"Right," Morales agreed. "I'm one of the main conspirators of the blowing up the Cuban plane. The historical responsibility, I admit, I bear on my back. I don't regret it, Chao."

Morales doubled down on the transport plane theory.

"Aviación de Cuba, first of all, is an agency of the Cuban Air Force. It is transporting the troops of the battalion from the interior, which are the ones that fought in Angola."

Morales made no mention of the flight carrying the North Koreans, but he reiterated the planes were used for the transport of special troops and equipment for Cuba's Ministry of the Interior. Obviously, to his mind, anyone killed during that operation was collateral damage—a military outlook certainly not exclusive to the efforts against Fidel Castro, but one echoed by those Kennedy memos that proposed the sinking of boatloads of innocent Cubans as justification for the invasion of Cuba. The needs of the many outweigh the needs of the few, as governments remind their people in not-so-subtle ways. Morales aligned himself with that mindset right there on TV.

In another shocking revelation on the show, Morales proclaimed Dr. Orlando Bosch's innocence in the operation, even though Morales himself placed handcuffs on the doctor after facilitating his travel into Venezuela in time for the bombing.

Francisco Chao confirmed Lozano placed the bomb on the plane but then wondered about Bosch's role.

"Ricardo [Lozano] is the one who puts the bomb on your orders?"

"Right."

"Orlando Bosch?"

"Orlando doesn't know about that, sir. Orlando Bosch knows absolutely nothing about that."

He exonerated Luis Posada next, relegating his role to procuring Ricardo Hernán Lozano, his old photographer, for the mission under false pretenses.

"You know what Luis Posada's responsibility is in the case?" Morales baited Chao. "That I asked him for a guide for Orlando Bosch [while in town] and he produced Hernán." Morales explained that

Lozano's recorded phone call to Posada after the bombing had gone unanswered, and when Lozano told Bosch that seventy-three dogs "went off a cliff," the doctor had hung up after stating he didn't know what that meant.

Morales then dangerously and publicly assigned culpability in the tragic bombing to multiple high-ranking officials. Though Morales had arrested Bosch, he claimed he did so at the request of Orlando Garcia Vasquez, the CIA agent he recruited for the top DISIP post. He claimed Garcia Vasquez carried out the plot with him, confirming what many in the international community had first suspected about DISIP's participation. But the chain of command responsible for the disaster, according to Morales, didn't stop there.

Morales accused Venezuelan President Carlos Andrés Pérez of being responsible as well. He said the president used Morales and his friends' assistance in efforts against Guyana as an excuse for their anti-Cuba missions.

"We were going to destabilize the government of Guyana," Morales told Francisco Chao.

"So do you think that Carlos Andrés Pérez was pursuing a patriotic motive by making this pact with a terrorist group?"

"When you make a pact with a terrorist group, you are not a patriot. You become a terrorist."

"So Carlos Andrés Pérez is a terrorist?"

"Correct," Morales said. "He is a participant in our terrorist operation."

Venezuelan government officials weren't the only ones with something to talk about after the show aired. In the extensive discussion of Morales's recruitment of Orlando Garcia Vasquez and the CIA's placement of Posada, Garcia Vasquez, and Morales in commanding positions in DISIP, the US agency was mentioned all over the program. Morales seemed to be in a mood to talk, clearly deciding his ties with all the *tres letras* were irreversibly severed.

Morales did not mention Flight 455's delayed takeoff from the layover. There were no excuses to be made. He positioned the loss of life as collateral damage, implicating anyone involved as participants in a deliberate act of terrorism. Was this Morales's last desperate grab for headlines after Tick Talks faded from the news? His increasing use of drink and drugs was noticeable, but had he really become that self-destructive? If not the whiskey, coke, and pills, then what would have caused him to seek out this spotlight?

Ego is the easy answer; it has historically been the sword on which many a samurai has fallen. But a better answer might be the end of a lifelong purpose. He lived his life fighting for a government that took him in, living in service of the endless missions it proposed, and he did not know how to function when it was over.

Morales's TV appearance and his repeated claims to be writing his memoir showed his desire to expose the secrets he knew. This was likely of great concern to anyone he had served. Maybe *En Una Hora* was just his first stop on the world's most dangerous book tour.

★★★

Rick returned to his father's condo, uneasy with how they'd left things. He'd been plenty justified in laying blame at his dad's feet—or hurling it at him—but he'd come on strong. Rick wouldn't accept anyone coming at him that way, justified or not, and he suspected his father felt the same.

On a Sunday in late November, Rick and Angel headed down to the Grove again.[620] They were welcomed into the condo this time with a proper introduction to Ricardo's girlfriend, Silvia, who made them coffee. Ricardo sat in the kitchen with the boys and made small talk, everyone engaged in placid, polite conversation. They didn't talk about the last visit, and Rick didn't ask for money. Instead, they just sat and enjoyed each other's company.

Ricardo stood and slid on his sandals. "Let's take a walk." He grabbed his handgun and tucked it in the rear of his waistband, then pulled his shirt over.

The three strolled Bayshore Drive, and Angel stayed mostly quiet, clearing the way for an authentic father and son exchange to evolve organically. They still weren't addressing past issues or present pain.

Rather, they just addressed each other. That seemed to be enough for the moment. They went nowhere important, said nothing important, but did it all beside each other, matching each other's steps.

When they returned to the condo, Ricardo turned to the boys.

"I want to take you both to dinner," he said. "We'll go out to Grove Isle, to a place I like there. The staff knows me and will get me out of there through the kitchen in case I have to make a speedy exit." He smirked, but the boys did not.

As the autumn sun descended and splattered the sky over Biscayne Bay with deep oranges and purples, Rick and Angel left. The boys weren't high that day—maybe they'd sensed this visit would be significant, one way or the other.

Rick would only speak to his father one more time. And it wasn't on Grove Isle.

Chapter Seventeen

Follow the Girl (1982)

Monday, December 20, 1982. Noon.

Francisco Chao Hermida met with his interview subject again at Centro Vasco restaurant early in the afternoon.[621] The location was popular with Miami Cubans—founded in 1962 by refugee Juan Saizarbitoria, it replaced the original Centro Vasco in Havana that was lost during the Cuban Revolution.[622] Nelson Alba and Leon DeValle, Chao's co-workers who produced Morales's appearance on *En Una Hora,* were lunching with him and debriefing about the newsworthy interview they'd recently aired.[623] They agreed there was likely even more in the well, and one of the journalists called Morales from the restaurant to book him for another televised interview.

They'd landed him at the right time—he was eager to discuss his operations and certainly held nothing back. When called and asked if he'd come back for more, not only did he agree but said he'd meet the group at the restaurant between one and two o'clock that afternoon. When he arrived, Alba noticed he was hyper and agitated. As they spoke, he began drinking Johnnie Walker Black heavily, ordering one double after the next as Alba's tab soon swelled to $125.

When discussing the next interview, Morales offered to share more about secret operations in Venezuela, but he also whet their appetite with a story about Miami police. He stated he was prepared to reveal the names of Miami police officers involved in drug trafficking.

Morales was becoming louder and more belligerent as he drank, at one point throwing his leg up on the table and revealing the Colt .38 blue steel revolver in his ankle holster.[624] He then got up to use the pay phone for what had to be the fourth or fifth time since sitting down;

he was all over the place. Upon returning to the table, he told them he was trying to get in touch with a lady he was planning to meet later, telling her to come to Centro Vasco.[625]

They wrapped up the long meeting, and Alba headed out around 7:30 while Ricardo stayed behind to meet his guest.

★★★

December 20, 1982. 9:00 p.m.

That week's *Monday Night Football* broadcast began on ABC-TV as the Cincinnati Bengals and San Diego Chargers prepared to square off. Frank Gifford, Howard Cosell, Don Meredith, and Fran Tarkenton began the broadcast and welcomed viewers to what would prove to be a real shoot-out between the quarterbacks.[626]

★★★

December 20, 1982. 9:30 p.m.

Nancy Cid, formerly Lamazares, met up with Morales and a friend, Juan Cecilio Fernandez, at Centro Vasco.[627] After a few drinks, Nancy was eager to head out, suggesting they go to Roger's on the Green, a restaurant and lounge in Key Biscayne. That didn't sit well with Ricardo, who told them he didn't want to go there. It would cause nothing but trouble.

The owner of Roger's on the Green, Rogelio Novo, had a silent partner in the restaurant named Juan Cid, a known pot dealer and recent ex-husband of Nancy.[628] Since splitting with Cid back in January, Nancy had become a real problem at the restaurant, acting like she still had a stake in the place just because her ex-husband did. She frequently left without paying a check, and Rogelio Novo had no choice but to take away her house account and ban her from the establishment. Her arrival there might be an issue that night.

Morales also knew that Novo and Cid were currently under federal investigation by the IRS for laundering proceeds from drug sales. Ricardo knew the appearance of the city's most famous informant might create a problem at Roger's, and with Cid's ex-wife, no less.

Despite Morales's rebuffing, Nancy was insistent.[629] Finally, he capitulated. Had Nancy actually been that persuasive, or did Ricardo just have a distracted refusal to smell the wolf's breath on the other side of the cottage door?

★★★

December 20, 1982. 10:00.

The trio left Centro Vasco and spent time cruising in Morales's wine-colored Cadillac. The ride to Roger's should've just been fifteen minutes, but Ricardo took the long route, contemplative.

★★★

December 20, 1982. 10:45.

Cherries Lounge was located on the ground floor inside Roger's. It had a rectangular bar to the right upon entry and a smattering of small round tables with wicker-backed chairs in a seating area to the left. Silver garlands were draped around the perimeter, decorative snowflakes dangled from the ceiling, and a Christmas tree stood in the corner of the lounge. Diners in the restaurant upstairs came down periodically to check the *Monday Night Football* score on the overhead TVs at the bar.

"AFC Playoff ramifications looming large for both San Diego and Cincinnati here. Cincinnati is behind here in the fourth, but driving. Second and ten now...Anderson drops back, plenty of time for a big one..."[630]

Owner Rogelio Novo was in the club that night with close associate Orlando Torres and some friends. Torres, a former Cuban police officer, had at times been described as Novo's personal bodyguard, which he denied.[631] He was working as a private detective and gun salesman at the time; he had known Novo for about twelve years and was admittedly "very close to him."[632]

Torres recognized a couple of patrons entering the lounge. He knew Nancy, of course, from spending considerable time in the place, and he recognized Monkey Morales from his numerous appearances on TV. Torres walked to Novo, who was standing at the bar, and pointed out the trio who'd just come in the door. Nancy was waving Novo over, who went reluctantly—Nancy sitting in his club meant trouble, but maybe he could keep some civility by saying hello. She introduced Novo to Morales, who he'd never met. Nancy was well aware that she was barred from the lounge, so that introduction to The Monkey might've been a message of sorts.

That's right, I'm here—do something about it.

Or perhaps it was something else entirely, something more nefarious. It was Nancy, after all. Not too many years ago she delivered Raul Diaz to her first husband's corpse, killed by her girlfriend's man. Maybe that introduction of Novo to Morales was an announcement for some other reason.

This is him.

Novo went over to the group but didn't pay much attention to Nancy, to which Morales took some exception.

"Don't you know her?" he asked Novo. "Isn't she your friend?"[633]

"He is not my friend," Nancy said. "*You* are my friend."

Novo told Morales if he was to spend time in his place he needed to show more respect, which was met with more snark from a drunken Ricardo, never one to lose a verbal joust, even when sober. After a testy exchange, Novo walked off. Morales watched him go.

"I ought to hit him in the back or the lung," he said to Nancy.[634]

People at the bar that night described Morales as loud and visibly intoxicated. At one point he even lifted his pant leg and showed the barmaid the gun in his ankle holster. He made his way over to Orlando Torres's table to greet a guest he'd known, Eugenio. When Morales sat, he leaned over and clumsily rested his elbow on Torres's knee, which he slid away, spilling Morales's drink.

"Anderson throws...uh oh!...picked off!" came from the TVs.[635]

Torres waved a waitress over and ordered Morales a new drink, but he stood.

"I'm not welcome at this table," Ricardo said and went back to the bar with Nancy and Fernandez, where he greeted a well-dressed Venezuelan named Raimundo.[636] He told Nancy he knew him from the "export business" in that country, though Raimundo also worked for the Venezuelan military. He knew Morales from his time in Caracas and had actually run into him earlier that afternoon in Centro Vasco when Ricardo was on one of his several trips to the pay phone. He'd declined Raimundo's offer for a drink, as he was busy entertaining the journalists. Then, by chance, perhaps, he ran into him again at Roger's.

Nancy waved Orlando Torres over to join her group at the bar. Based on his previous interaction with Morales as well as all he'd seen and read about him, Torres moved his gun from his back waistband around to the front for easier access before heading over. Nancy greeted Torres with an embrace, and, strangely, Morales followed suit. Torres then felt Morales slide his hands around his side and back, frisking him.[637] Torres pulled back, and Morales grabbed his tie.

"That's disrespectful," he told Ricardo, playing it off like he was offended by a gay advance rather than being thankful he hadn't felt the gun.[638] Torres walked off to the other side of the bar.

Within ten minutes, Nancy's group gathered their things to leave when their friend Juan Fernandez told them he thought the tension was growing too intense in the bar. They started for the door, but Morales couldn't leave without one last dig.

"Hey, you got any coke?" he called out to Torres as the entire lounge looked over.

As the front door closed, Torres told Novo "The *maricons* (faggots) have left," and it was done.[639] A night fraught with tension was over, but not before the bar manager saw Nancy leaving with a glass from the bar. She grabbed a plastic cup and headed out after her.

★★★

December 20, 1982. 11:40 p.m.

Moments after leaving, Morales returned, walked to Torres, and asked about his parting epithet. Torres pointed up to the football game.

"I was talking about the game."

"Yeah, Howard, I would just call this a bad throw by Anderson. I'm not sure what he was looking at. He was under pressure and I don't think he saw Fox coming at all."[640]

Novo saw the confrontation and approached, causing Morales to turn and exchange words with Novo instead. Ricardo squared up to him, turning his back to Torres.

"This is what killed Fouts in the regular season when they sacked him six times. He's waiting for his offensive line to pick up the blitz and he's getting blind side strikes like this."[641]

★★★

December 20, 1982. 11:41 p.m.

Outside in the valet parking area, Nancy was carrying on about being accosted for leaving with a glass. The bar manager retrieved the glass and poured Nancy's drink into a plastic cup.

A single gunshot rang out from inside the bar, and everyone in the lot froze. Patrons came scampering out, one couple passing by Juan Fernandez and muttering in panicked broken English.

"They kill him."

Inside, Morales lay beside the bar, blood streaming from his head and pooling on the faded, striped carpeting. Metro-Dade police cars soon swarmed the scene and detained twenty-five people to interview.

Paramedics from Fire Rescue Unit 15 began to treat him for a single gunshot wound to the head. He was breathing but totally unresponsive.

"Sixty-six completions by both quarterbacks, that's a record...and the clock will run out."[642]

★★★

December 21, 1982. 12:30 a.m.

Lead investigator Detective Steve Roadruck and Sergeant Frank Wesolowski were the first homicide detectives to respond to the scene.[643] The detectives processed the scene at Roger's with crime scene techs and collected a single .32 caliber shell casing in the process. They then began the process of interviewing everyone who remained at the lounge. Some were diners eating in the restaurant upstairs, some were musicians playing for them, others were busy in the kitchen, and some were patrons sitting in the lounge. All of them had one thing in common—none said they'd seen the shooting.

Raul Diaz was in bed watching *On Golden Pond* with his girlfriend when he got a call from Jim McGee, writer at *The Miami Herald*.[644] McGee told Diaz the news, and the detective was soon in touch with the homicide department and on his way to Mercy Hospital.

Morales had been his most valuable asset and his friend for a time. He was a source of as much value as he was frustration for Diaz, with the last few years being the most difficult. He'd kept away, even when Morales called upon him.

While the events of that night might've been inevitable, as Diaz drove to the hospital he rifled through all of their time together, work as well as the social times.

He might've even recalled the 1976 failed attempt by a city commissioner's thugs to lure Morales into a bar fight to justify their shooting him. How could a good investigator not have?

Orlando Torres was also on a late night drive, cruising the southwest section of Dade County, disassembling his .32 caliber Walther handgun and tossing the parts in various canals he passed.[645]

★★★

Annette was awakened in the middle of the night by a commotion in the living room.[646] She left her bedroom to find her normally stoic Uncle Pucho sobbing uncontrollably as Yolanda stood by him, trying to process everything.

"No lo creo, no lo creo," he kept repeating. "I can't believe it, I can't believe it."

The twenty-year-old walked to her uncle and instinctively embraced him, and he collapsed in her arms, repeating his distressed mantra. Yolanda looked to her daughter and told her the news. The horror of what had befallen Uncle Richard, combined with the weight of a fifty-five-year-old man crying for his baby brother in her arms, flooded the girl with grief.

Rolando "Pucho" Morales had drifted from Ricardo in recent years due to the drug business. Pucho had an uncompromisable value system, and his choice to step away from his brother was not lightly considered. It became apparent that Ricardo needed help; he was bouncing all over the place, leaving Pilar, then living with Quesada before witness protection moved him elsewhere. As far as Pucho knew, Ricardo had no steady place to lay his head after that, crashing with Mollie for a while and then some other woman on Bayshore Drive, so he opened his door to him. Pucho had kept Morales—plus his arsenal of about twenty-five guns of all shapes and sizes—with him at his Fontainebleau Boulevard condo for the past few months. He saw Ricardo's chaotic life up close, and though there were times it didn't feel right, Pucho was still his older brother—the older brother, others would tell him, Ricardo always wanted to be like.

Rick answered the ringing phone at Magda's house on Tuesday morning. It was his friend Angel who was working at Mercy Hospital as a respiratory therapist.

"Yo, I think your dad is here," he said. A shooting patient had come in overnight with the name Guillermo, but there was talk around the hospital that it was actually Monkey Morales.

When police removed Morales's wallet the night before, the two IDs inside—a New York driver's license and a Texas ID—showed the name Guillermo Anibal Martinez.[647] Though Nancy reported his real name to the responding officers, the hospital didn't get that word until after they'd received him. At 1:15 a.m., Detectives Rimondi and Perez were at the hospital when they learned from the ubiquitous and seemingly omniscient Miami crime reporter Edna Buchanan that the patient was actually Monkey Morales.[648]

★★★

By mid morning there was a contingent of family assembled in the hospital waiting room, eager for any information about Ricardo's condition. Yolanda, Annette, and Pucho joined Magda, Rick, Raul, and Sylvia initially. Pilar arrived with her two daughters at some point as Ricardo lay in the ICU, still comatose. Police were stationed at the hospital's main entrance to keep the family away from the bloodthirsty press outside.

Rick and his brother Raul arrived at Mercy Hospital together. Upon entering, Angel met them in the lobby.

"Everyone is saying it's The Monkey," Angel said.

Rick and Raul thanked him and sat with family members and waited for news; periodically, a hospital worker would swing by and give Yolanda or Pucho an unofficial update. Everyone in Miami knew who Morales was, and the workers seemed eager to be helpful and connect with the family in some way. Yolanda appreciated each update, but she was preoccupied by a woman seated off to the side beside the pay phones. It seemed each time the family received some news, the woman got up and made a call.

Annette could read her mother as well as anyone; even when Yolanda kept her fountain of opinions locked behind her lips, it seeped out of her face. That woman by the phones was pissing her mother off for some reason. When Yolanda was distracted, Annette slunk over to the phone bank, pretended to use a phone, and waited for the woman's next call.[649] Annette was talking to herself into a receiver when the stranger got up again and dialed.

"No change," she said into the phone. "He's still alive." She hung up and sat back down. The woman wasn't interacting with anyone from the family; she was just trying to blend into everything else going on in the lobby.

The family paced, worrying and wondering what was going on, but Rick wasn't having any of it. He was convinced this was a last-ditch effort to make his dad disappear, maybe some witness protection bullshit that would land him in Spain with a new name while they all cried over an empty casket. Their feelings had never been considered before, so why would this be different? No one had been allowed to see Ricardo yet, and Rick wasn't sure they ever would.

The doctors approached the family later that afternoon. Despite everyone that had come into Ricardo's life in his four decades traversing the globe, there stood the few who shared DNA with him, now finally called to the forefront. It was time for the inevitable discussion that the kin of anyone kept alive by artificial means must have with doctors. There was no brain activity in Morales, and that left only one humane option. The family was allowed to say a last goodbye.

Rick stepped into the room beside his siblings and mother and looked to a man he barely recognized in the bed. His face was bloated from the gunshot trauma, and he was sporting a mustache for the first time anyone could remember.

Rick approached the bed, still unsure about who he was looking at.

"Is that even him?" he wondered aloud.

"It's him," Magda confirmed.

Each person took their place bedside and had their final solemn moment with Ricardo. Rick's emotions were swirling. What to say to a man who he'd barely known, especially when Morales wanted it that way? His father had hurled insults at him but then welcomed him into the condo and made dinner plans, just like when he abandoned Rick as a child then showed up at football practice and promised to pick him up the next day. His father never picked him up and, well, that dinner on Grove Isle was now fucked as well. The constant seesaw journey had Rick sick. He would offer his father a final word, a closing sentiment.

Rick leaned over.

"Now who's the fucking *qualupero?*"

"Get out!" Magda yelled. He did, and the rest of the family followed as Dr. Ploaza stepped in and terminated supportive treatment.

Rick walked ahead of everyone, back down to the lobby, and joined the group that was speculating about what might've happened the night before. They compared snippets of what they'd gleaned from hospital staff, police, and anyone else they interacted with. Rick informed them the hospital was pulling the plug, and a silent wave washed over them. Someone in the group suggested they tell the lady who'd just walked over to the phone bank.

"Who?" Rick asked, looking across the lobby.

"That lady we were talking to, Nancy. She said she was with your father last night."

Rick started toward her as she hung up, having made her final call. She went toward the exit, gliding past police and press, her head down. Rick called out to her.

"Are you Nancy?"

She didn't look up.

"I'm Ricky's son."

She kept walking, faster now.

"I'm sorry," she said, though she didn't turn.

"What happened?"

"I'm sorry."

"Hey!" He sped up, closer to her now. "What happened?"

"I'm sorry."

"Who did it?"

"I'm sorry."

"Weren't you there?"

He kept asking questions and she kept apologizing all the way to her car, which she got in, closed the door like she didn't even hear him, and left the lot. Rick stood alone then slowly headed back inside.

Did Ricardo hear him earlier? What else did he hear while lying in that mystical limbo?

Thanks from Cuban exiles?

Fury of seventy-three airline passengers?

A whimper from a scared little girl handed to Congolese soldiers?

She was the only mystery in his life. Morales brought all things to very definitive conclusions in his missions. Not everyone was happy, but they knew where they stood. But what happened to that little girl that clung to his back in the jungle? He'd given her away into a mystery.

At 1:32 p.m. on December 21, at age forty-three, Ricardo Morales Navarrete followed her into the grandest mystery of all.

★★★

Ricardo had been shot from behind at relatively close range, just behind the right ear. Based on X-rays, the lodged bullet lay in the upper portion of his skull, strangely suggesting an upward trajectory as if the gun had been fired from below.

On the investigation front, police spoke to those present that night with little success. Most didn't notice an altercation, and only one person said they saw the shooting—Nancy Cid. She was brought from Roger's to the homicide department and interviewed by Det. John LeClaire at 1:45 a.m. on the night of the shooting. She detailed her activities with Morales and Fernandez that night and said she'd witnessed the conflict between Rogelio Novo and Morales.

The report of her statement reads: "Nancy Cid then observed an argument between Rogelio Novo who was holding a firearm and Morales who wasn't holding a firearm. She advised she heard several shots as she was approximately fifteen feet away from the argument. She observed Rogelio Novo shooting the firearm and observed Ricardo Morales fall to the ground..."[650]

Nancy's witness statement was the only one with a visual account of the shooting, so Novo became the sole suspect for the time being.

At 3:10 a.m. on the night of the shooting, Detective Roadruck finally interviewed Juan Fernandez, the friend who was with Nancy and Ricardo. He confirmed the tension in the club that night, as well as the exchange outside with the bar manager and the plastic cup. But he indicated he didn't think Nancy had followed Ricardo back into the club.

The following morning, detectives were unable to locate Novo at his address, and his wife said she thought he went to New York the previous day.[651] They spent the morning trying to track down his car and locate his stepson with no luck. At noon, Novo's attorney Frank Furci left a message for Detective Roadruck stating his client was not responsible for the shooting they were investigating nor did he have any information regarding it.[652] Further, Furci informed Roadruck that he advised Novo not to speak with police in reference to the incident.

Assistant State Attorney Sam Rabin told the detectives they didn't have enough to make an arrest. Roadruck then called Furci, who agreed to make his client available only if an arrest was imminent.[653]

A background check of Novo revealed an arrest the previous year for carrying a concealed firearm. They probed further and found the weapon was an automatic, blue steel .32 caliber Walther, which matched the caliber of the shell casing found beside Morales.

On Wednesday, two days after the shooting, Nancy was interviewed again at the homicide offices.[654] She retold her account of events, though some details in her story changed. She now stated that she hadn't been inside the bar when the shooting occurred but rather was entering the lobby at the time. She only saw Morales fall to the ground in front of Novo, who was holding a gun. He passed her on his way out, said he didn't know what happened, and left. Detectives showed Nancy photos of two guns—a .38 caliber with a two-inch barrel and the Walther Novo was arrested with. She identified the Walther as the one she saw Novo with. She told the detectives she was "mistaken and confused" when giving her initial statement on the night of the shooting.

Detectives found Orlando Torres's felony record, which included aggravated assault, carrying a concealed firearm, and assault and battery.[655] He became a person of interest for the detectives.

Beyond the names given by patrons of Roger's on the Green, investigators who knew Morales's story were likely aware the case could go almost anywhere. The more they opened up Morales's life, the more arteries would've been shown to them, with many extending beyond Miami. His recent appearance on Channel 39's *En Una Hora* detailing the Cubana Airlines plot certainly presented a host of things for agencies to probe. His scheduled return appearance to the show, one that promised to reveal the names of Miami police officers involved in the city's drug trade, was a path that might've also borne fruit, as by the end of the '80s nearly 10 percent of the Miami Police Department had been either suspended or fired from involvement in drug-related scandals.[656]

But how earnestly would the investigators follow these avenues opening up to them? On the day of Morales's death, just a day after the shooting with barely an investigation underway, *The Miami News* quoted Sergeant Wesolowski saying, "It is simply a bar argument and a shooting. With all the homicides we have, I can't worry about Morales's entire life. As long as I'm satisfied that it's a shooting in a bar fight, that makes a little less work for me. I could go on forever following his life and his enemies."[657]

★★★

Detectives kept raking the local soil, eventually getting Orlando Torres to homicide for an interview on January 10. He arrived with his attorney, a private detective, and an interpreter provided by the State Attorney's office. He detailed his version of the events of December 20, stating he'd known only Nancy personally and had only known of Ricardo Morales from TV. He understood him to be "a killer who had killed many people."[658]

Torres confirmed he owned a .32 caliber Walther PP and did carry it on his person, concealed in his waistband. He stated he had experience with handguns from his time as a policeman in Cuba and while working at a Miami gun shop. He purchased the firearm legally from Continental Gun Shop, and he claimed he gave a .32 caliber automatic handgun to his longtime friend Rogelio Novo as a gift.

Torres confirmed details the police obtained from other witnesses, including how he accidentally spilled Morales's drink and was patted down by him. He admitted to calling Morales a *maricon* as he was leaving and that Morales returned to confront him. When he did, Novo stepped over and, according to Torres, was struck in the chest by Morales, causing Novo to fall backward. Given Novo's recent heart surgery, Torres became concerned, and he acted when he saw Morales lean down for his ankle-holstered weapon. Torres admitted to pulling his own weapon and firing a shot into Morales's head from a couple feet away. Fearing retaliation from any of Morales's dangerous associates, Torres stated he'd bolted from the scene and disposed of the weapon in parts around Dade.

Police couldn't ignore that Torres's statement lined up with some pieces of the puzzle, like the curious upward trajectory of the bullet shown by the X-ray. That was consistent with Morales being shot while bending down for his weapon. Torres's account of the evening and Morales's behavior prior to the incident also seemed consistent so he wasn't arrested, but the "subject" line on subsequent police reports replaced Rogelio Novo's name with Orlando Torres's.

The investigation continued, with Novo coming into homicide on January 13 with his new superstar attorney, Roy Black. Before beginning, Black advised Detective Roadruck that "no questions concerning [Novo's] relationship with Juan Cid or the ownership of Roger's on the Green would be directed toward his client as both these topics are currently under federal investigation."[659] Novo confirmed his tenuous relationship with Nancy due to her split from Cid and her subsequent behavior in the club. He detailed the events of the night leading up the final confrontation, which he claimed was about Morales objecting to being called a homosexual.

He said Morales squared up to him, shoved him, and then went for the gun at his ankle, which Novo knew to be there from what his barmaid told him earlier in the night. Novo said he heard a shot but didn't see Torres fire, but he assumed he had because he was the only person near him. Novo said he went home and called his attorney not out of guilt, but because "people don't move around this town without one."

Novo also turned in his .32 caliber weapon for testing, and police eliminated it from the investigation.[660]

As days went on, investigators worked the witness statements. Novo and Torres's story seemed to stand, any hidden motives notwithstanding, and on January 20, *The Miami Herald* reported Torres would likely not be arrested in the case.

"Based on what I've got, it's probably justifiable homicide," Roadruck said.[661] Without anything more concrete that connected Morales to Torres, Novo, and Cid's club, what else did they really have?

The case remained open. Investigators worked Torres's confession, testing his unused ammunition that his attorney gave the police, and they conducted more extensive background checks with prior employers.

As they did, an unexplored motive emerged on February 20 from over two thousand miles away. An article in *The Arizona Republic* newspaper about Irv Berger, the new owner of the MISL professional soccer team the Phoenix Inferno, alleged that he'd never actually owned the team.[662] Rather, the article posited, he was simply a front for underworld "heavy Cubans."

"The group," the article stated, "consisted of Manuel Espinosa, Juan Cid, Rogelio 'Roger' Novo, Emilio Palmar, and Julio Eiroa, according to four people close to the Inferno and documents obtained by *The Republic*." The article said Cid and Novo were currently "under investigation by law enforcement authorities in the laundering of money obtained from drug sales, according to a Miami police lieutenant and a federal Drug Enforcement Administration official."

The most stunning detail emerging from the article involved The Monkey:

"Morales, 42, who was identified as an informer for a number of intelligence and police agencies, including Miami's 'Operation Tick Talks' drug investigation, was expected to testify during a federal grand jury in Miami regarding Cid and Novo's finances, Miami police said."

Morales's murder at Novo and Cid's club in an alleged "bar fight" now had a more solid lead attached to it than the utterance of a pejorative. A couple of months later on May 5, Assistant State Attorney Rabin met with top police brass, including Roadruck and Captain Don Matthews, regarding the article and Morales's reported participation with any federal agencies that police didn't know about.[663] Rabin asked Roadruck to contact the FBI regarding the possibility.

When the detective contacted the Bureau, he was informed by Agent Dennis Lacina that Morales was now "strictly persona non grata in the FBI office and not being used as any type of information source."[664]

Roadruck next spoke with IRS investigator Raul DeArmas.[665] He contacted DeArmas because he and his agency were responsible for bringing Morales into the Witness Protection Program for his participation in their case against Jose Alvero-Cruz. DeArmas and his agency were also bringing their investigation of Cid to a federal grand jury. DeArmas responded to Roadruck and said he could only give limited information about the active case, but he stated that Ricardo Morales was not scheduled to testify against Juan Cid or anyone else.

Reverend Manuel Espinosa, mentioned beside Juan Cid and Rogelio Novo as one of the "underworld" figures behind the Phoenix Inferno, had become a significant presence in the Cuban community. Back when Mimi was working for him, he'd made waves as a public voice advocating for the loosening of blockades against Cuba—a position that did not sit well with the militant anti-Castro community. As a result, the portly, bearded activist had been shot at, sued, and bombed before he suddenly abandoned his stance on Cuba.[666] His appearance on Channel 39 shortly after Morales's death piqued the investigators' interest.

In his sit-down interview, Espinosa claimed to have done an independent investigation of Morales's murder and found it was linked to a conspiracy, but he stopped short of airing anything specific.[667] On May 10, Roadruck visited Espinosa's office and asked what he knew about the case. He said that when he last spoke with Morales, he claimed to be working with DeArmas in the IRS's Operation Greenback, which was directed against Juan Cid. Espinosa also said he spoke with Juan Cid on December 23, where he admitted to having Ricardo killed. The reverend gave the name of a witness to the conversation and further went on to say that Nancy and Juan Cid were seen drinking together at Menage Lounge in Coconut Grove two days after the shooting. It was Espinosa's opinion that Nancy had set Morales up for Cid. Police obtained a copy of the Channel 39 tape, but it was only a teaser for the contents he would eventually relay to the police. He did not reveal specifics of the perceived plot due to fear for his life.

The *Arizona Republic* article reporting the business arrangement between Espinosa, Novo, and Cid established Espinosa had the opportunity to be privy to such a conversation, provided he and Cid actually had one. But with Cid and Novo under investigation, was this just Espinosa's attempt to distance himself from them, or possibly to lay the foundation for a plea bargain if he was eventually snagged into the federal probe?

In June 1983, Espinosa still stood as the only person subpoenaed by Assistant State Attorney Rabin for a grand jury review. As a result, Roadruck wrote to Rabin his formal recommendation from the law enforcement side, stating, "This investigator in review of the case has determined that based on information received as of this date, no charges would be filed on subject Torres...this investigator has determined that this case be exceptionally cleared at this time."[668]

Shortly after his death, Ricardo Morales was quickly and quietly cremated, with half his ashes spread on Biscayne Bay by Pucho, and the other half placed in a mausoleum with his mother, Ines, when she passed only a few months later. For a soldier and operative serving US government agencies for so long, it was an undignified send-off. There was no twenty-one gun salute by uniformed soldiers, and no one triangulated an American flag to hand to Ines Morales Navarrete Gonzalez. There actually wasn't a funeral at all. No one likely ever thanked Ricardo Morales for his service—an impolite oversight in today's society valuing the sacrifice of so many. Ricardo's sacrifice was invisible.

Chapter Eighteen

Endless Possibilitees

Every generation has their landmark tragedy, measurable by one's memory of where they were when they heard the news. JFK's assassination is a common one, followed by the Space Shuttle *Challenger* explosion and the 9/11 attacks. For Miamians who read the news during the Cuban exile wave, the murder of the imperishable Ricardo Morales serves as one of those moments.

But shouldn't an espionage story of an international spy end in a web of intrigue? Despite our need as spectators to have all stories arrive at a definitive conclusion, those that *don't* often outlive those that *do* in our minds. Thirty-five years after Morales's death, on December 20, 2017, documentary producer Alfred Spellman wrote a lengthy profile of Morales for *Medium* called "Ricardo 'Monkey' Morales, the Most Interesting Man in Miami, Was Gunned Down 35 Years Ago Today."[669] In just the past few years, Morales's story has been profiled on Spyscape's *True Spies Podcast* and NPR radio's *Full Disclosure* with Roben Farzad, and both shows dedicated an entire episode to him. Most recently, Rick Morales Jr. appeared on Rob Reiner and Soledad O'Brien's podcast *Who Killed JFK?* to explore the role of the Cubans and possibly Morales himself in the assassination.

As with the unsolved mysteries of the world, Morales's murder conjures up a host of theories. If you were to focus on what took place in Roger's that night, limited in scope to the players immediately involved, you have the same theory that homicide investigators reached—a chance encounter, a slur, and ultimately a confrontation. Even further, that story could be bent a little to include Nancy bringing Morales there, initially against his will, because she was asked to do so, whether or not she knew the reason. There were a thousand clubs in Miami—why Roger's, given the history?

Was Nancy Cid asked to deliver Morales? If so, who would've been close enough to her to do ask her to do so? Morales had been placed in Witness Protection by Raul DeArmas for his cooperation in the IRS case against Alvero-Cruz. But DeArmas was also bringing Rogelio Novo and Juan Cid to a grand jury in an unrelated case. Did word on the street conflate the two IRS cases, perhaps erroneously reporting that DeArmas placed his star witness in the Marshalls' program to testify in his Novo/Cid case? That would certainly warrant a second look given what happened to Ricardo in Novo and Cid's club.

Then there is the issue of the Jose Alvero-Cruz case itself. Even if the two IRS investigations hadn't been confused, Morales's testimony in the Alvero-Cruz trial might've put a target on him. Since launching the grand jury investigation against Alvero-Cruz, Jerry Sanford had received a number of death threats, disclosed to him by Miami Police Special Investigations Unit detectives DC Diaz and Sebastian Aguirre.[670] Detectives Diaz and Aguirre reported receiving information that Alvero-Cruz had put a $1 million contract on Ricardo Morales's head.

One looking for a more international spy story could focus on the allegations Morales had just publicly leveled against DISIP, its commander Orlando Garcia Vasquez, and Venezuelan President Andrés Pérez himself. Morales's appearance on *En Una Hora* about Flight 455 aired just a few weeks before the shooting. This placed the bombing, which occurred six years prior, back in the news with specific accusations.

Morales was also profiled in feature articles for *Harper's* and *Newsday* that year, each outlining his journey through the international agencies. Both articles positioned Morales as not so much a soldier but as a criminal who'd exchanged his government work for absolution of sin—the ultimate professional informant. That was not the business card to be carrying around in 1982 Miami if longevity was in one's plans.

Nor was writing a book.

After his death, Morales's attorney John Komorowski revealed the book was in the outline stage and would have been "very explosive."[671]

"He was up in New York in the beginning of November talking to publishers," Komorowski said. "He was talking to two or three, playing each one off the other. That was his style."

If news of his book had spread—and Morales was being anything but tight-lipped about it—that would've opened another door for investigators. It's reasonable to assume he would've written about meeting Oswald and the JFK assassination in the terms he'd told his sons. There were individuals and agencies in the US that would've preferred the book never see the light of day.

Jerry Sanford very likely had the best answer when asked who could have killed Ricardo Morales.

"How many points does a compass have?" he replied.[672]

Morales's brother-in-law and fellow anti-Castro operative, Hector Cornillot, said of the confrontation at Roger's, "It was an assassination. They were waiting for him."[673]

"Life is a con game, and they were great con people," Cornillot said of the operatives of that era. "They would gain your trust, your faith, you would give them the shirt off your back; they would take it and kill you. And Nancy was as good as Ricardo."

Those in law enforcement weren't beyond such speculation either, despite the case being cleared. Retired Chief Raul Martinez said of the circumstances, "I thought for sure it was a hit from the many enemies on the many fronts he had created, through the many years he played the spy/narco/informant game."

Detective Diosdado Diaz was more direct. "Bullshit. It was a fucking hit."[674]

Retired Lieutenant Raul Diaz, the closest person to Morales carrying a badge, also thought there might be more to it.

"He had many balls up in the air," Raul said. "And some of the balls that were up in the air were smarter than him, more powerful than him, and better placed."[675]

Venezuela, for example?

"Yes, Venezuela," Diaz said.

Morales had spoken with the well-dressed Venezuelan importer/military official named Raimundo that night in Roger's. The extent of their connection and his exact role with the Venezuelan military remains unknown, but his presence in the club on that night is something to consider, especially since Morales's *En Una Hora* interview implicated DISIP in Flight 455's fate.

Beyond the basic question of who would've wanted him killed, one must wonder how Morales's experience and caution could've been so easily usurped. Komorowski called him "a real life James Bond. He's been on every side there's been. Everything he does is for a reason—he's got a master plan…you think a guy as professional as he is, how's he ever going to get in a bar fight?"

Chief Martinez echoed that sentiment. "It's hard to believe, as astute as Monkey was, that someone got the best of him."[676]

Is it our innate tendency toward conspiracy that makes us think there was more at play on December 20, 1982? Or can we just not accept that a life so infused with danger, secrets, and betrayal could end in a stupid bar fight?

Either way, Morales's all-consuming purpose was self-preservation in a career of scattered landmines. He served many but mostly lived in service of self; had he not, he would've been swallowed long before that Monday night at Roger's on the Green. Inside Morales there was more mission than man for many years—often to the disdain of those who loved him—until the missions evaporated.

And without mission, we die.

Chapter Nineteen

Epilogue

The demise of someone looming so large comes with long-lasting reverberations for those around them. That was the case for Rick; his father's death brought his misdeeds into the limelight in full force. Scant was any mention of Brigade 2506 or Operation 40. His media presence in recent years had been about those other things in Miami that sell faster.

Rick's emotional process to rectify his father's life and death would be difficult enough without the snickering and side-eyed glances from people as he passed. One night he and a date were in line at the movies when some teenagers behind him sang "Shot the Monkey" under their breath, replacing the word "shock" from the famous Peter Gabriel song. He'd have to learn to ignore it as best he could.

While his father's death could've served as closure for Rick, it only pushed him farther out onto the fringe. An aunt of his had recently married a Peruvian man, and Rick began hanging out with the man's two nephews, both in their early twenties. The brothers barely spoke English, so Rick was asked to show them around and help them find a job, since he seemed to have a lot of time on his hands.

Turned out Rick's new uncle had more than adequate work lined up for the guys when he began importing raw quaalude powder from a connection in Colombia. In short time, Rick and his new cousins set up an unfurnished house in Miami with a press in the garage. They were soon turning powder into pills and moving them into West Palm Beach, their designated territory.

As luck would have it, the guys had hooked up with a major pot dealer named Alfredo at the swanky club La Notte. He knew people in need of pills and blow, and soon the cousins began rolling heavy. Rick would swing in and out, doing deals here and there with them. On one of his visits, his uncle turned to him with a proposition—Rick could come in full-time, not just on sporadic runs. He was family and showed he could be trusted as a member of the organization as it grew.

Rick stood in that empty house in Kendall which had grown to include not just pills and coke, but now guns too. A lot of them. Something was whispering in Rick's ear, and in a moment of uncommon clarity, he realized that if he accepted the offer, he'd be accepting responsibility to do things that might get people killed. Maybe himself. He told his uncle and cousins that he wanted to stay a freelancer.

By 1985, the Peruvian group was distributing cocaine outside Florida with a repeated route to Detroit. Rick handled a few of those flights, moving two kilos each time and returning to Miami International Airport with $64,000 in cash stuffed into every available inch of clothing on his body. By all accounts he was succeeding, ducking a couple of close calls along the way, and making good money. But he wasn't enjoying any of it.

"I know I can get caught at any moment," he said, "and it'll prove everybody right."

When his aunt left her new Peruvian husband and told Magda what was going on, Rick's mom started harping on him to quit the business. Magda reminded her son that he was headed for jail. He knew deep down that she'd end up being right.

One night, a cousin of his Peruvian relatives named Yoyo called Rick and asked him to come and help with a job. He knew Yoyo to be an enforcer, standing six foot nine and nearly three hundred pounds, and wondered why the hell he was needed. When Rick pulled up to the designated apartment, there was something immediately familiar with the NW 7th Street complex. He'd passed it a million times, but this time it triggered a recollection. He realized he'd pulled into the development where his father shot Eladio Ruiz on his doorstep a dozen years ago. A shudder went through him as he walked toward Yoyo's unit, his senses beginning to signal trouble. He was on alert before, but now his body began to fight his every step.

What the fuck? It was probably just because he'd been reminded of his father. He shook it off and continued.

Once he arrived, Yoyo led him inside. He closed the door behind them and didn't offer his hand, but rather an Uzi submachine gun.

"Hold onto this," he said.

"Why?"

"I'll tell you in a minute. Go sit down."

Rick sat on the couch with the weapon on his lap and listened to Yoyo's plan. A connection of his had ripped him off for two kilos, and the dude was on his way over. Yoyo planned to confront him and just needed Rick to stand there with the gun, hoping to coax a confession.

Then what?

Rick sat on Yoyo's couch awaiting the guest for three hours, each passing minute drilling more doubt into his head. Something was up. He wasn't this stupid—everything about the night felt manufactured.

Is this the feeling his father had ignored at Roger's on the Green?

Rick kept playing along, waiting for a moment in time to open up and show him an escape route. When Yoyo was in the bedroom at one point, Rick slid the clip out of the gun and ejected the bullet from the chamber. He threw the ammunition on the other side of the room, laid the gun on the couch beside him, and walked out the door. Once outside, he ran to his car and peeled out.

The next day, Rick got a call from one of the cousins.

"Hey, you hear what happened?"

His cousin told him that a guy they knew as "Chapulin" had ripped off Yoyo and showed up to his apartment last night. He knocked on the door and was sprayed with gunfire right on the doorstep. Yoyo emptied an entire clip into him.

Rick took a step back as ice water coursed through him. Yoyo the monstrous enforcer didn't need Rick's help at all; he needed a patsy.

How many bullets could one dodge before intuition failed? Rick didn't put much stock in all that spiritual bullshit from the old ladies in his family, but if ever there was a sign from above, this was it. He chose to obey it and quit both the drug business and Miami forever.

★★★

Rogelio "Roger" Novo was found shot to death on a deserted stretch of road in Pembroke Pines on January 12, 1985.[677] Police Chief John Tighe said he was killed elsewhere and dumped there, and the investigation ruled out robbery as a motive. Novo was shot once in the head, and he had gold jewelry and over one hundred dollars in cash on him when found. The case sat on the books as a longtime unsolved Miami murder.

Rolando "Pucho" Morales was deeply affected by the loss of his younger brother. The silent man of honor, respected by all and never one to stray from the law, confessed to his sister Yolanda on his deathbed that he'd killed Roger Novo. He claimed to have shot him, put him in the trunk of his car, and dumped him in South Broward County.

Rudy "Redbeard" Rodriguez never harbored any resentment toward Carlene Quesada, despite going to jail because of him. "He saved my life," is how Rudy put it, in light of the escalating violence in Miami's drug business at the time of his arrest.[678] He served his time and remained in Miami upon release.

When Carlene fell ill in 2018, Rudy took his former partner in and cared for him during his final days, completing a family bond that dated back more than seven decades when they came to the US together.[679] Carlene passed away on October 12, 2019 at the age of seventy-seven.

Rudy Jr. got out of the drug business without ever doing time. He and the other children of the OGs moved on to other pursuits after Rudy and Carlene were arrested, with Rudy, Jr. becoming a supervisor at Miami International Airport. He's retired now, and today he and his wife live a scaled-down life, raising animals on a farm in the middle of nowhere in Florida.

"I'm just a hippie, man," he said.

Rafael Villaverde and his boat have still not been found.

Jerry Sanford put his experiences in espionage circles to work and penned two novels, *Miami Heat* and *The Lost Spy*, as well as a nonfiction book detailing his own travails in Miami called *Odyssey into Politics*.

His experiences prosecuting, defending, and associating with South Florida's most notorious figures were a source of great strain. Sanford maintained, "Although many people would dispute this statement, I considered [Morales] to be a remarkable man."[680]

Raul Diaz retired from the police force in 1983 after heading the CENTAC-26 task force. During his tenure he participated in the investigation to bring down Griselda Blanco and the most dangerous Colombian cartel operating in the US. Diaz underwent too great a toll, personally and professionally, and he hung it up at the age of thirty-six to found his own private detective agency.

Raul Martinez climbed the ranks of the department, becoming lieutenant in 1982 then major in 1985.[681] He became an assistant city manager in 1998 and was appointed chief of police in 2000. He retired in 2003.

After serving nine years in prison, Hector Cornillot escaped while on a work detail. He was eventually recaptured and went on a forty-day hunger strike, which resulted in a reduced sentence. You may have met him as today, at age eighty-five, as he drives for a popular rideshare company in Miami. Hector still maintains that the "medals of the revolutionary are prison and death," and he can take solace that both he and his brother-in-law each got theirs.

Annette didn't celebrate Thanksgiving for ten years after her Uncle Richard's death. That holiday in 1982 was the last time she saw him, where he rather heroically, of course, caught the falling turkey as it slid off the platter her mother was carrying. Annette remained in Miami, became a school teacher, and just recently retired. For decades she quietly carried the hope that her most cherished uncle would live again beyond the smattering of sensationalistic snippets in modern media.

Her sister Lynette was completing her PhD at Princeton when her uncle was killed. She plowed through the resultant family upheaval and remained in New York, eventually becoming an art historian, curator, and professor in Spanish Renaissance and Latin American and Italian Art. She no doubt reminded her students not to leave their jackets unattended.

After hearing Pucho's deathbed confession about Rogelio Novo, Yolanda lived until age ninety-five occasionally saying, *"Yo tengo que vivir mucho mucho tiempo, hasta que está gente gentuza se muera"*—vowing to "live a long time to see every one of those scumbags die."[682] In 2018, Annette informed her she'd heard Nancy Cid had been diagnosed with Alzheimer's, to which Yolanda replied that it didn't count—she was still alive.

Yolanda passed away in August 2020, two years before Nancy.

Magda buried her third husband in 2001, and she currently lives in Colombia with her male companion of twenty plus years. She prefers not to think about the past.

Rick landed in a small town in Michigan where his longtime girlfriend had grown up, and they married in 1991. Most of the Moraleses splintered after Ricardo's death and only maintained the most irregular of contact, if any. Rick presently doesn't have a relationship with either his brother Raul or sister Sylvia.

In 2021, Rick had a direct message sitting in his Twitter inbox from a Robert Morales.

Are you my brother?, it said.

Is Monkey your dad?, Rick replied.

Yes.

Then you are.

After having not seen each other since their impromptu judo classes nearly forty years earlier, Rick and Roberto reconnected, talking on the phone about family, their father, and everything that happened in the years before the COVID-19 pandemic. After talking for a few months, Rick and his wife flew down to Florida to meet with Roberto who, at just fifty-two years old, was in failing health and sat on a waiting list for a new kidney.

Rick called Roberto's case worker at the Mayo Clinic in Jacksonville and volunteered his kidney to give his half brother, though Rick's sugar levels were too high at the time. He altered his diet drastically, looking to lower his numbers as soon as possible, when Roberto got a call telling him to be in Jacksonville within forty-eight hours—a kidney had become available from another source.

Roberto underwent successful surgery that saved his life. After getting out of the hospital and back to health, he flew to Michigan with his wife and daughter to spend time with Rick, his wife, and their two grown children. There's a lot to talk about when you lose track of someone for four decades and still share one gargantuan, unifying thing. There were plenty of lost years, but who knows if either of them would've been prepared to forge a relationship prior to that moment, given all they'd seen and heard about their father. Maybe that was the perfect time to build something positive, life-affirming, and even life-saving, had Rick's blood work been different.

Something rather beautiful came out of that DNA.

Post Script

On April 17, 2025, Roberto Morales was killed by a mass shooter's bullet on the campus of Florida State University, where he worked. He leaves behind a wife and daughter, and innumerable people who knew and loved him on the campus and off. He was 57.

He can write his final chapter in this book here, courtesy of his last text to the authors from February 8, 2025. "My whole life up until I reconnected with Ricky, my father's life has been a mystery to me. My mother raised me under a shade of secrecy regarding the old man and I guess because there are many things he did that she didn't want me to know. You and Ricky have shined a spotlight on him and I can finally have a real understanding of who he was and who she was. I have nothing but love and gratitude for you. Thank you again and I hope to meet you one day and have a single malt and a Cohiba to celebrate."

It'll be a little later than we'd hoped, but it'll happen. If they allow smoking.

Endnotes

Introduction

1 John Katzenbach, "Monkey Morales Speaks No Evil," *Miami Herald*, 5/20/82, p. 1D.
2 "Tick-Talks Hearing Testimony Ends," *The Miami Herald*, 5/21/82, p. 2C.
3 John Cummings, "License to Kill," *Newsday*, 6/30/82, p. 13.
4 Katzenback, "Monkey Morales Speaks No Evil," p. 1D.
5 John Rothchild, "The Informant," *Harper's*, 1/82, p. 29.

Chapter One

6 CIA Dispatch from Chief of Station JMWAVE to Chief of Special Affairs, "Typic/Operational PRQ1 Part I: Ricardo Anibal Morales Navarrete," 2/13/64.
7 Magda Morales, interview with author, 3/11/24.
8 CIA, "Typic/Operational PRQ1 Part I: Ricardo Anibal Morales Navarrete," 2/13/64.
9 Ricardo Morales, Deposition, Part II, State of Florida v. Alfredo Arias, et al., 4/5/82, p. 28, 29.
10 CIA Information Report, "Elements of the Cuban Intelligence Community as of June 1960," Report ***CS CI 3/764,016, 2/20/61.
11 CIA, "Elements of the Cuban Intelligence Community as of June 1960," 2/20/61.
12 Morales, Deposition, State of Florida v. Alfredo Arias, 4/5/82, p. 22.
13 Ibid., p. 23.
14 Ibid., p. 24.
15 CIA Weekly Summary, "Fidel Castro and the Cuban Revolution: the First Decade," 2/7/69, p. 4.
16 Britannica, "Cuban Revolution," https://www.britannica.com/event/Cuban-Revolution.
17 CIA Memorandum, "Political Murders in Cuba—Batista Era Compared with Castro Regime," 1/21/63, p. 1.
18 Tony Perrottet, "When Fidel Castro Charmed the United States," Smithsonian Magazine, 1/24/19, https://www.smithsonianmag.com/history/when-fidel-castro-charmed-united-states-180971277/
19 Ibid.
20 Britannica, "Cuban Revolution."

21 Jennie Mazucco, "Modern Latin America, web supplement for 8th Edition," Brown University Library.
22 Britannica, "Cuban Revolution."
23 Ibid.
24 Ibid.
25 Mazucco, "Modern Latin America."
26 Britannica, "Cuban Revolution."
27 Ibid.
28 CIA Weekly Summary, 2/7/69, p. 4.
29 CIA Weekly Summary, 2/7/69, p. 7.
30 Alan Gomes, "Americans Have New Hopes to Reclaim Property Seized by Cuba 50 Years Ago," *USA Today*, 7/30/15.
31 Ibid.
32 Perrottet, "When Fidel Castro Charmed the United States."
33 Annette Bosch, interview with author, 4/24/20.
34 Lynette Bosch, interview with author, 4/16/20.
35 Lynette Bosch, 4/16/20.
36 Hector Cornillot, interview with author, 4/1/24.
37 Rubén Gallo, "Missing in Havana," The Brooklyn Rail, 6/22.
38 Hector Cornillot, 4/1/24.
39 Morales, Deposition, 4/5/82, p. 17.
40 CIA, "Typic/Operational PRQ1 Part I: Ricardo Anibal Morales Navarrete," 2/13/64.
41 Morales, Deposition, 4/5/82, p. 46.
42 Ibid.
43 CIA Dispatch from Chief, JMWAVE to Chief, WH Division, "Operational/JMATE/AMOT Ricardo Morales Navarrete," 1/20/61.
44 95th Congress House Select Committee on Assassinations, "Appendix to Hearings Vol X: Anti Castro Activities and Organizations; Lee Harvey Oswald in New Orleans; CIA Plots Against Castro; Rose Cheramie," 3/79, p. 57.
45 CIA, "Operational/JMATE/AMOT Ricardo Morales Navarrete," 1/20/61.

Chapter Two

46 Phil Buchen, White House Report, "Castro," 6/01/75, p. 8.
47 Inspector General Kirkpatrick, "Inspector General's Survey of the Cuban Operation," 8/61, p. 6.
48 Kirkpatrick, "Inspector General's Survey," p. 682.
49 Ibid., p. 7.
50 Ibid., p. 685.
51 Ibid., p. 17.
52 Ibid., p. 20.

53 Bay of Pigs Brigade 2506 Museum Website, "Who We Are," https://www.bayofpigsbrigade2506.com/the-history.
54 Dem Price and Theodore A. Ediger, "The Total Disaster That Was the Bay of Pigs," *Sunday Star,* 4/14/63.
55 Price and Ediger, "The Total Disaster That Was the Bay of Pigs."
56 Ibid.
57 Arthur Schlesinger Jr., Special Assistant to the President, Memo to President John F. Kennedy, "CIA Reorganization," John F. Kennedy Presidential Library, John F. Kennedy Papers, National Security File, Departments and Agencies, Box 271, Folder, *CIA 5/1961–8/1961,* 6/30/61.
58 Price and Ediger, "The Total Disaster That Was the Bay of Pigs."
59 George Volsky, "Cuban Exiles Recall Domestic Spying and Picketing for CIA," *The New York Times,* 1/4/75.
60 CIA Memo from JMWAVE to BELL, "WAVE Attempting to Organize Recruiting Mechanism," Agency file ***80T01357A, 4/6/61.
61 Hector Cornillor, interview with author, 6/6/24.
62 Gilbride, *Matrix for Assassination,* p. 159.
63 Spartacus Educational, "Frank Fiorini (Sturgis)," https://spartacus-educational.com/JFKsturgis.htm.
64 Frank A. Sturgis, Testimony to US House Select Committee on Assassinations, Miami, FL, 3/20/78, p. 28.
65 Sturgis, Testimony to HSCA, p. 29.
66 Buchen, White House Report, "Castro," p. 9.
67 Gen. Edward Lansdale, "Program Review by the Chief of Operations, Operation Mongoose", 1/18/62, https://history.state.gov/historicaldocuments/frus1961-63v10/d291.
68 Ibid., p. 11.
69 Ibid.
70 Ibid., p. 13.
71 Volsky, "Cuban Exiles Recall Domestic Spying and Picketing for CIA."
72 Carlos Martinez, "Cuban Raider's Own Story on Attack," *The Miami Herald,* 6/24/63.
73 Volsky, "Cuban Exiles Recall Domestic Spying and Picketing for CIA."
74 US Department of State, Office of the Historian, "Milestones 1961–1968/The Cuban Missile Crisis," https://history.state.gov/milestones/1961-1968/cuban-missile-crisis.
75 US Department of State, "Cuban Missile Crisis."
76 Maxwell D. Taylor, Chair of the Joint Chiefs of Staff, Memo to President Johnson, US Department of State, Office of the Historian, "Foreign Relations of the United States, 1964–1968, Volume XXII, Dominican Republic; Cuba; Haiti; Guyana," 3/21/64.
77 Ibid.

Chapter Three

78 US Department of State, Office of the Historian, "Foreign Relations of the United States, 1964–1968, Volume XXIII, Congo, 1960–1968," https://history.state.gov/historicaldocuments/frus1964-68v23/d1.
79 US Department of State, "Foreign Relations of the United States, Congo, 1960–1968."
80 Ibid.
81 Deputy Director of Security, Memo to Chief CI/OA, 4/2/64.
82 CIA, "Draft Cable Bio of Ricardo Morales Navarette," National Archives RIF***104-10177-10230.
83 Morales, Deposition, 4/5/82, p. 12.
84 Betsy Palmer, CIA File Review, National Archives, 7/21/78, p. 2.
85 CIA, Report of Covert Assessment, National Archives, 6/3/64, https://www.archives.gov/files/research/jfk/releases/104-10177-10244.pdf.
86 Morales, Deposition, 4/5/82, p. 89.
87 Glenn Garvin, "Anniversary Recalls Congo Rescue by Miami Cubans," *Miami Herald*, 11/15/14.
88 Don Hollway, "Mad Mike and His Wild Geese," Historynet, 2/8/19, https://www.historynet.com/mad-mike-and-his-wild-geese/.
89 Holloway, "Mad Mike and His Wild Geese."
90 Ibid.
91 Ibid.
92 Palmer, CIA File Review, p.3.
93 Morales, Deposition, 4/5/82, p. 92.
94 Chief of Station, CIA Memo to Deputy Chief/WH/SA, 9/1/64.
95 Morales, Deposition, 4/5/82, p. 9.
96 Bruce Cheever, DC/WH/SA CIA Memo to Chief CI/OA, 10/2/64.
97 CIA, Memo from WAVE station to BELL, "AMBUD-1," 6/15/61.
98 Ibid.
99 Garvin, "Anniversary Recalls Congo Rescue by Miami Cubans."
100 Ibid.
101 Ibid.
102 Ibid.
103 Ibid.
104 Ibid.
105 WM Knott, CIA Memo to Chief, Alien Affairs Staff, RIF***: 104-10122-10147, National Archives, 11/24/64, p. 1.
106 CIA, Classified Message, 12/1/64, https://documents3.theblackvault.com/documents/jfkfiles/NARA-Oct2017/NARA-Nov9-2017/104-10122-10185.pdf.

107 WM Knott, CIA Memo to Chief, Alien Affairs Staff, "Ricardo Anibal Morales Navarrete (AAC-1142)-***380858(C)/Alberto Perez Martinez (AAC-1143)-***223124(C)," 12/10/64.
108 Palmer, CIA File Review, p.3.
109 Ibid.
110 Memorandum of Agreement, No. 16, p. 1.
111 Brittanica, "The Congo, Bolivia, and death of Che Guevara," https://www.britannica.com/biography/Che-Guevara/The-Congo-Bolivia-and-death.
112 Volsky, "Cuban Exiles Recall Domestic Spying and Picketing for CIA."
113 Ibid.
114 Ibid.
115 Volsky, "Cuban Exiles Recall Domestic Spying and Picketing for CIA."
116 Wikispooks,https://wikispooks.com/wiki/Jos%C3%A9_Sanjen%C3%ADs_Perdomo.

Chapter Four

117 Hilton Cordoba and Jose Carrillo, "Neighborhood Change in Miami's Little Havana; A Demographic Analysis from 1970 to 2000," Florida Atlantic University, Department of Geosciences.
118 Lance Dixon, "How did Miami's Little Havana become the home for Cuban immigrants? We took a look at the history," *The New Tropic*, 4/25/19, https://thenewtropic.com/miami-little-havana-cuban-history/.
119 Dixon, "How Did Miami's Little Havana become the home for Cuban immigrants?"
120 US Citizenship and Immigration Services, "Refugee Timeline," https://www.uscis.gov/about-us/our-history/stories-from-the-archives/refugee-timeline.
121 Morales, Deposition, 4/5/82, p. 126.
122 Ibid., p. 125.
123 Ibid.
124 Miami Dade Police, Annual Report 2021, "History of the Miami Dade Police Department," p. 9.
125 Don Bohning, "Bosch: Often at Loggerheads With Law, Exile Had Always Remained Free," *The Miami Herald*, 10/12/68.
126 95th Congress House Select Committee on Assassinations, "Appendix to Hearings Vol X," 3/79, p. 90.
127 Don Bohning, "Exile Arms Seized to Protect Area," *The Miami Herald*, 1/10/65, p. 16.
128 Bohning, "Exile Arms Seized to Protect Area."

129 SAV Miami, FBI Memo to Director, "Lee Harvey Oswald/IS-R-Cuba/Buded 6/1/64," https://www.maryferrell.org/showDoc.html?docId=218083***relPageId=2.
130 Cornillot, interview with author, 6/6/24.
131 Ibid.
132 CIA, Information Report, "Executive Committee of the 30th of November Revolutionary Movement in Exile," 10/8/63, p. 1.
133 Cornillot, interview with author, 6/6/24.
134 Ibid.
135 Gene Miller, "Cigar Box Bomb Attached to Ship," *The Miami Herald*, 10/19/66, p. 1.
136 Morales, Deposition, 4/5/82, p. 118.
137 Henry Reno, "Bomb's Blast, Blaze Gut Hialeah Grocery," *The Miami Herald*, 7/24/64.
138 Morales, Deposition, 4/5/82, p. 130.
139 Ibid., p. 132.
140 Ibid., p. 121.
141 Ibid., p. 122.
142 UPI, "Banana Boat Spared Blast of Crude Bomb," *Tampa Bay Times*, 10/19/66.
143 Morales, Deposition, 4/5/82, p. 122.

Chapter Five

144 Ismael Rodriguez, "Epicure Market Closes For Good, But Leaves A Legacy," *BRG International*, 9/22/17.
145 Robert Hardin and Jack Greene, "'Reluctant' Witnesses Talk in Bookie Bombing Probe," *The Miami Herald*, 6/23/67.
146 Jim Savage, "Luck Keeps Target Alive," *The Miami Herald*, 7/14/67.
147 Ricardo Morales, Deposition, Part III, State of Florida v. Alfredo Arias, et al., 4/6/82, p. 7.
148 Morales, Deposition, 4/6/82, p. 10.
149 Ibid., p. 11.
150 Ibid.
151 Ibid., p. 13.
152 Ibid.
153 Nicholas Pileggi, *Casino: Love and Honor in Las Vegas* (Simon & Schuster, 1995), p. 24.
154 Frank Rosenthal, "How to Beat the Ponies," https://www.frankleftyrosenthal.com/tips_and_tricks/ponies.php.
155 Pileggi, *Casino: Love and Honor in Las Vegas*, p. 25.
156 Ibid.
157 "Playing All the Angles," *Chicago Tribune*, 1/24/95.

158 "Frank 'Lefty' Rosenthal Obituary," *Telegraph UK*, 12/4/08, https://www.telegraph.co.uk/news/obituaries/3550837/Frank-Lefty-Rosenthal.html/1000.
159 FBI, Records Vault, "Frank Rosenthal file Part 01," p. 38, https://vault.fbi.gov/frank-rosenthal/frank-rosenthal-part-01-of-02/view
160 Morales, Deposition, 4/6/82, p. 17.
161 Ibid.
162 Phil Doherty, *The Miami Police Worksheet* (Xlibris, 2012), p. 185.
163 Morales, Deposition, 4/6/82, p. 28.
164 Ibid., p. 31.
165 Doherty, *The Miami Police Worksheet,* p. 185.
166 Ibid.
167 Dave Nelson and Jon Nordheimer, "Two Bombs Rip Home of Underworld Figure," *Miami Herald,* 8/22/67.
168 David Sears, "How Three Amateur Jewel Thieves Made Off With New York's Most Precious Gems," *Smithsonian Magazine,* 2/25/14.
169 John Katzenbach, "Ex-Terrorist Says He Shot Key Figure in Big Jewel Theft," *Miami Herald,* 5/13/82, p. 3B.
170 Katzenbach, "Ex-Terrorist Says He Shot Key Figure in Big Jewel Theft."
171 Morales, Deposition, 4/6/82, p. 18.
172 Mark Florio, interview with author, 2/6/24.
173 Nelson and Nordheimer, "Two Bombs Rip Home of Underworld Figure."
174 Morales, Deposition, 4/6/82, p. 24.
175 Doherty, *The Miami Police Worksheet,* p. 185.
176 William Roemer, "Samuel M. Giancana," FBI Report to Director, Agency File ***92-3171-2107, 9/27/67, p. B.
177 Roemer, "Samuel M. Giancana," p. B.
178 Morales, Deposition, 4/6/82, p. 35.
179 Jane Ann Morrison, "Spilotro was merely a killer; Lefty mastered the more frightening Glare," *Las Vegas Review-Journal,* 10/18/08.
180 Alexander R. Hammer, "Lum's Alters Terms in Caesars Palace Purchase," *New York Times,* 9/15/70.

Chapter Six

181 FBI, Memo to Director, "Bombing Activities by Cuban Exiles, Bombing Matters," File ***CR-174-649-652, 11/8/68, p. 2–9.
182 Robert James Dwyer, FBI Report, "Unknown Subject; Bombing of the Soviet Embassy," File ***174-300, 4/15/68, p. 2.
183 SAC Miami, FBI Memo to Director, "UNSUB Bombing of B-25 Cargo Aircraft," 3/28/68, p. 4.
184 FBI, Memo, "Bombing Activities," p. 10.

185 Carlos Martinez, "Refugee Held in Bombing of Business," Miami Herald, 2/15/68, p. 29A.
186 SAC Miami, "UNSUB Bombing," p. 1.
187 Ibid.
188 Jack Roberts, "High Goes to Mexico on Rollason Mission," *The Miami News*, 1/10/65, p. 18.
189 FBI Deputy Director for Plans, Memo to Director, "Cuban Power (Power Cubano)," 3/26/68, p. 1.
190 Lynette Bosch, interview with author, 6/7/20.
191 Annette Bosch, interview with author, 6/25/24.
192 Rolando Morales, interview with author, 3/15/24.
193 Milt Sosin and Bob Wilcox, "Miami Exile Charged with Terror Bombings," *The Miami News*, 2/14/68.
194 Morales, Deposition, 4/5/82, p. 81.
195 Sosin and Wilcox, "Miami Exile Charged with Terror Bombings."
196 Dwyer, "Unknown Subject; Bombing of the Soviet Embassy," p. 4.
197 Ibid., p. 6.
198 Ibid., p. 5.
199 US v. Bosch trial transcript, US District Court, Miami, FL, 11/7/68, p. 353.
200 US v. Bosch, p. 357.

Chapter Seven

201 Paul Hendrickson, "Of Burning Ambition and Orlando Bosch," *Washington Post*, 5/12/88.
202 95th Congress House Select Committee on Assassinations, "Appendix to Hearings Vol X," 3/79, p. 89.
203 95th Congress HSCA, "Appendix to Hearings Vol X," p. 89.
204 Ibid., p. 91.
205 Ibid., p. 89.
206 "Bosch: Often at Loggerheads with Law, Exile Had Always Remained Free," *The Miami Herald*, 10/12/68.
207 Hendrickson, "Of Burning Ambition and Orlando Bosch."
208 Ibid.
209 George Davis Jr., FBI Memo to Director, "MIRR," File ***97-4474-245, 11/12/65, p. 18.
210 Davis Jr., "MIRR," p. 18.
211 Ibid.
212 US v. Bosch trial transcript, US District Court, Miami, FL, 11/7/68, p. 238.
213 US v. Bosch, p. 251.
214 Ibid., p. 246.

215 LJ Gallo, US Coast Guard Memo to Commander, Eighth CG District (OLE), "Suspected Bombing of M/V Granwood, investigation of," 6/14/68, p. 1.
216 SAC, MM FBI Memo to Director, "Explosion in Engine Room of British Freighter Granwood," 6/7/68.
217 Michael Crane, FBI Memo to Director, "Explosion Aboard Japanese Freighter 'Mikagesan Maru' Gavelston, Texas," File ***45-1159, 8/16/68, p. 1.
218 John R. Ackerly and Michael E. Crane, FBI Memo to Director, File ***45-101814-21, 6/12/68.
219 FBI Memo to Director, "Unsub: Explosion in Engine Room of British Freighter "Granwood" on High Seas, 25 Miles from Key West, Florida," 5/4/68.
220 US v. Bosch, p. 412.
221 Ibid., p. 256.
222 Ibid., p. 255.
223 Ibid., p. 258.
224 Ibid., p. 260.
225 Ibid., p. 267.
226 SAC, FBI Report to Director, "Explosion, Caribbean Venture, Evil, Metal Fragments, Cuban power," File ***MM 45-1168, 8/30/68.
227 US v. Bosch, p. 276.
228 Ibid., p. 289.
229 Ibid., p. 298.
230 SAC, FBI Memo to Director, "Unsub; Explosions on Spanish Registry Vessel SS Coromito," 9/13/68.
231 SAC, FBI Memo, Unsub; Explosions on Spanish Registry Vessel SS Coromito."
232 US v. Bosch, p. 313.
233 Ibid., p. 315.
234 Ibid., p. 322.
235 Ibid., p. 337.
236 Michael E. Crane, FBI Report, "Orlando Bosch Avila, et al.," 10/3/68, p. 8.
237 Crane, "Orlando Bosch Avila, et al.," p. 16.
238 Ibid., p. 9.
239 Ibid., p. 11.
240 Dan Bohning, "FBI Arrests 9 Cubans in Attack on Freighter," *The Miami Herald*, 10/12/68.

Chapter Eight

241 John C. Phelps, Deposition, State of Florida v. Hector Cornillot Llano, Dade County Criminal Court, 12/14/71, p. 3.
242 Bernardo Perez, Deposition, State of Florida v. Hector Cornillot Llano, Dade County Criminal Court, 1/7/72, p. 5.
243 Dade County Sheriff's Office, Hector Cornillot Arrest Warrant, 10/14/70.
244 Gene Miller and Joe Crankshaw, "Man Held, Questioned In Bombing Incident," *The Miami Herald*, 6/19/76, p. 1B.
245 State of Florida, Criminal Court of Dade County—Uniform Commitment to Custody of Division of Corrections, 5/5/72.
246 Hector Cornillot, interview with author, 6/6/24.
247 Ibid.
248 Ibid.
249 Miller and Crankshaw, "Man Held, Questioned In Bombing Incident."
250 Morales, Deposition, 4/7/82, p. 12.
251 CIA, Intelligence Information Cable, Dominican Republic to Miami, "Recruitment of Cuban Exiles by Aton Costanzo Palau to Jain Ranks of the Forces of General Imbert and General Wessin y Wessin," 6/10/65, p. 2.
252 Directorate General, Madrid, Spain Ministry of Government, Memo, "Cubans, Rolando Masferrer Rojas and Julio Constanzo Palau," 8/22/70.
253 CIA, "Recruitment of Cuban Exiles by Aton Costanzo Palau," p. 2.
254 CIA, Intelligence Information Cable, "Possible Imminent Departure of a 60 Man Commando Team from Miami, Florida to the Dominican Republic to Assist General Antonio Imbert Barreras," 6/10/65, p. 1.
255 SAC, FBI Memo to Director, "Aton Costanzo Palau; Gerald Patrick Hemming, et al., Neutrality Matters, Internal Security—Dominican Republic," 6/11/65, p. 4.
256 Bob Wilcox and Dick Holland, "Exile Gunned Down on Street Here," *Miami News*, 11/23/68.
257 Morales, Deposition, 4/6/82, p. 76.
258 Ibid., p. 79.
259 Ibid.
260 I-1 CIA, Memo to Argo Iris, "Francisco Varona Alonso, aka Varona," 10/6/68, p. 1.
261 I-1 CIA, Memo, "Francisco Varona Alonso, aka Varona," p. 1.
262 Ricardo Morales, Deposition, Part IV, State of Florida v. Alfredo Arias, et al., 4/7/82, p. 19.

Chapter Nine

263 "Police Chief Stresses Community Relations," *The Miami Herald*, 6/12/70, p. 7B.
264 Associated Press, "Miami Police Campaign Fails to Lure Negroes," *Orlando Sentinel*, 1/19/70, p. 10.
265 Morales, Deposition, 4/7/82, p. 14.
266 Ibid., p. 10.
267 Raul Diaz, *Reasons We Serve* Podcast, "Episode 11: Retired Raul Diaz Miami Police Department," 4/30/23.
268 Raul Diaz, interview with author, 2020.
269 Maria Anderson and Steve Velasquez, "Pedro Pan: A Children's Exodus from Cuba," Smithsonian National Museum of American History, 7/11/17, https://www.si.edu/stories/pedro-pan-childrens-exodus-cuba.
270 FBI, Memo, "Max Lesnik; Internal Security—Cuba; Possible Obstruction of Justice," Miami, FL, 5/18/73, p. 12.
271 Diaz, interview with author, 2020.
272 Leman L. Stafford Jr., FBI Memo to Miami office, "Cuba Libre," 10/10/60, p. 1.
273 "Spanish Magazine Begins Sales in Major U.S. Cities," *The New York Times*, 8/20/72.
274 FBI, Memo, "Max Lesnik; Internal Security—Cuba; Possible Obstruction of Justice," Miami, FL, 4/5/73, p. 1.
275 FBI, Memo, "Max Lesnik," 5/18/73, p. 3.
276 Ibid., p. 4.
277 FBI, Memo, "Max Lesnik," 4/5/73, p. 4.
278 Ibid., p. 5.
279 SAC, Miami (105-3492) FBI memo to Acting Director, FBI (105-64869), "Max Lesnik; IS—Cuba; Possible Obstruction of Justice," 4/5/73, p. 1.
280 Joe Broadus, "Police Seek Witness in Murder Case After Defendant is Slain at His Door," *The Miami Herald*, 8/2/73.
281 Raul Diaz, interview with author, 2020.
282 Raul Diaz, interview with author, 5/17/24.
283 Diaz, interview with author, 5/17/24.
284 Ibid.
285 Morales, Deposition, 4/6/82, p. 90.
286 Ibid., p. 86.
287 Diaz, interview with author, 5/17/24.
288 Morales, Deposition, 4/6/82, p. 87.
289 Diaz, interview with author, 5/17/24.
290 Ibid.
291 Joe Broadus, "Police Seek Witness in Murder Case After Defendant is Slain at His Door," *The Miami Herald*, 8/2/73.

292 Morales, Deposition, 4/6/82, p. 89.
293 Milt Sosin, "Cuban 'Informer' Quizzed in Slaying," *Miami News,* 8/2/73, p. 1A.
294 Sosin, "Cuban 'Informer' Quizzed in Slaying," p. 6A.
295 Diaz, interview with author, 5/17/24.
296 Ibid.
297 Ibid.
298 Edgar B. Martegani, CIA Memo to Chief of Station Miami, "Ricardo Morales Navarrete," 6/9/72.
299 William P. McSweeney, CIA Dispatch to Chief, Western Hemisphere Division, "Rybat Typic PLMHABYSS/AMDESK-1," 11/8/72, p. 1.
300 McSweeney, "Rybat Typic," p. 2.
301 Ibid.
302 Ibid., p. 3.
303 Ibid., p. 1.
304 CIA, Intelligence Information Cable, "Additional Potential Embarrassment for the Venezuelan Government in Connection with the Status of Ricardo Morales Navarrete," 11/23/76, p. 2.

Chapter Ten

305 Special Assistant for Coordination of Foreign Narcotics Information, CIA Memo to John Warner, "Cuban Exiles Involved with DEA," 3/17/76, p. 3.
306 Special Assistant, "Cuban Exiles Involved with DEA," p. 3.
307 Morales, Deposition, 4/5/82, p. 105.
308 Ricardo Morales, Deposition, Part IB, State of Florida v. Alfredo Arias, et al., 4/2/82, p. 46.
309 Morales, Deposition, 4/2/82, p. 46.
310 Ricardo Morales, Deposition, Part IA, State of Florida v. Alfredo Arias, et al, 4/2/82, p. 56.
311 Frank Greve, "Police Informer Escapes Blast," *The Miami Herald,* 7/3/74.
312 FBI, Report from Miami Office, "Orlando Bosch Avila; Internal Security—Cuba," Agency file ***105-2856, 4/27/73, p. 2.
313 FBI, Report, "Orlando Bosch Avila," p. 7.
314 Ibid.
315 Hilda Inclán, "Bosch Declares War On Castro," *The Miami News,* 6/18/74.
316 Inclán, "Bosch Declares War On Castro."
317 Greve, "Police Informer Escapes Blast."
318 Roberto Morales, interview with author, 3/27/74.
319 Ibid.
320 Ibid.

321 Ibid.
322 Annette Bosch, interview with author, 6/25/24.
323 Morales, Deposition, 4/5/82, p. 62.
324 Morales, Deposition, 4/5/82, p. 60.
325 Morales, Deposition, Part 1A, 4/2/82, p. 46.
326 Morales, Deposition, 4/2/82, p. 64.
327 Lynette Bosch, interview with author, 4/11/20.
328 "The Perfect Hideout: Jewish and Nazi havens in Latin America," The Wiener Holocaust Library, https://wienerholocaustlibrary.org/exhibition/the-perfect-hideout-jewish-and-nazi-havens-in-latin-america/.
329 Rachel Donadio, "Following the Trail of a Nazi Mass Murderer Who Was Never Caught: A Review of The Ratline," *The New York Times*, 2/2/21.
330 Morales, Deposition, 4/2/82, p. 53.
331 Jerome Sanford, personal diary/notes, given to authors by subject.
332 Michael Ray, "Carlos the Jackal," Brittanica, updated 5/3/24, https://www.britannica.com/biography/Carlos-the-Jackal.
333 Farzad, *Hotel Scarface: Where Cocaine Cowboys Partied and Plotted to Control Miami* (Berkley, 2018), p. 181.
334 D. Benitez, "Investigation into the bombing of the Social Security Office—Case No. 3-86," MPD Report, 12/4/75.
335 Terrell Snowden, "Found Explosive Device," MPD Police Report, 12/3/75.
336 Ofc 0173, "Bombing (Federal Building)," MPD Police Report, 12/3/24.
337 Rick Abrams and Milt Sosin, "Security Tightened in Mystery Bombings," *Miami News*, 12/4/75, p. 7A.
338 Abrams and Sosin, "Security Tightened in Mystery Bombings."
339 Ibid.
340 Ibid.
341 Ibid.
342 Rick Abrams and Hilda Inclán, "'I Warned Rogers Trouble Possible,' Mayor Ferre Says," *The Miami News*, 12/5/75, p. 6A.
343 Abrams and Inclán, "'I Warned Rogers Trouble Possible.'"
344 Ibid.
345 Ibid.
346 Joseph Dawson, FBI Report, "MIBOM," 12/16/75.
347 Ian Glass, "Bomb Explodes Here at Airport Locker; Caller Warned EAL," *Miami News*, 10/17/75.
348 Carlos J. Licea, "Miami Bombings 'Like Havana, 1958,'" *Miami News*, 12/5/75, p. 5A.
349 Licea, "Miami Bombings 'Like Havana, 1958.'"

350 Taylor Branch and Eugene M. Propper, *Labyrinth* (Penguin Books, 1983), p. 141.
351 Deputy Director for CIA Operations, Memo to FBI Director, Intelligence Division, "Rolando Otero-Hernandez; aka Rolando Otero, Rolando Papillon," 5/5/76.
352 Ricardo Morales, Deposition, Part VI, State of Florida v. Alfredo Arias, et al., 4/12/82, p. 29.
353 Raul Diaz, interview with author, 5/17/24.
354 Ibid.
355 Morales, Deposition, 4/12/82, p. 26.
356 Gloria Marina and Ron Sachs, "Bomb Suspect Enjoys Dominican Hospitality," *The Miami Herald*, 1/22/76.
357 Ibid.
358 Ibid.
359 Don Bohning, "Bomb Suspect Flees to Venezuela; Will Press Extradition, US Says," *The Miami Herald*, 1/24/76.
360 Branch and Propper, *Labyrinth*, p. 133.
361 Bohning, "Bomb Suspect Flees to Venezuela."
362 Branch and Propper, *Labyrinth*, p. 134.
363 Ibid., p. 135.
364 Ibid., p. 137.
365 CIA, File on Rolando Otero, National Archives, File ***104-10220-10028, p 29.
366 Branch and Propper, *Labyrinth*, p. 142.
367 Ibid., p. 163.
368 Diaz, interview with author, 5/17/24.
369 Ibid.
370 Gaeton Fonzi, House Select Committee on Assassinations Memo to Tanenbaum, "Otero Leads," 5/17/77, p. 2.
371 "Acquitted on Bomb Charges, Otero Faces County Charges," *Orlando Sentinel*, 8/25/76, p. 50.
372 Robert James Dwyer, FBI Memo, "Internal Security-Cuba," Bureau File ***109-584 (HSCA National Archives, 2/8/96), p. 2.
373 Hilda Inclán, "Bosch Declares War on Castro," *The Miami News*, 6/74, p. 3.
374 Dwyer, "Internal Security-Cuba," p. 2.
375 Branch and Propper, *Labyrinth*, p. 260.

Chapter Eleven

376 Nora Gámez Torres, "Cuban Exile Told Sons He Trained Oswald, JFK's Accused Assassin, at CIA Training Camp," *The Miami Herald*, 10/29/21, p. 14A.

377 "The President John F. Kennedy Assassination Records Collection," The National Archives, https://www.archives.gov/research/jfk.
378 Deb Riechmann, "Trump Boasted He'd Open All JFK Files, but Now Says He Can't," Associated Press, 4/26/18, https://apnews.com/trump-boasted-hed-open-all-jfk-files-but-now-says-he-cant-2f48d57f9ee045d98eb784d2295288ef.
379 White House, Memorandum for the Heads of Executive Departments and Agencies, "White House Memorandum Regarding Disclosure of Information in Certain Records Related to the Assassination of President John F. Kennedy," 12/15/22, https://www.whitehouse.gov/briefing-room/presidential-actions/2022/12/15/memorandum-on-certifications-regarding-disclosure-of-information-in-certain-records-related-to-the-assassination-of-president-john-f-kennedy/.
380 Ann Louise Bardach, "The Story of Marita Lorenz: Mistress, Mother, CIA Informant, and Center of Swirling Conspiracy Theories," *Vanity Fair,* 11/93.
381 Sturgis, Testimony to HSCA, 3/20/78, p. 41.
382 Bardach, "The Story of Marita Lorenz."
383 Sturgis, Testimony to HSCA, 3/20/78, p. 157.
384 Thomas Maier, "Inside the CIA's Plot to Kill Fidel Castro—With Mafia Help," Politico Magazine, 2/24/18, https://www.politico.com/magazine/story/2018/02/24/fidel-castro-cia-mafia-plot-216977/.
385 Erik Hedegaard, "The Last Confessions of E Howard Hunt," *Rolling Stone,* 4/2/07.
386 Lance Morrow, "44 Years Later, a Washington, D.C. Death Unresolved," *Smithsonian Magazine,* 12/08, https://www.smithsonianmag.com/history/44-years-later-a-washington-dc-death-unresolved-93263961/.
387 Stephen Neukam, "Robert Kennedy Jr. Sees 'Overwhelming Evidence' CIA Involved in JFK Assassination," *The Hill,* 05/08/23, https://thehill.com/blogs/blog-briefing-room/3993563-robert-kennedy-jr-sees-overwhelming-evidence-cia-involved-in-jfk-assassination/.
388 Nora Gámez Torres, "Cuban Exile Told Sons He Trained Oswald, JFK's Accused Assassin, at a Secret CIA Camp, *The Miami Herald,* 10/29/21, p. 14A.

Chapter Twelve

389 Raymond Aguiar, "De las Pruebas," 10/21/05.
390 CIA, Memo to Miami/San Juan, "Unsubs; Bombing of Cubana Airlines DC-8 Near Barbados, West Indies, October 6, 1976; Neutrality Matters-Cuba-West Indies," 10/76, p. 39.

391 Morales, Deposition, 4/5/82, p.151.
392 Harold H. Saunders, FBI Memo to Secretary, "Re: CASTRO, FIDEL, SPEECH, ALLEGATIONS, CIA INVOLVEMENT, CUBANA AIRLINER, BOMBING," 10/18/76, p. 5.
393 Saunders, FBI Memo, p. 3.
394 Nora Gámez Torres, "Drugs, Spying, and Terrorism: CIA Files Offer Insight on Life of Luis Posada Carriles," *The Miami Herald*, 11/15/17, https://www.miamiherald.com/news/local/community/miami-dade/article184844308.html.
395 CIA, Memo, "Unsubs; Bombing of Cubana Airlines DC-8," p. 39.
396 Jonathan Franklin, "Pinochet Directly Ordered Killing on US Soil of Chilean Diplomat, Papers Reveal," *The Guardian*, 10/8/15, https://www.theguardian.com/world/2015/oct/08/pinochet-directly-ordered-washington-killing-diplomat-documents-orlando-letelier-declassified.
397 Morales, Deposition, 4/5/82, p.106.
398 Ibid.
399 Luis Posada Carriles, *Los Caminos del Guerrero* (Self-published, 1994). (Passages translated and reprinted in article: https://baracuteycubano.blogspot.com/2011/01/luis-posada-carriles-escribe-sobre-la.html.)
400 Derek Bolton, "North Korea's Nuclear Program," The American Security Project, 8/12, https://www.americansecurityproject.org/ASP%20Reports/Ref%200072%20-%20North%20Korea%E2%80%99s%20Nuclear%20Program%20.pdf.
401 Bolton, "North Korea's Nuclear Program," p. 2
402 Ibid.
403 Morales, Deposition, 4/5/82, p. 102.
404 CIA, Memo to Director, "Unknown Subjects; Suspected Bombing of Cubana Airlines DC-8 Near Barbados, West Indies, October 6, 1976, Neutrality Matters-Cuba-West Indies," 11/76, p. 5.
405 Clarence M. Kelley, Memo from FBI Director to Henry Kissinger, 11/5/76, p. 2.
406 Oscar King, Report of Statements to Police, Trinidad and Tobago Police Service, 10/27/76.
407 CIA, "Unknown Subjects," 11/76, p. 6.
408 Branch and Propper, *Labyrinth*, p. 101.
409 Ibid., p. 100.
410 Saunders, FBI Memo to Secretary, p. 6.
411 CIA, Report, "Possible Plans of Cuban Exile Extremists to Blow Up a Cubana Airline," 6/21/76.
412 King, Report of Statements to Police, 10/27/76, p. 4.
413 Branch and Propper, p. 100.
414 CIA, Memo to Director, 11/76, p. 5.

415 Tim Weiner, "Cuban Exile Could Test U.S. Definition of Terrorist," *New York Times*, 5/9/05.
416 FBI Director, Memo to Legats: Caracas, Buenos Aires, Mexico City, "RADIO WQBA INTV NAVARRETE RICARDO MORALES," 10/22/76.
417 FBI Director, Memo to Legats: Caracas, Buenos Aires, Mexico City, 10/22/76.
418 Ibid.
419 Ibid.
420 Ibid.
421 Branch and Propper, *Labyrinth,* p. 101.
422 Ibid., p. 167.
423 FBI Director, Memo to Legats: Caracas, Buenos Aires, Mexico City, 10/22/76.
424 Ibid.
425 Taylor Branch and John Rothchild, "The Incident," *Esquire Magazine,* 3/1/77, p. 55.
426 Branch and Rothchild, "The Incident."
427 Roberto Morales, interview with author, 3/21/24.
428 Branch and Rothchild, "The Incident."
429 CIA, Memo to Director, 11/76, p. 8.
430 CIA, Cable to FBI, "Potential Embarrassment for the Venezuelan Government Due to Possible Exposure of Proof That Ricardo Morales Navarrete is a Venezuelan Security Official," 11/9/76, p. 4.
431 CIA, Cable to FBI, "Potential Embarrassment for the Venezuelan Government," p. 1.
432 Deposition of Ricardo Morales, Part IB, State of Florida v. Alfredo Arias, et al., 4/2/82, p. 43.
433 Branch and Rothchild, "The Incident."

Chapter Thirteen

434 James Kelly, "South Florida: Trouble in Paradise," *Time Magazine,* 11/23/81.
435 "$109 Million in Drug Money Ends Up in Miami Banks," *Santa Cruz Sentinel,* 6/8/80, p. 7.
436 "$109 Million in Drug Money Ends Up in Miami Banks," p. 7.
437 Ibid.
438 Ibid.
439 Ibid.
440 Drug Enforcement Administration, Report, "Drug Enforcement Administration History: 1975–1980" p. 44, https://www.dea.gov/sites/default/files/2021-04/1975-1980_p_39-49.pdf.

441 DEA, "Drug Enforcement Administration History: 1975-1980," p. 44.
442 James M. Markham, "Florida Is Becoming Drug Traffic Center," *New York Times*, 5/1/72.
443 DEA, "Drug Enforcement Administration History: 1975-1980," p. 45.
444 Markham, "Florida is Becoming Drug Traffic Center."
445 Ibid.
446 Chuck Volpe, interview with author, 7/24/24.
447 Owen Band, "The Spy Left Out in the Cold: Bay of Pigs Vet Bernardo de Torres Died Alone," *Miami New Times*, 5/13/19, https://www.miaminewtimes.com/news/bernardo-de-torres-bay-of-pigs-veteran-kennedy-assassination-spy-is-dead-11166861.
448 Joshua St. Clair, "*Tiger King's* Mario Tabraue Was Sentenced to 100 Years in Prison. Then He Got Out.," *Men's Health*, 5/27/20, https://www.menshealth.com/entertainment/a31955789/who-is-mario-tabraue-netflix-tiger-king/.
449 Owen Band, interview with author, 6/18/24.
450 Volpe, interview with author, 7/24/24.
451 Morales, Deposition, 12/16/80, p. 9.
452 Humberto Becerra, interview with author, 6/21/24.
453 Ricardo Morales, Deposition, Part VIII, State of Florida v. Alfredo Arias, et al., 4/14/82, p. 25.
454 Morales, Deposition, 4/14/82, p. 25.
455 Mollie Scruggs, interview with author, 6/19/24.
456 "Inside the Scarface Hotel," Messynessy, 9/20/18, https://www.messynessychic.com/2018/09/20/inside-the-scarface-hotel/.
457 Rudy Rodriguez Jr., interview with author, 7/12/24.
458 Rothchild, "The Informant," p. 34.
459 Rodriguez Jr., interview with author, 7/12/24.
460 Ibid.
461 Scruggs, interview with author, 6/19/24.
462 Rodriguez, Jr., interview with author, 7/12/24.
463 Humberto Becerra, interview with author, 3/27/24.
464 Morales, Deposition, 12/16/80, p. 9.
465 Edna Buchanan, "Drug Raid Nets $913,000 Cash," *The Miami Herald*, 3/26/78.
466 Morales, Deposition, 12/16/80, p. 10.
467 Lynette Bosch, interview with author, 6/25/24.
468 Annette Bosch, interview with author, 6/25/24.
469 Raul Martinez, interview with author, 7/9/24.
470 Ibid.
471 Helga Silva and Hilda Inclán, "Drug Suspect Morales Also FBI Target," *Miami News*, 4/7/78, p. 5A.

472 John Cummings, "License to Kill," *Newsday*, 6/30/82, p. 15.
473 Rodriguez Jr., interview with author, 7/12/24.
474 Humberto Becerra, interview with author, 3/27/24.
475 "Judge Orders Lawmen to Leave Morales Alone," *The Miami Herald*, 4/26/78, p. 4A.
476 Silva and Inclán, "Drug Suspect Morales Also FBI Target," p. 5A.
477 Annette Bosch, interview with author, 7/16/24.

Chapter Fourteen

478 John Rothchild, "The Informant," *Harper's*, 1/82, p. 36.
479 Al Messerschmidt, "Judge Bars Wiretap Information in Drug Case," *Miami Herald*, 7/27/78, p. 2C.
480 Messerschmidt, "Judge Bars Wiretap Information in Drug Case," p. 2C.
481 Raul Martinez, interview with author, 7/9/24.
482 Danny Goodgame, "Jury Acquits Former Spy in Pot Case," Miami Herald, 7/30/78, p. 1D.
483 Morales, Deposition, 12/16/80, p. 12.
484 Rodriguez, Jr interview with author 7/12/24.
485 Ibid.
486 Humberto Becerra, interview with author, 3/27/24.
487 Morales, Deposition, 12/16/80, p. 13.
488 Ibid.
489 Morales, Deposition, 12/16/80, p. 14.
490 Ibid., p. 15.
491 Ibid.
492 Ibid.
493 Rodriguez Jr., interview with author, 7/12/24.
494 Rothchild, "The Informant," p. 36.
495 Sanford, diary/notes.
496 Ibid.
497 Ibid.
498 Ibid.
499 Ibid.
500 Jerome Sanford, *Odyssey Into Politics: Jerry Sanford vs. the Miami Herald* (Outskirts Press, 2012), p. xvi.
501 Morales, Deposition, 12/16/80, p. 17.
502 Ibid., p. 19.
503 Raul Diaz, interview with author, 5/17/24.
504 Humberto Becerra, interview with author, 3/27/24.
505 Ibid.
506 Farzad, *Hotel Scarface*, p. 63.
507 Ibid.

508 Becerra, interview with author, 3/27/24.
509 Farzad, *Hotel Scarface,* p. 64.
510 Rodriguez Jr., interview with author, 7/12/24.
511 Rothchild, "The Informant," p. 36.
512 Ibid.
513 Sanford, diary/notes.
514 Joe Crankshaw, "Alleged Kingpin Seeks to Testify," *The Miami Herald,* 10/26/79, p. 2D.
515 Crankshaw, "Alleged Kingpin Seeks to Testify."
516 Becerra, interview with author, 6/21/24.
517 Ibid.
518 Morales, Deposition, 12/16/80, p. 22.
519 Ibid., p. 23.
520 Ibid., p. 24.
521 Becerra, interview with author, 6/21/24.
522 Ibid.
523 Sanford, diary/notes.
524 Jerome Sanford, Memo to JV Eskenazi, "Possible Threats," 1/8/80.
525 Sanford, diary/notes.
526 Ibid.

Chapter Fifteen

527 Morales, Deposition, 12/16/80, p. 28.
528 Ibid., p. 29.
529 Jerome Sanford, personal diary/notes.
530 Ibid.
531 Ibid.
532 Sanford, *Odyssey Into Politics,* p. 41.
533 Morales, Deposition, 12/16/80, p. 33.
534 Ibid., p. 34.
535 Ibid.
536 Ibid., p. 30.
537 Gary Moore, "Operation Tick Talks Gave Inside Glimpse of Drug Smuggling World," *St. Petersburg Times,* 6/1/82, p. 1.
538 Morales, Deposition, 12/16/80, p. 36.
539 Moore, "Operation Tick Talks Gave Inside Glimpse of Drug Smuggling World."
540 Ralph de la Cruz and Christine Evans, "Car Bomb Injures Convicted Smuggler," *The Miami Herald,* 8/18/90, p. 3B.
541 Morales, Deposition, 12/16/80, p. 35.
542 Ibid., p. 38.
543 Ibid., p. 39.
544 Ibid., p. 40.

545 Farzad, *Hotel Scarface*, p. 3.
546 Morales, Deposition, 12/16/80, p. 40.
547 Rothchild, "The Informant," p. 38.
548 Morales, Deposition, 12/16/80, p. 40.
549 Ibid., p. 41.
550 Sanford, diary/notes.
551 Roberto Morales, interview with author, 3/21/24.
552 Morales, Deposition, 12/16/80, p. 1.
553 Ibid., p. 3.
554 Ibid., p. 4.
555 Raul Martinez, interview with author, 7/14/24.
556 Ibid.
557 Helga Silva, "Tick Tapes: They Were Taken at Their Word," *The Miami Herald*, 10/20/81, p. 3B.
558 Raul Martinez, interview with author, 7/14/24.
559 Morales, Deposition, 4/6/82, p. 57.
560 Raul Martinez, interview with author, 7/9/24.
561 Raul Diaz, interview with author, 7/13/24.
562 S. Roadruck, Supplementary Report, Case ***439528-C, Metro Dade Police Dept, 12/22/82, p. 11.
563 Morales, Deposition, 4/2/82, p. 37.
564 Raul Martinez, interview with author, 7/14/24.
565 Sanford, *Odyssey Into Politics*, p. 85
566 Humberto Becerra, interview with author, 6/21/24.
567 James Kelly, "South Florida: Trouble in Paradise," *Time Magazine*, 11/23/81.
568 Kelly, "South Florida: Trouble in Paradise."
569 Ibid.
570 Ibid.
571 Karen Juanita Carrillo, "The Mariel Boatlift: How Cold War Politics Drove Thousands of Cubans to Florida in 1980," History.com, 9/20/20, www.history.com/news/mariel-boatlift-castro-carter-cold-war.
572 Carrillo, "The Mariel Boatlift."
573 Ibid.
574 Ibid.
575 Helga Silva, "Mariel Crime has Peaked Officials Say," *The Miami Herald*, 4/23/82, p. 18A.
576 Kelly, "South Florida: Trouble in Paradise."
577 Ibid.
578 Carrillo, "The Mariel Boatlift."
579 Silva, "Mariel Crime has Peaked Officials Say."
580 Ibid.
581 Raul Martinez, interview with author, 7/27/24.
582 Diaz, *Reasons We Serve*, "Episode 11."

583 Drug Enforcement Agency, Report, "History: 1980-1985," p. 52, https://www.dea.gov/sites/default/files/2021-04/1980-1985_p_49-58.pdf.
584 Nicholas Griffin, *The Year of Dangerous Days: Riots, Refugees, and Cocaine in Miami 1980* (Simon & Schuster, 2020), p. 65.

Chapter Sixteen

585 Morales, Deposition, 4/2/82, p. 25.
586 Ibid., p. 30.
587 Ibid., p. 29.
588 Morales, Deposition, 4/13/82, p. 27.
589 John Katzenbach, "Drug Dealer Tried to Bribe Him, Officer Says," *The Miami Herald*, 5/4/82, 1B.
590 Joan Fleischman and John Katzenbach, "Cop Relieved of Duty Over Drug-Dealer Link," *The Miami Herald*, 5/14/82, 4C.
591 Moore, "Operation Tick Talks Gave Inside Glimpse of Drug Smuggling World," p. 1.
592 Helga Silva, "Tick Tapes: They Were Taken at Their Word," p. 3B.
593 Ibid.
594 John Katzenbach, "State Ordered to Hand Over Intelligence Data on Police", *The Miami Herald*, 5-12-82, p. 2B.
595 Heather Dewar, "Police Not Probing Zamora, Officers Say," *The Miami News*, 5/14/82, p. 5A.
596 John Katzenback, "State Agent Didn't Believe Informant," *The Miami Herald*, 5/18/82, p. 1B.
597 John Katzenbach, "Tick-Talks Case Warrant Issued," *The Miami Herald*, 4/7/82, p. 3B.
598 Jay Ducassi, "Facing Charges, Villaverde Resigns Post," *The Miami Herald*, 8/7/81, p. 6D.
599 Ducassi, "Facing Charges, Villaverde Resigns Post," p. 6D.
600 Jim McGee and Fabiola Santiago, "Tick-Talks Defendants Were on Trip," *The Miami Herald*, 4/4/82, p. 1B.
601 McGee and Santiago, "Tick-Talks Defendants Were on Trip," p. 1B.
602 Ibid.
603 Raul Martinez, interview with author, 7/9/24.
604 Ducassi, "Facing Charges, Villaverde Resigns Post," p. 6D.
605 Ibid.
606 Ibid.
607 Heather Dewar, "Monkey Morales Admits Murder and 15 Bombings," *The Miami News*, 4/28/82, p. 1A.
608 John Katzenbach, "Monkey Morales Speaks No Evil," *The Miami Herald*, 5/20/82, p. 1D.
609 Farzad, *Hotel Scarface*, p. 172.

610 Katzenbach, "Monkey Morales Speaks No Evil."
611 Branch and Rothchild, "The Incident," *Esquire Magazine*, p. 36.
612 Verne Williams, "Wiretap Ruling Toughens Task for Police," *Miami News*, 9/18/82, p. 7A.
613 Williams, "Wiretap Ruling Toughens Task for Police."
614 Verne Williams, "Reno Drops Tick-Talks; 30 Will Go Free," *Miami News*, 9/28/82, p. 1A.
615 Williams, "Reno Drops Tick-Talks; 30 Will Go Free," p, 1A.
616 Sanford, *Odyssey Into Politics*, p. xxi.
617 Ibid.
618 Jerome Sanford personal diary/notes.
619 "Ricardo El Mono Navarrete," *En Una Hora*, YouTube, 10/15/16, https://www.youtube.com/watch?v=NiSBUn8csTw&t=5163s.
620 Angel Villamil, interview with author, 9/30/24.

Chapter Seventeen

621 S. Roadruck, Supplementary Report, "Nelson Alba interview," Case ***439528-C, Metro Dade Police Dept, 5/15/83, p. 2.
622 Susan Orlean, "The Homesick Restaurant Run by Cuban Refugees," *The New Yorker*, 1/7/96, https://www.newyorker.com/magazine/2021/09/06/magazine19960115the-homesick-restaurant.
623 Roadruck, "Nelson Alba interview."
624 S. Roadruck, Supplementary Report, "Cecilio Juan Fernandez interview," Case ***439528-C, Metro Dade Police Dept, 12/22/82, p. 8.
625 Roadruck, "Nelson Alba interview," p. 2.
626 *Monday Night Football*, National Football League (ABC-TV, 1982).
627 Roadruck, "Cecilio Juan Fernandez interview," p. 8.
628 S. Roadruck, Supplementary Report, "John Mack interview," Case ***439528-C, Metro Dade Police Dept, 12/24/82, p. 4; Bob Nightingale, "Inferno Linked to Underworld," *The Arizona Republic*, 2/20/83, p. A12.
629 J. LeClaire, Supplementary Report, "Nancy Hernandez Cid interview," Case ***439528-C, Metro Dade Police Dept, 12/26/82, p. 3.
630 *Monday Night Football*, ABC-TV.
631 Al Messerschmidt, "Restauranteur Ordered to Testify," *The Miami Herald*, 7/28/83, p. 3D.
632 S. Roadruck, Supplementary Report, "Orlando Torres interview," Case ***439528-C, Metro Dade Police Dept, 1/11/83, p. 2.
633 Roadruck, "Nancy Hernandez Cid interview," p. 5.
634 Ibid., p. 5.
635 *Monday Night Football*, ABC-TV.

636 S. Roadruck, Supplementary Report, "Raimundo Bruno Torres interview," Case ***439528-C, Metro Dade Police Dept, 1/30/83, p. 1.
637 Roadruck, "Orlando Torres interview," p. 4.
638 Ibid.
639 Ibid.
640 *Monday Night Football*, ABC-TV.
641 Ibid.
642 Ibid.
643 Steve Roadruck, interview with author, 8/26/24.
644 Raul Diaz, interview with author, 8/7/24.
645 Roadruck, "Orlando Torres interview," p. 4.
646 Annette Bosch, interview with author, 6/25/24.
647 S. Roadruck, Supplementary Report, "Narrative summary," Case ***439528-C, Metro Dade Police Dept, 12-23-82, p. 11.
648 Roadruck, "Narrative summary," p. 2.
649 Annette Bosch, interview with author, 6/25/24.
650 Roadruck, "Nancy Hernandez Cid interview," p. 11.
651 Roadruck, "Narrative summary," p. 12.
652 Ibid., p. 13.
653 Ibid.
654 Roadruck, "Nancy Hernandez Cid interview," p. 6.
655 Roadruck, "Narrative summary," p. 3.
656 Kim M. Lersch, "Drug Related Police Corruption: The Miami Experience," in *Police Misconduct: A Reader for the 21st Century, 2001*, ed. Michael J. Palmiotto, p.132-144, https://www.ojp.gov/ncjrs/virtual-library/abstracts/drug-related-police-corruption-miami-experience-police-misconduct.
657 Tom Duboco, "Morales Killed in Argument Over Her Drink, Friend Says," *The Miami News*, 12/23/82, p. 4A.
658 Roadruck, "Orlando Torres interview," p. 2.
659 S. Roadruck, Supplementary Report, "Rogelio Novo interview," Case ***439528-C, Metro Dade Police Dept, 1/16/83, p. 2.
660 Roadruck, "Rogelio Novo interview," p. 1.
661 Al Messerschmidt, "Macho Pride May Have Killed Morales," *The Miami Herald*, 1/20/83, p. 1D.
662 Nightingale, "Inferno Linked to Underworld," p. A12.
663 S. Roadruck, Supplementary Report, "Recommendation," Case ***439528-C, Metro Dade Police Dept, 6/13/83, p. 1.
664 S. Roadruck, Supplementary Report, Case ***439528-C, 5/11/83, Metro Dade Police Dept, p. 2.
665 Roadruck, 5/11/83, p. 2.
666 RA Zaldivar, "Espinosa Levels New Round of Charges," *The Miami Herald*, 2/3/81, p. 4B.

667 Roadruck, 5/11/83, p. 2.
668 Roadruck, "Recommendation," p. 1.

Chapter Eighteen

669 Alfred Spellman, "Ricardo 'Monkey' Morales, the Most Interesting Man in Miami, Was Gunned Down 35 Years Ago Today," *Medium*, 12/20/17, https://medium.com/@AlfredSpellman/ricardo-monkey-morales-the-most-interesting-man-in-miami-was-gunned-down-35-years-ago-today-9f5270e4b6ba.
670 Jerome Sanford, Memo to US Attorney JV Eskenazi, "Possible Threat," 1/8/80, p. 2.
671 Richard Mauer and Luisa Yanez, "Morales is 'Brain Dead'; Cops Have Prime Suspect," *The Miami Herald*, 12/22/83, p. 4A.
672 Mauer and Yanez, "Morales is 'Brain Dead.'"
673 Hector Cornillot, interview w author, 6/6/24.
674 Farzad, *Hotel Scarface*, p. 183.
675 Raul Diaz, interview with author, 5/17/24.
676 Raul Martinez, interview with author, 7/9/24.

Chapter Nineteen

677 Joan Fleischman and Jim McGee, "Slain Restauranteur Feared He Might Be Killed, Pal Says," *The Miami Herald*, 1/15/85, p. 1B.
678 Rodriguez Jr., interview with author, 7/12/24.
679 Ibid.
680 Jerry Sanford, personal letter to Rick Morales, 12/8/22.
681 Raul Martinez, interview with author, 7/27/24.
682 Annette Bosch, interview with author, 8/15/24.

Acknowledgments

The authors would like to thank the following for their assistance in bringing this complicated and expansive story to life after six years of work. Morales's living relatives were critical in constructing his story from each of their unique experiences and perspectives: Ricardo's beloved nieces Lynnette and Annette Bosch; nephew Rolando Morales; ex-wife Magda; brother-in-law Hector Cornillot; and son Roberto Morales.

Throughout his life, Ricardo made many professional acquaintances who helped us color much of the story: retired law enforcement officers Lt. Raul Diaz, Chief Raul Martinez, and Det. Steve Roadruck; Mutiny Club workers Owen Band, Chuck Volpe, and Mollie Scruggs; business acquaintances Humberto "Super Papi" Becerra and Rudy Rodriguez, Jr; attorneys Jerome Sanford and Brad Komorowski; and Rick Jr's childhood friend Angel Villamil.

The voluminous amount of research required for accuracy in reporting was made much easier by some consultants who came through in a pinch: authors Roben Farzad and Taylor Branch; Rick Hirsch, retired *Miami Herald* editor; Jerri Williams, retired FBI agent; Michael Miceli, esq; Mark Florio, US Navy SEAL 1990-1996.

All of it would've been for naught if not for the people who got it into your hands, namely Debra Englander, Caitlin Burdette, and the team at Post Hill Press, as well as our agent Colleen Oefelein. Thank you all.

Rick: Presenting my father's life story and my place in it for all to see was a deeply personal decision—I'd never even told my grown children the stories they read in this book. So many others found the story daunting and elusive, but not Sean Oliver. He was all-in and determined to tell the story of an infamous man, good and the bad, as it really was.

None of this would have been possible without the love and support of my family—my wife Cheri and children Corey and Jordyn—without whom I doubt I would have survived. They are my world and I would have been lost without them.

Me and my extended family have spent years digging around the darkest corners of Miami (and my mind) to give readers a glimpse into what that world entails and the price a family pays.

Sean: As much as my wife considers stacks of FBI and CIA documents creating obelisks throughout our house lively decor, I'm sure she's happy to now have a more minimalist design. Until the next one. And that's why she's been my artistic lifeline for a quarter century, and my partner in all things great and small.

My daughters Mia and Lana have been on the journey as well, and live as artists in their own right. They knew from the earliest age that art is truth, and their ABCs stood for Always Be Creating. They couldn't have made me more proud.

Lastly, to anyone who instilled a love of reading in me from my mother Eileen to the other teachers who posited steadfastly that the secret to life is written in the pages of bound things, I thank you humbly. Everything I write is because of you.

About the Authors

SEAN OLIVER: Sean has never carried out a contract bombing, but he is the author of eight books and a 2021 Writer's Digest Writing Competition winner in the script category. He is an actor and voice artist with over a hundred major motion picture and TV credits. He currently teaches in New Jersey where he lives with his wife and two daughters.

RICARDO MORALES, JR: Rick is the second of Ricardo Morales Navarrete's four children. He has appeared on radio and podcasts for NPR, Actualidad Radio 1040 AM, *Spyscape, The Opperman Report,* and Rob Reiner and Soledad O'Brien's *Who Killed JFK.* He is a father of two and lives in Michigan with his wife Cheri and cat Buddy.